Y0-BZK-176

THIS BOOK IS FOR YOU IF . . .

You've been curious about Jewish mysticism and what it has to offer.

You have read other books on Kabbalah and found them confusing.

You are interested in how the teachings of Kabbalah relate to other religious teachings.

You want to develop an overall framework for Jewish spiritual practice.

You would like to find new ways of thinking about God and the Divine in the world today.

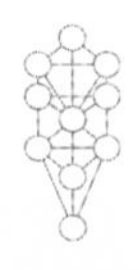

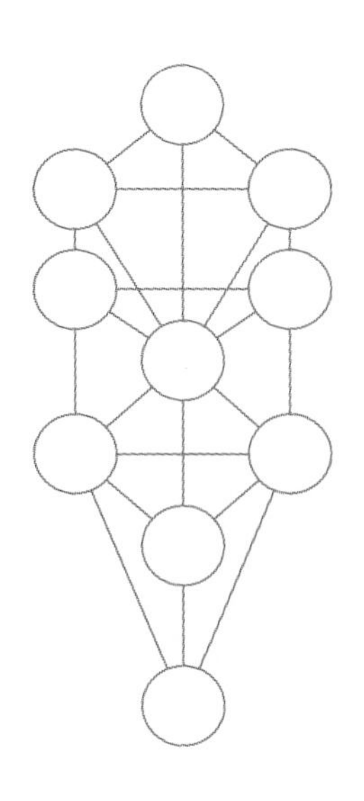

The Gift of Kabbalah

Discovering the Secrets of Heaven, Renewing Your Life on Earth

TAMAR FRANKIEL, Ph.D.

For People of All Faiths, All Backgrounds

JEWISH LIGHTS PUBLISHING

WOODSTOCK, VERMONT

The Gift of Kabbalah:
Discovering the Secrets of Heaven, Renewing Your Life on Earth

Library of Congress Cataloging-in-Publication Data

Frankiel, Tamar, 1946–
The gift of Kabbalah : discovering the secrets of heaven, renewing your life on earth / Tamar Frankiel.
p. cm.
Includes bibliographical references.
ISBN 1-58023-108-X
1. Cabala. 2. Mysticism—Judaism. 3. God. 4. Spiritual life. 5. Self-actualization (Psychology)—Religious aspects. I. Title.
BM525.F747 2001
296.1'6—dc21

2001000063

10 9 8 7 6 5 4 3 2 1

Manufactured in the United States of America

For People of All Faiths, All Backgrounds
Published by Jewish Lights Publishing
A Division of LongHill Partners, Inc.
Sunset Farm Offices, Route 4, P.O. Box 237
Woodstock, VT 05091
Tel: (802) 457-4000 Fax: (802) 457-4004
www.jewishlights.com

Contents

Acknowledgments

My own personal discovery of Kabbalah was not planned in any way. As I look back, I see that strange quality of a spiritual journey—one does not make decisions about it, not really. One finds oneself pulled, drawn forward, as if by an ineffable force. Perhaps there is no better example of causation from the future. In a person's life, of course, the future is not yet defined. The actual future depends on one's actions. But the fact that *something* is there, pulling one forward, is not to be doubted. So it was with my journey into Jewish spirituality, which involved descending (as the mystics say) into mysticism and the intricate world of Kabbalah.

I am very grateful to God for the direction my life has taken. And I also want to thank those whom God provided along the way to bestow gifts and offer the gentle pushes I needed to move forward.

My professors in graduate studies at Miami University and the University of Chicago gave me skills in research and critical thinking that have supported me throughout the years, even though many of them would be surprised at the kinds of treasures I chose to mine with those skills. My rabbinic teachers, largely from Chabad-Lubavitch and Breslov, have been the best guides I could imagine through the concepts of Jewish mysticism because they were willing to teach and re-teach basics. They are too many to mention, but I must thank Rabbi Chaim Dalfin, who first taught me *Tanya,* Rabbi Chaim Citron, who modeled a meaningful approach to textual analysis, and Rabbi Avrohom Czapnik, who inspired me with his way of bringing out practical implications of each mystical insight. I am fortunate also to have been able to work with Rabbi Aaron Parry on other projects; some of what I learned from him has been incorporated here.

I am grateful also for all those who are working so diligently to translate and interpret materials that have been inaccessible for so many decades and centuries. The number of books on Jewish mysticism available in English to the average reader today would simply astound our ancestors. Especially, I want to mention Rabbis Chaim Kramer, Avraham Greenbaum, and the Breslov Research Institute, whose work in disseminating Rabbi Nachman's teachings is a model of excellence, combining thoroughness with a passion for spiritual truth. My anchor through all these studies has been the wisdom of Rabbi Abraham Isaac Kook. Paulist Press published an edition of selections of his writings more than twenty years ago, which my husband and I received as a wedding present—now the most-thumbed book in our library. A few more selections have become available in English since then, and I have also been fortunate to study pieces of his original Hebrew writings. When more of his work is translated, surely he will be regarded as one of the great visionaries of our time.

Some of these currents began to flow more surely together a few years ago. In 1996, I met Connie Kaplan and became an avid student of her teachings about dreams and soul contracts. I became more and more certain that the information she was transmitting supported and enhanced my work in Jewish mysticism. When she began her work in Creation Spirituality with Matthew Fox and his colleagues in 1998, she spoke to me about the exciting work of mathematical cosmologist Brian Swimme and biologist Rupert Sheldrake. A while later, my colleague and friend at Claremont School of Theology, Ann Taves, introduced me to David Griffin, whose work on parapsychology and philosophy fascinated and encouraged me. Later, it turned out that Swimme and Sheldrake had contributed to one of Griffin's books on postmodern thought—my circles were connecting! I had the opportunity to teach courses on theology and Jewish mysticism at the University of California, Riverside, which helped more pieces of the puzzle come together.

In the meantime, working on two books on prayer with Judy Greenfeld deepened my studies in the practical aspects of mysticism. She, along with Randi Rose, Toba August, and Joyce Kirsch, listened patiently to my early attempts to expound on the Kabbalah's teachings about the *sefirot* as I was struggling to understand and integrate them into my life. Other students in seminars I taught with Judy and Connie gave me valuable feedback on my work. I am deeply indebted to all these people. I am painfully aware of not being able to footnote many of the insights I have gained from the oral teachings of Connie Kaplan, but I encourage readers to seek out her work, more of which will be published in coming years.

A few more thanks are due: to my Kabbalah class in the summer of 2000, who helped me fine-tune the presentation—especially to Dena Glaser, Sara Lansill, and Leah Schnall; to Randi, Sara, and Ann Brener, who read early versions of the manuscript; to my editor, Donna Zerner; and to Stuart Matlins, Sandra Korinchak, Emily Wichland, and all the staff at Jewish Lights, who helped bring this work into final production.

One caveat: I do not pretend to be an authority on Kabbalah, only an explorer with a few talents to contribute. I can say that I have thought deeply about Jewish mystical teachings and brought to bear the knowledge that is available to me at present, without attempting to make it acceptable to any particular party or denomination. Of course, I take full responsibility for any errors of fact or interpretation.

I hope this book will enable its readers to see God, the universe, and each of us participating in the unfolding of creation. My great desire is that we all can live from a vision of "unbroken wholeness," to use physicist David Bohm's phrase—the ultimate vision of the universe. In that way, we can perhaps hope to fulfill what the rabbinic tradition identified as the human task: to "make a dwelling-place" for God; or, as the Hasidic masters say, to infuse the entire world with Godliness.

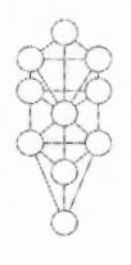

A Note on the History of Kabbalah

Kabbalah, the popular term for Jewish mysticism, comes from a Hebrew root that means "to receive"; thus Kabbalah is the received tradition. It originated, probably several centuries B.C.E., in the study of esoteric aspects of the written Torah (the first five books of the Bible), the contemplation of prophetic visions like those of Ezekiel and Isaiah, and apocalyptic traditions. Specific rabbis were known to be teaching mystical theology and practice in the first centuries C.E. Some leading scholars think that the Gnostics of the early Christian era (ca. 100–200 C.E.) developed their ideas from a core Jewish mystical tradition that existed by the first century. We have Jewish mystical texts that date back probably to the second or third century C.E., but we know very little about the transmission and interpretation of these texts. From the fascinating teachings that have come down to us, it is highly likely that the mystics limited their teachings to small circles because they were concerned about being considered culturally and even politically subversive in a variety of ways.[1] Yet in the long run, their thought was highly influential. The traditional Jewish prayer book, first compiled in the eighth century C.E., still incorporates important mystical ideas.

Whatever the reasons for the original secrecy, Kabbalah in a variety of interpretations became better known in the Middle Ages, even though its teachers still emphasized oral, teacher-to-student transmission. Among the best-known works circulating among the mystical masters of Europe were the *Sefer Yetzirah* (originally from the third century) and the *Bahir* (eleventh century). Major schools of mysticism existed in Germanic territory, in southern France, and in Spain, where the *Zohar* was published in the late 1200s. A major biblical commentator, Moshe ben Nachman, or Nachmanides (known in Jewish scholarship by the acronym Ramban) was one of the Spanish mystics; he frequently refers to mystical teachings in his commentary. After the expulsion of Jews from Spain in 1492, mysticism traveled with the exiles to Italy, the Balkans, and the Land of Israel.

By the mid-sixteenth century, a number of outstanding scholars and mystics had settled in Safed (pronounced *s'fat*), a small town in the Galil (northern Israel). Their presence attracted more individuals with similar inclinations, and soon Safed became the world center of Jewish mystical piety. When a remarkable rabbi named Isaac Luria arrived there in 1589, he quickly became the acknowledged master of the group and spent the next three years, until his death, consolidating, explaining, and elaborating the mystical heritage. "Lurianic mysticism" became the basis for most Jewish mysticism down to the present day.

Political and economic changes led to the decline of Safed in the next century, but teachings spreading from the village continued to engage the interest of more than a small elite. The next great eruption of mysticism came in the form of a popular movement in the 1600s led by Shabbatai Tzvi, an erratic teacher whose disciples believed to be the Messiah, but who converted to Islam to escape death. After this debacle, many rabbis discouraged the teaching of mysticism to the general populace, and invoked again the traditional prescription of secrecy. Great mystics were carefully watched and sometimes forbidden to publicize their teachings. For example, about a hundred years later, Rabbi Moshe Chaim Luzzatto (whose acronym is the Ramchal) taught a devoted group of disciples in Italy, but when contemporary rabbinic leaders learned that he believed some of his students to be incarnations of great past leaders, and one to be a potential messiah, he was forbidden to teach. He moved to Amsterdam but again met discouragement. Nevertheless, a number of Luzzatto's works were accepted and are today much respected in the history of mysticism.[2]

Most mystics stayed underground. According to one tradition, a circle known as the "hidden ones" carried on the teachings of the Ari—the "Lion"—Isaac Luria, for nearly two hundred years in Eastern Europe. In 1740 a member of this circle emerged into public view in the Ukraine, saying that it was now time to reinvigorate mystical teachings among the general populace. His name was Israel ben Eliezer, known as the Baal Shem Tov. His teachings, transmitted by his disciples and theirs in turn, sparked a flame of piety across Eastern Europe.

The members of this movement were known as Hasidim (or Chassidim, meaning "the devout ones"). They taught love of God, joy in worship, and the ability of every Jew to be connected to God through prayer and service—whether or not a person was learned according to rabbinic criteria. Although this way of transmitting mystical teachings also had opponents, Hasidism grew to become a major influence on the piety of the Jews of Eastern Europe. In addition, many great non-Hasidic scholars continued to study Kabbalah. In the nineteenth century, even among the non-Hasidic groups, a young man who showed intellectual promise and a desire to inquire into esoteric meanings might be given a copy of the *Zohar*—one of the classic mystical texts—when he was still a teenager.[3]

Unfortunately, the persecutions and pogroms of late nineteenth-century Russia decimated many Jewish communities. Most dramatically, in the Holocaust perpetrated by Nazi Germany in the mid-twentieth century, ninety percent of Eastern Europe's rabbis were slaughtered. Still, the Hasidic traditions and some of the masters of Hasidic teachings survived and brought their message to the United States, in waves of immigration that began at the end of the nineteenth century. Until the 1950s, access to the traditions was confined mostly to the Orthodox enclaves of major cities, for all the Hasidim were Orthodox, as were Sephardic Jews who also maintained a strong mystical tradition. Martin Buber, who was originally from a Hasidic tradition, had begun to translate traditional tales and sayings, but it was the Lubavitch sect of Hasidim known as Chabad (tracing its roots to the town of Lubavitch in Russia) that began to spread the teachings to assimilated and non-Orthodox American Jews. Both through its official rabbinic representatives and through teachers who were trained in Chabad but left the confines of the group, mystical teachings became far more accessible even to Jews uneducated in tradition. The important Jewish Renewal movement, which attracted young Jews in major cities beginning in the 1970s, encouraged serious study of mysticism as well as other aspects of Jewish tradition. By the end of the twentieth century, a wide variety of Jewish groups had exposure to Kabbalah and were including mysticism, at least occasionally, as part of their teachings.

Meanwhile, the American public had demonstrated a growing interest in spirituality since the 1960s, an interest that increased dramatically in the 1990s. Most of that interest was directed toward Eastern thought, especially Hinduism and Buddhism, or to theosophical and occult traditions that had previously been of interest only to an elite minority. But non-Jews also became interested in Kabbalah. This was not entirely a new development; as we will see in Chapter 1, non-Jews have sought spiritual insight from kabbalistic traditions before. But as awareness of Kabbalah spread through the mass media, popular interest in Kabbalah grew larger than ever.

At present, different approaches to Kabbalah are available. In traditional Hasidism, as well as in neo-Hasidic groups that deemphasize observance of Jewish law, mystical interpretations are incorporated as part of general Jewish learning. Studying mystical teachings while learning Bible, prayer, and Jewish law is the most integrated approach. I encourage everyone who reads this book to incorporate that kind of study into their spiritual practice. But, for the beginner with a strong interest in mysticism, the relevant books are very difficult because they require familiarity with many basic Jewish texts and concepts, and often with Hebrew words and letters. Another alternative that has emerged in recent years is groups that specialize in Kabbalah for a general audience, but one must be careful because some of these groups are of doubtful authenticity and even use questionable methods to gain adherents. A third approach is reading books by non-Jewish kabbalists (note that many are older works, recently reprinted to satisfy current demand). Most of these are interlaced with intricate esoteric interpretations from other theosophical traditions and cannot be said to present Jewish Kabbalah. Finally, in very recent times a number of writers, including myself, have begun the effort of making the concepts of mystical Judaism available for the general reader who does not possess deep knowledge of Jewish tradition. Hopefully, these books will encourage dialogue among spiritual practitioners in Judaism and in other traditions as well.

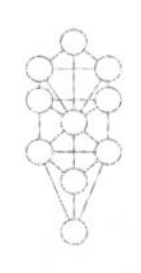

PART I

SEEKING A NEW VISION

1 Opening the World of Kabbalah

The need to reach the rock-bottom of truth, the desire to know the very source and origin of life, this is a religious urge that impels man beyond the physical, the material, in his longing for a transcendental truth. This is the inquiry that would encompass the whole of life, down to its root.

—Rabbi Mordecai Miller[1]

From Concealment to Revelation

A hidden tradition. Esoteric, complicated, dangerous. Only a few could study it, and it was carefully guarded from the unlearned and outsiders.

This is the reputation of Kabbalah, as the ancient tradition of Jewish mysticism is known. Today, however, its basic teachings are available to the general educated public. Movie stars study Kabbalah. You can pick up at your local bookstore numerous books that introduce the basic vocabulary and conceptual structure of Kabbalah. Other books offer insights on Jewish meditation. Academic works purport to reveal the psychology or social history of mysticism.

Yet if you think about it, this sudden accessibility is a little suspicious. If Kabbalah was so secret for so long, how can we approach it so easily now? If it is so difficult, how can it be made simple enough for a popular audience? And if it has been around for millennia, why is it coming to the fore at this time? Is there something special about the resurgence of Jewish mystical tradition among the many religious theories and many forms of meditation and self-improvement available today?

Kabbalah has been hidden to a considerable degree, and the fact that it is coming into public vision now is no accident. The Jewish mystics have taught that although all spiritual teaching goes back to the original Divine revelation encapsulated at Mount Sinai (Exodus 20), the particular form in which a teaching appears is appropriate to its era and its audience. There is a rabbinic saying: "God provides the remedy before the disease." The appearance of Kabbalah in public means that Jewish mysticism has something unique to offer, a power for healing the spirit as we move into a radically new future.

Many thinkers now acknowledge that the dominant inherited thought systems of the modern West no longer are sufficient to nourish human and planetary life. As a result, various forms of ancient spirituality, formerly esoteric and inaccessible, are now being translated into terms comprehensible to a popular audience. We do not yet know exactly how to do this translation. Some of the richness of complex traditions like Kabbalah is undoubtedly lost in the process of popularization. But if the wisdom of the core teachings can be preserved and transmitted, the tradeoff is worthwhile. We—collective humanity—must rethink and reimagine our world and our personal lives along spiritual lines.

Kabbalah offers truly unique insights that enable us, as the *Sefer Yetzirah* says, to probe into the realities of the world.[2] Moreover, it presents its truths in an expansive and unusually comprehensive framework. Many books talk about holistic perspectives, but Kabbalah makes clear that holism must be integrated with an appreciation of plurality and diversity. It also insists that we view our personal journeys in the larger context of what is happening in God's world, for that is the only way to avoid creating another mystical narcissism. Kabbalah thus enables us to see the depth dimension in all aspects of life, from family relations to politics and technology.

This book will provide you with guideposts in understanding Kabbalah. As you absorb the lessons of Jewish mysticism, you will be able to think in new ways—as a citizen of the cosmos—and align your life with the greatest spiritual aspirations of humankind.

Remembering Who We Are

Let's start with a basic question: Why is it that human beings encounter so many problems in life? Why are we beset with war and racism, political and ethnic conflicts, disharmony with our environment, and shattering events in our personal lives? Kabbalah tells us that the ultimate cause of our problems, from our personal lives to the widest range of humanity, is forgetting who we are. We have forgotten our true selves and our true purpose. This teaching brings us some good news: In our deepest core, we do know who we are. When we rediscover it, we will recognize it because it is not alien to us. This teaching comes ultimately from the Bible, which clearly states that human beings are made in the Divine image—that is who we truly are. Our purpose is to become clear mirrors of Divinity. Sometimes we see glimpses of our true inner selves, our Divine selves. But most of the time, in our haze of half-knowing, we create layer upon layer of delusion about our lives.

Strangely enough, the Jewish mystics also say that our forgetting is necessary so that God's purpose in creating the earth can be accomplished. If we remembered with clarity why we are here, we would not have free choice. We would simply be robots programmed to do what we were told. But if we are truly to manifest Godliness we cannot be robots, because one of the characteristics of the Divine is the ability to create freely. Thus, by obscuring our origins, God was able to give us free choice—to choose whether or not to manifest as loving, creative images of the Divine.

This is simply the nature of earthly existence according to Kabbalah. Many other forms of mysticism agree. Robert Frost, in a little-known poem called "The Trial of Existence," writes of the forgetting that accompanies earthly incarnation. He puts the words in God's mouth very poignantly:

> . . . Always God speaks at the end,
> "One thought in agony of strife
> The bravest would have by for friend,
> The memory that he chose the life;
> But the pure fate to which you go
> Admits no memory of choice,
> Or the woe were not earthly woe
> To which you give the assenting voice."[3]

We volunteered for earthly service, but part of the package is that we cannot remember doing so. That is what makes life such a challenge.

Along with forgetting who we are comes another problem: self-doubt. Our uncertainty about what we are doing here distorts everything in our culture. We live in a time when human beings have achieved more than people of previous centuries could even dream. On the surface, we appear to be a species of self-confident, assured creatures. But our culture reveals the opposite: Books, newspaper columns, talk shows, and self-help groups constantly address the issue of self-esteem. Group rivalry and ethnic conflict escalate to shore up weak social identities. Why are we so insecure? To use a New Testament image, we have built our houses on sand instead of rock. The sand is the idea that we are separate, independent individuals, desperately competing in an alien world. The rock is our connection to God. When we are not in touch with the ultimate Source that can give us a picture of our true worth, we will slip and slide into the sea of false knowledge that inundates our information age. What we need is the deep knowledge of ourselves as truly created in the image of God. We must experience ourselves as creative, loving, and profoundly connected to each other and to the rest of creation.

The idea that we are made in the image of God is such an awesome thought that we hide it from ourselves. The great modern Jewish philosopher Abraham Joshua Heschel wrote sadly, "The man of today shrinks from the light."[4] We may say, "Well, maybe we're made in the Divine image," but then we counter by saying, "We can't really know God. So what good is it anyway?" Kabbalah emphasizes, on the contrary, that while we may not be able to know God's essence, we can think about God and understand how teachings about the Divine plan apply to our lives.

Kabbalah teaches us directly about Godliness, about Divinity. Scholars have called it a "theosophy," which means "wisdom about the Divine." Only when we have a grasp on the meaning of Divinity and Divine purpose can we possibly understand what we are here for. Intellectual work is thus an important part of Kabbalah. If we ask questions and are told "you just have to accept it," that's insufficient. We can't just recite words and phrases that are meaningless to us. We may not be able to understand everything, but at least we have to put in the effort. While traditional religious virtues like faith and trust are important categories in Judaism generally and in Kabbalah in particular, we must also be willing to embark on a journey that will stretch the mind.

Often social customs and pressures discourage us from this effort. Most established religious traditions have tried to place limits on people's search for the deeper truths. Religious authorities often believed that esoteric wisdom was dangerous to the social order, because religious enthusiasm could often be manipulated by the unscrupulous (as indeed it has). Historically, mysticism has also been seen as dangerous to those in power, as mystics who believe in the Divine image in everyone have tended to be concerned about equity and justice. As a result, many of us have been taught to believe that one has to be a very saintly person to be truly "in the image of God." It's beyond the reach of ordinary folk. Different religious traditions have put this belief in different ways. Some say that only one person was really Godly, and all we can do is rely on what that person said and did thousands of years ago. Others say that we can reach a level equivalent to divinity, but it takes a person a multitude of lifetimes. Still others tell us that we can do it, but we have to give up worldly pleasures, become asectics, and cut off our ties to the world.

These views are all contrary to the teachings of Jewish mysticism. All of us have the gifts we need to reflect the image of God, each in our own unique way. The very fact that we have arrived here, in human incarnation, tells us that we have the courage to take on the task. Although Kabbalah teaches that we may reincarnate in different bodies to accomplish our soul's mission, we always have the possibility of completing that mission in our present lifetime. Moreover, Kabbalah was not cultivated in an atmosphere completely separated from daily life. Judaism never had monks and nuns who withdrew from ordinary life to nourish their spirituality. Most rabbis, including many kabbalists, worked for a living at some trade or business. If they wanted to be close to God, they had to spend time at it, but most had to do it while they were living a normal life.

Today, although we are busy and often preoccupied with day-to-day matters, many of us actively desire to have our entire lives permeated with spirituality. We want to work at creating our lives around a higher ideal. The teachings of Kabbalah are appropriate because Judaism says that our "temple" is the home as well as the synagogue or religious institution; that marrying and raising children is just as holy as having a separated spiritual life; that caring for our bodies and minds is as important as spiritual experience.

Of course special times and activities such as retreats and purifications can be helpful as part of a spiritual practice. Mystics in Judaism as in other traditions were known to depart from the normal person's routine—for example, by sleeping less or fasting more. But Judaism holds that, for most people, separations from the world should be temporary and limited, enabling us to refresh our connection to Spirit. We must then return to the world and integrate what we have received. This is the point of our effort, for the ultimate goal is that *the whole world will become a vessel for Divinity.* When humans reach the point of "From my flesh I will see God!" as Job says (19:26), the purpose of creation will be realized. We will have remembered and fully realized our Divine image.

Kabbalah provides a unique system for enabling us to do this. It continually tries to point us to the deeper levels of everything we do. Nothing in the world is outside its purview. Kabbalah teaches, for example, that our true Divine purpose can never be completely forgotten. If we look with a compassionate eye at our lives and at the society we live in, we can perceive that most people are indeed striving for spiritual greatness but have expressed that striving only in partial, truncated ways. Science's quest for power over nature, an individual's aspiration for wealth and honor, our desperate searches for love and pleasure are all part of the same effort. They are all part of Divinity—love, power, honor, and delight are all attributes of God. But in our society they are usually cut off from their ultimate Source, so they do not give full satisfaction.

For Kabbalah, everything is a metaphor that provides access to ultimate reality. Problems that arise on one level can be resolved on another. And at each point, we are thrown back to the question "How can we manifest Godliness? How can we be Divine?"

Is Kabbalah Only for Jews?

God isn't only for Jews, so neither is Kabbalah. While there are some aspects of Kabbalah that are almost impossible to understand without absorbing a great deal of Jewish tradition, Kabbalah as a theosophy is primarily about understanding what God is (as far as we can understand) and who we are as refractions of the Divine image. Because of this, it is important for all peoples.

Yet, according to the popular conception among Jews, you couldn't study Kabbalah unless you were forty years old, married, and male—and, traditionally, Jewish. What these criteria meant was that a student should be mature, well grounded in the basics of Judaism (including Talmud), and stable in his personal life. Because a strong grounding in biblical and Talmudic texts was presupposed, women were not included. Women were taught the portions of Torah necessary to live a Jewish life, which was a considerable amount of learning, but they generally did not have access to Talmudic learning or extensive biblical commentaries. Rules also restricted certain kinds of kabbalistic interpretation and use of Divine names. All these restrictions would apply to non-Jews even more.

There were good reasons for the restrictions. If one studied kabbalistic texts without an appropriate background, one could easily misinterpret them. An uneducated interpreter would be like a person trying to fill a doctor's prescription without going to pharmaceutical school—even if you could read the writing, you wouldn't understand the code. Nevertheless, restrictions on some teachings were gradually lifted beginning around the twelfth century, and writings of masters of Kabbalah slowly became accessible to the literate Jewish population. At certain periods in the Middle Ages mystical teachings became quite widespread. Admittedly, widespread in medieval and early modern times did not mean what it does today. When books had to be copied painstakingly by hand, they were expensive and scarce. The writings of the mystical masters were more difficult than biblical Hebrew, and some were in Aramaic. Even after the printing revolution of the sixteenth century, the literate Jewish population who could read those languages well was largely limited to males. The subject matter of the mystical writings was highly esoteric, including many intricate interpretations of Hebrew letters and words and their numerical value. Nevertheless, over the centuries, the general concepts of Jewish mysticism gradually became available to those who sought them. The concepts of medieval Kabbalah were familiar to some Christian scholars and mystics. By the time of the Renaissance, those teachings were regarded as part of the general heritage of Western mysticism—some Christians even used them to support Christian doctrine! Kabbalah was also influential in the theosophical movements that emerged in nineteenth-century Europe and North America (and which may have influenced Robert Frost).

In short, Kabbalah in the general sense has not always been limited to Jews, and some of the basic concepts of Kabbalah, such as we will study in this book, can be understood without intensive Jewish education. More intricate teachings are difficult to access from outside of Judaism, and it is probably wise to be suspicious of anyone who says they are teaching deep mysteries to people without background in Judaism. It is also the case that many Jewish scholars still insist on limiting most Jewish teachings, including Kabbalah, to Jews. Some even teach, on the basis of certain mystical traditions, that Jews have a different kind of soul from non-Jews. While I don't subscribe to that viewpoint, I would be misleading my readers if I didn't acknowledge its existence.

Even if one could have defended such a viewpoint in earlier times, I believe that it is no longer relevant. We are part of one world, and we all need to understand each other at the deepest levels. Opening up the insights of our mystics can be a significant step in that direction. By learning something about Kabbalah, you can deepen your insight into the highest teachings of your own tradition, whether you are Jewish or a practitioner of another spiritual approach.

How Kabbalah Can Help You

Kabbalah is exciting because it is so multidimensional. Ever since I began my studies with rabbis from Hasidic traditions that were shaped by Kabbalah, I was fascinated by its conceptual structure. Soon I learned that people in these traditions—primarily Lubavitch and Breslov—were practicing various forms of meditation, which I had thought was only for Hindus and Buddhists. At the same time, I saw an intense devotion to what I had always loved about Judaism, namely, an insistence on applying spirituality to practical action in the world. As I continued my own studies, I discovered teachings about physical health, emotional development, childhood education, and relationships. And in each case I found that when my teachers explained the issue in depth, they were drawing me back to that single focus: Bring God into the world. You and I, each one of us personally, has the job of bringing God in, daily, nightly, weekly, yearly. All of us, collectively, are creating the body of God.[5] The task was awesome and challenging, and at the same time delightful and deeply meaningful.

That task is what I want to introduce to you in the chapters that follow. Kabbalah is a theology that gives rise to a cosmology and an anthropology. As a theology, it presents God as active, in dynamic interaction with the created world. As a cosmology, it shows how the world emanates from God. As an anthropology, it is a map of humanity in our effort to approach the Divine and to bring Divinity into our corner of the cosmos. In Chapter 2, I will offer an overall perspective of this cosmology and anthropology, and introduce the basic vocabulary that we will use. This vocabulary may not be familiar, but will become almost second nature by the time you reach the end of the book. Several alternative translations of the Hebrew terminology are in use; I have adapted them to convey, as best as possible, the various levels of Divine manifestation that Kabbalah is trying to express.

Then, in Part II, we will examine in greater detail the kabbalistic map of Divinity, the way that God expresses Godself in the world. I call this "The Unfolding of Creation." The three chapters in this section look at the kabbalistic "Tree of Life" from the top down. An especially exciting aspect of this side of our study is that kabbalistic teachings seem to run parallel to some of today's most advanced scientific cosmologies, and I will allude to some of these parallels.

Kabbalah involves not only study and contemplation of the Divine, but also self-reflection and prayer to incorporate this knowledge into our own lives. In order to accomplish this, we must review our personal and collective history in light of the Kabbalah's anthropology. I call this process "The Path of Remembering," and describe it in Part III. In these three chapters we will re-examine the kabbalistic map with its segments considered in reverse order from the study of creation. This will enable you to look at your own personal life, from infancy to the present, to see how you have moved on a spiritual path, and where you need to go.

At various points in our discussion, I will point you to Part IV, in which I suggest a variety of practices that will help you contemplate and absorb into yourself the ideas we are considering. I chose these from among many practices I have tried because they are extremely powerful. If you practice them conscientiously, they will eventually transform you.

While we will be focusing on understanding, it is important to remember that Kabbalah is implicitly a path of action, one that enables us to transform the world. The traditional prescription of *mitzvot,* or "commandments," whether for Jews or non-Jews, have been understood in Kabbalah to be expressions of a Divine embodiment in the world.[6] The Hebrew word *mitzvah* is related to an ancient root that means "connection." We connect to our Divine Source by doing certain acts and abstaining from others. It is not that an external force demands obedience from us; rather, we know deeply, inwardly, that something calls us to a higher way of life. As the Torah says, "It is very near to you, in your mouth and in your heart to do it" (Deuteronomy 30:14). Although we will not undertake the study of *mitzvot* in this book, we must remember that through certain kinds of action and non-action, we express the Divine will that wants to be acting through us. Those acts manifest the Divine embodiment in the world, enabling us to join in the Divine delight that comes from uniting act and intent, spiritual consciousness and physical reality.

Studying Kabbalah can profoundly affect your experience of life itself. When you begin to take it seriously, you will find yourself looking beyond appearances, going beneath the surface of things. You will see yourself and others differently; you will discover that you are able to interpret what happens to you on many levels. Ultimately, you will begin to see yourself as a vessel for Divine energy, not only a reflection of the Divine image, but also a co-creator with God. And you will have practical methods to remind you of your own Divine potential.

The path of Kabbalah is a wondrous journey. It's one I've been on for more than twenty years, and I'm still fascinated by each facet of life that is illuminated by integrating this mode of study and practice into my life. This book offers you the first steps, a kind of explorer's guide, to discover various ways this path can enrich your life. I invite you to enter upon the exploration with me—to walk through a door with a great light on the other side. That light is the gift of Kabbalah.

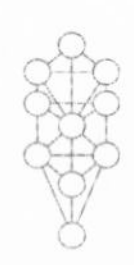

2 Kabbalah and the Image of God

Where Is the Real World?

A great rabbi of one of the European schools of learning said that the greatest secrets of Kabbalah are secrets only until they are known. Once you understand them, they are as simple and open as the palm of your hand.

This is true of the first basic principle of Kabbalah: *The world you see is not the real world.* More precisely, the world *as you see it* is not the real world. Kabbalah does not hold that the world we see is an illusion. However, our sight is limited. This is no secret—it is an obvious truth. We know that the world is much larger and more complex than it appears at first sight. In addition, all the inventions we have created to expand the range of our senses, from microscopes to radar telescopes, are also limited. The world that we can perceive is a mere slice of a multidimensional world beyond our senses and even beyond our mathematics.

In Kabbalah we learn that the world is a partial manifestation of a much larger ultimate reality, which we call "God." The kabbalists called that reality *Ein Sof,* the "There-Is-No-End" or the Infinite.

Perhaps the idea that God is infinite appears to be an obvious truth as well. In the Western world it is customary to refer to God as the Creator, and multitudes believe that the entity we call God created the world, in one way or another. But here we are saying something a little bit different. The *Tanya,* a classic book of modern mysticism, expresses it in this way: The-Blessed-Holy-One is not separate from creation even for a moment.

One metaphor used by some contemporary scientists is that the world is a hologram, or holographic image, of the Divine. A hologram is a picture taken by laser light that has certain peculiar properties. When exposed on the appropriate kind of photographic film, the hologram shows the full picture of the object in three dimensions. If you cut the film in half, each half will also show the full picture of the object in three dimensions, unlike a normal photo, which if cut in half shows only the top half in one slice and the bottom in the other. In a holographic image the only difference from the original will be that the half-picture is slightly less focused than the whole one. If you continue snipping the film into smaller and smaller pieces, each tiny piece will still contain the image of the entire original object. However, the smaller the pieces are, the fuzzier they will be.

In this metaphor, the laser light is God's light projecting an image of God, and the created universe is the picture or hologram representing God. Each entity within the universe is one of the snippets of film. Each contains *all* the elements of Divine manifestation (for which we will learn the terms later on). All of God is included in any part of creation. Thus the holographic image, though separate from the original, contains all the information that the original contained.

However, the fuzziness means it is not always equally easy to see God. God's signature may not be so clear in a piece of gravel from the driveway, for example. We may think it is clearer in a rainbow, or in a sunset over the ocean; and it may radiate more to us through a newborn baby than in our next-door neighbor. Nevertheless, each is its own refraction of Divinity.

The fact that reality is a refraction of God's light provides us with our religious metaphors. A piece of rock may represent one metaphor for God—indeed, religious texts sometimes call God a "Rock"—*Tzur Ha-Olamim,* Rock of Worlds, or Rock of

Ages. We can imagine God's firmness, strength, and immovability as we think of a rock. When we speak of God's purity, however, we might use the image of the fresh innocence of a newborn baby. God offers us metaphors for Divinity in every aspect of our lives. We can see them if we look.

At the same time, we must recognize that our finite minds cannot comprehend in any precise way the relation between God and creation. Perhaps the best we can say is that the universe is God unfolding Him-Her-Itself.[1] All the information we have about the world—the mirror image of yourself in the mirror, the feelings you have as you greet the sun in the morning, the latest scientific theory you read about in the newspaper—are shadows or holographic snapshots or metaphors of God. They make up our universe, which is constantly expanding as we get more pictures.

One of the names for God in the Bible is "I will be what I will be." This implies that God is in the process of manifesting in the world. Still, much of God is concealed and, according to Kabbalah, there are different levels of manifestation and concealment. While every entity in the universe is constructed of the Divine elements, not all of those elements are manifest in every being. Stones do not reveal life force, for example, and plants do not demonstrate mobility. The human being is called in the Bible "the Divine image" because Adam, the first (male/female) human being, and all his/her descendants, revealed the greatest possible range of Divine attributes on earth.

As a result each human being, without exception, carries the stamp of Divinity. With all our differences, even with being split into six billion people incarnated on this planet, each of us is still a complete hologram of God.

The only problem is, like the tiny hologram, each of us is somewhat fuzzy. It's hard to see God's image clearly. Because it is blurry, some of our Divine nature is, as Kabbalah terms it, "concealed." That concealment presents us with our life task: to become "revealed," to be a clear, radiant image of the Divine.

The Turkey Prince

Unfortunately, the world in its present state does not tell us we are Divine or that our life work is to radiate Divinity. Instead, its regular and repeated message is that we are poor, struggling creatures who must compete to survive, and acquire as much as we can. A famous story from a Hasidic master, Rabbi Nachman of Breslov, illustrates this point.

> A royal prince once became mad and thought that he was a turkey. He felt compelled to sit naked under the table, pecking at bones and pieces of bread like a turkey. The royal physicians gave up hope of ever curing him of his madness, and his father, the king, suffered tremendous grief.
>
> A sage then came and said, "I will undertake to cure him."
>
> The sage undressed and sat naked under the table next to the prince, pecking at crumbs and bones. "Who are you?" asked the prince. "What are you doing here?"
>
> "And you?" replied the sage. "What are you doing here?"
>
> "I am a turkey," said the prince.
>
> "I am also a turkey," answered the sage.
>
> They sat together like this for some time, until they became good friends. One day, the sage signaled the king's servants to throw him shirts. He said to the prince, "What makes you think that a turkey can't wear a shirt? You can wear a shirt and still be a turkey." With that, the two of them put on shirts.
>
> After a while, the sage signaled the servants again, and they threw him a pair of pants. Just as before, he said, "What makes you think that you can't be a turkey if you wear pants?"
>
> The sage continued in this manner until they were both completely dressed. Then he signaled again, and they were given regular food from the table. Again the sage said, "What makes you think that you will stop being a turkey if you eat good food? You can eat whatever you want and still be a turkey!" They both ate the food.

> Finally the sage said, "What makes you think that a turkey has to sit under the table? Even a turkey can sit at the table."
>
> The sage continued in this manner until the prince was completely cured.[2]

The turkey prince is a metaphor for each of our lives. You can probably think of many times when you realized you were so narrowly focused on getting what you wanted that you missed seeing something beautiful or appreciating someone in your life. This narrowmindedness is part of the human condition. We spend most of our time going after things that we think will satisfy us, but we don't even notice the great palace of our beautiful planet, or the banquet table of gifts set before us. We do not know that we are truly royalty, made in the Divine image. We are governed by our lower appetites—what Kabbalah calls our animal souls—and cannot see beyond our immediate needs and pleasures.

Collectively, we are completely immersed in a narrow version of reality. Even if we were able to peek out above the tablecloth, we would probably only see the beautiful silver and crystal on the table. A few of us might be so tuned in that we could hear the conversations going on among the nobility. A very tiny group might be able to gaze around and see the intricate designs of the tapestries or glimpse the architecture of the palace beyond. But almost all of us would miss the most beautiful sight of all—the radiance of the loving face that belongs to the King, the owner of the palace, court, and banquet.

In reality, the world is much grander than we imagine; our perspective can be so much broader. Also our potential for spiritual bliss is much greater than anything we can imagine on the physical plane. But we can be coaxed into seeing that grander perspective only a little bit at a time, like the prince putting on the royal garments one by one. Kabbalah, too, asks us to proceed step by step, trying on each garment and getting used to it. The wise man waved no magic wand, nor did he teach the prince to chant mystical words to be free from his affliction. Patiently, he helped him work his way into it, until he was cured of his narrow delusions.

And, the prince did not have to give up what he wanted to be. He could still be a turkey as long as he wanted. Each of us has our own nature, which will not be overruled but rather transformed. From a childhood version of who we want to be—an astronaut, a police officer, a doctor, or a turkey—we build our ideals. From the apparent accidents of our birth, our family, our traumas and successes, our unique form emerges, yearning to be filled with higher purpose. The idiosyncrasies that mark our specialness, even the mysterious aspects of ourselves will all come to fruition, in ways we cannot imagine, in our ultimate spiritual reality.

Revealing Divine Light

The prince (or princess) is the Divine image within each of us. The King, of course, is God. The effort to get up from under the table is our striving toward the essential Godliness, the uniqueness of our God-given soul, that each of us deeply desires to manifest. The scriptures say, "Be holy as I am holy" (Leviticus 11:44). This is similar to the message of many traditions, that the goal of the human being is to imitate God, or be like God (or Christ, or Buddha, or another near-divine model).

The biblical creation story tells us that we started out being Godlike; human beings were made "in the image of God." But Adam and Chava (Eve) let themselves be convinced that they were not good enough. The story of the serpent in the Garden tells us that they were unwilling to believe that everything was complete and good just as it was. He persuaded them that an external act, eating the fruit of the forbidden tree, would make them more like God. In short, doubt and confusion came into human existence. Ever after, we have been trying to make ourselves into something other than who we are.

In a sense, Adam and Chava were too uncertain, too fragile to hold the Divine glory. That sense of fragility echoes a kabbalistic explanation of the creation story. According to the master kabbalist of sixteenth-century Safed, Rabbi Isaac Luria (1520–1572), the Divine Light gave form to the world by emanating ten vessels, or *sefirot* (pronounced *suh-fee-ROTE*), and then pouring light into them. But the original light was too powerful and it shattered the vessels, scattering shards of light throughout the universe. Those shards make up our present world. Each shard is now covered with a *klipah,* or shell, and the human task is to crack open the shell to reveal the light. The shell is the facade, the light inside is true being. On the human level, the shell is our persona or ego, the front we show to the world. The light inside is our soul, our unique refraction of the Divine image.

The task—the *tikkun,* or "correction," of the original error of Adam and Chava—is to separate the good and evil that have been mixed in the world. This separation happens every time we make a choice for the good. If human beings do this consistently, the evil in the world will disappear, because it exists only so long as humans nourish it with their energy.[3]

Kabbalah adds another dimension to this teaching. It is not just a matter of making a series of good choices, as though we have a checklist in front of us through our lives. This would be rather disheartening, since our choices are so numerous that we could hardly be confident of making them all correctly. Rather, we have the possibility of re-creating ourselves as beings that shine with an inner light. We can become more and more in tune with our Divine Source so that our daily choices come from the pure core of our being. For Judaism teaches that every soul is pure in essence; there is no incorrigible flaw in any soul.

We can imagine each human as a beautiful old lamp into which a rich, shining oil is poured, so it looks like a rainbow filling the vessel. But the lantern is crusted over and nearly full of a coarse brown sediment. Once the oil is inside, you cannot see it at all because of the dark residue. If you start spooning out the

God's light has no limits; the limitation lies only in the recipient, whose "windows" are darkened by his own baseness.
—Rabbi Eliyahu Dessler[4]

sediment and cleaning the inner surface, you will begin to see the radiant oil even though sediment remains on the bottom. The more you spoon out and clear away, the more of the liquid you will be able to see. This is a gradual process of refinement that suggests a way to do spiritual work. When we discover something is blocking our manifestation of the Divine image, we clear it out, and more of our true inner light can shine.

Yet even as we contemplate this possibility of refining ourselves, we ask whether it is possible. Can we really overturn our turkey habits and become royalty, filled with Divine purpose? Society often reinforces our inner suspicion that only a rare individual can be Godfilled, by sanctifying certain types of people and ignoring others. Please erase from your inner tapes the belief that only certain people can achieve closeness to God or unification with their true Divine image. It is completely possible that an ordinary person can do this. Kabbalah, like all of Jewish tradition, has always been rooted in daily life. We need only to fill our own life with the light of goodness. Just as a shoe is formed on a last, we need only follow the shape of our own soul. Remember: Your coming into the world is itself a work of courage. As Frost wrote, if we could see life from a heavenly perspective, we would realize that those who come to earth are heroes:

> The tale of earth's unhonored things
> Sounds nobler there than 'neath the sun;
> And the mind whirls and the heart sings,
> And a shout greets the daring one.[5]

Fortunately, we have help along the journey. We have a map that will guide us through the territory of the soul, the map that has been called the "Tree of Life."

Mapping the Divine Energies

The ordinary world is really only the lowest level—"under the table"—of a great cosmic palace. Similarly, human beings are not simply what we appear to be. We are not equivalent to our physical bodies, for example. The bodies we experience are dense manifestations of a deeper structure known as the Tree of Life or Tree of the *Sefirot*. *Sefirot,* as we saw above, is the term for the original vessels into which Divine light was poured. Although those original vessels were shattered, their form was reconstructed and became the basic template for the next creation that ensued. *Sefirot* in most kabbalistic discussions alludes to centers of radiant Divine energy. They correspond to what are often called "attributes" of God. They are the ways in which God has chosen to manifest Divinity in the world, but they are very much hidden.

Thus, if we speak of a *sefirah* (singular form) of, for example, *Tiferet*-Splendor, we mean that God manifests in the world through what we perceive as splendor, which we often associate with extraordinary beauty or harmony. The word "splendor" attempts to grasp something of that particular mode of God's self-revelation. But we should not be too attached to the precise wording; the words merely point in the direction of something that must be discovered in deeper investigation.

The difficulty of capturing God's manifestation in words tells us that the *sefirot* also represent levels of concealment. Kabbalah teaches that the Divine Light is so intense that if it were presented to us directly, we could not see it at all—in fact, we could not exist. As we saw, in a previous creation the vessels were shattered by the intensity of pure Divine Light. Similarly, the biblical tradition records God telling Moses, "No one can see My Face and live" (Exodus 33:20).

Nevertheless, the mystics have helped us by articulating some of the dimensions of this concealment. The received tradition of Kabbalah speaks of four "Worlds," from the first emanation of the Divine Light down to the physical world in which we live. Briefly, they are called *Atzilut,* or Emanation (from God); *Beriah,* or Creation; *Yetzirah,* or Formation; and *Asiyah,* or Action. Each of those worlds corresponds to a letter of God's holy four-letter name. Each world has levels within it: Each has ten *sefirot,* and each of those *sefirot* has ten levels within it. The lowest energy level of one world becomes the highest energy level of the next.[6] Each world, and each level within the worlds, is a veil that masks Divinity. Probably a true map of the revelation of Divine energies, if one could be drawn, would be as complicated as the descriptions of DNA structures used in biology. But it is not necessary to be able to know all the intricacies in order to benefit from the perspective of Kabbalah, just as one need not understand physics to benefit from electricity.

We will use a simple model of ten basic *sefirot.* The body is one of the veils that these Divine qualities wear, and the *sefirot* are often portrayed as arrayed along the shape of a human body.

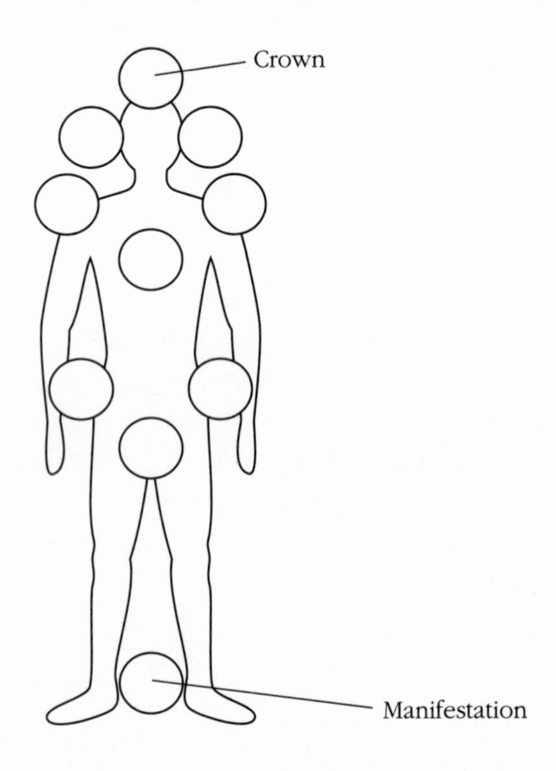

On this model, the level closest to the Divine is at the top, portrayed above the head (like the crown chakra described in the teachings of yoga). The level that manifests in the physical world is represented as at the feet.

Another mode of picturing the *sefirot*—used more in medieval times than in recent centuries—is a set of concentric circles. In this model, the level closest to the Divine is the central circle, and its light radiates through all the levels to the outermost circle, which is the physical world in which we live and act.

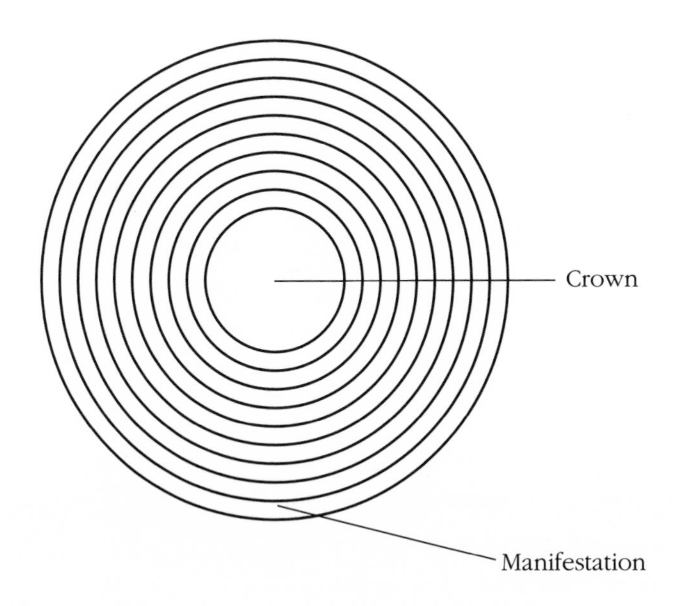

The first model is the one most commonly used today, and it is the one we will adopt in this book. It can be most easily understood if we organize the ten *sefirot* into three triangles. The diagram on the following page shows the traditional connections among the *sefirot,* with the triangular relationships highlighted in bold. You will see this diagram, and segments of it, frequently throughout the book. Seen as a tree, the roots are in heaven, and the flowers and fruit are arrayed along the branches below.

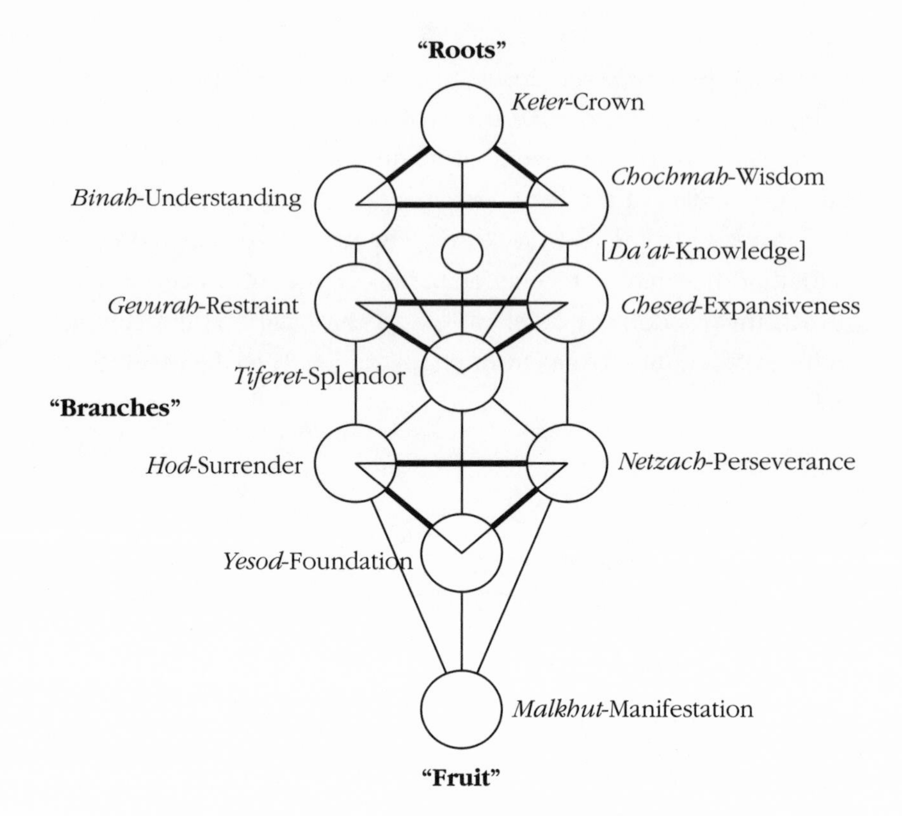

We will discuss the entire map from two different perspectives. The first perspective is from the top down: how the Divine energies transform and manifest themselves proceeding from God's emanation of Divine Light to the world as we know it. I am calling this perspective the "Unfolding of Creation." In the second half of this book, I will describe the *sefirot* as also the "Path of Remembering." This approach will view the *sefirot* as a multiplicity of voices. This mode of understanding will take us on a more circuitous route, beginning at the bottom of the diagram and moving up the tree in terms of stages of development, but also spiraling through the *sefirot* to indicate their interrelationships. Ultimately, this process will bring us into the depths of our hearts, where we unify our human selves with the Divine. Hopefully, moving along the paths of the Tree in both these ways will make it easier for you to understand how the *sefirot* apply to different areas of your life.

Now it is time to add the names of the *sefirot*. You will probably want to memorize and review them often, as they are part of the basic vocabulary of Kabbalah. Then we will go to the beginning—the Head—to start our course through the Divine creative process. In the meantime, you may want to begin doing a meditation that will help you get a feeling for the various levels of the *sefirot*. Go to the Meditative Visualizations in Part IV and do the meditation entitled "The House of the Worlds" (p. 180).

THE TEN SEFIROT

HEBREW	ENGLISH	POSITION ON BODY	MEANING
Keter	Crown	crown of head	Divine spark; will; soul
Chochmah	Wisdom	right temple	first emanation of Light; spark of inspiration; seed of thought
Binah	Understanding	left temple	nourishing the spark into a flame, the seed into an organism
[Da'at]*	Knowledge	brain stem and spinal cord	"Eleventh *sefirah*"—unifying and connecting knowledge
Chesed	Expansiveness	right shoulder and arm	lovingkindness; Divine grace and universal support
Gevurah	Restraint	left shoulder and arm	discipline; limitation; strength of character
Tiferet	Splendor	heart and solar plexus	harmonic balance of tendencies; the "bolt" that unites and binds all the *sefirot*
Netzach	Perseverance	right hip and leg	energetic initiative; stamina

(continued next page)

THE TEN SEFIROT—*continued*

HEBREW	ENGLISH	POSITION ON BODY	MEANING
Hod	Surrender	left hip and leg	acceptance; yielding
Yesod	Foundation	womb and genitals	processing and transmitting energies of the preceding *sefirot*
Malkhut	Manifestation	feet and lips (as organ of speech to outside world)	"Kingship," *Shekhinah;* the final impression made on the physical world; Divine presence immanent in the world

**Da'at* is included in many kabbalistic schemas as an alternate to *Keter,* because *Keter* is regarded as beyond description. See pp. 47–49.

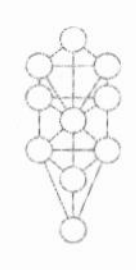

PART II

THE UNFOLDING OF CREATION

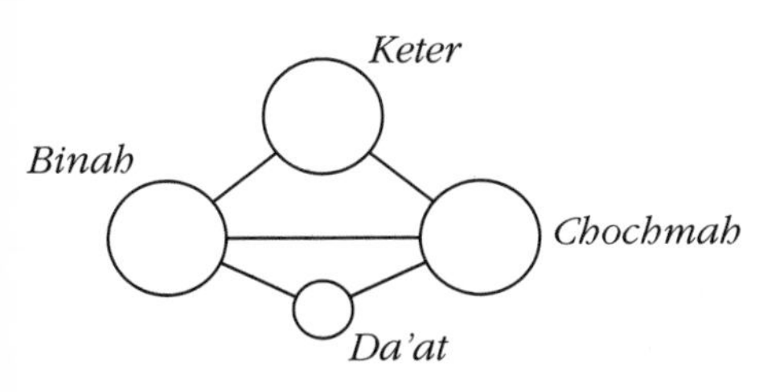

3 Divine Mind

With wisdom God founded the earth,
with understanding God established the heavens
and with God's knowledge the depths are broken up.
—PROVERBS 3:19–20

The Divine Sea of Consciousness

Kabbalah teaches that the universe begins with a thought of God—or rather, an arising of will, something that comes even before a thought. We might imagine this as a flicker of desire that arose in the Infinite Allness-Nothingness, what the mystics call *Ein Sof,* the Endless. Scientists have described the beginning as a wave or ripple in an infinite sea of energy, intensifying to become that unimaginably hot point from which the universe was born. That first ripple was will, the desire to create. It is called *Keter*-Crown.

Every time that will rippled through the emerging cosmos, each wave was a new occurrence of potential, which is called *Chochmah*-Wisdom. As waves interacted and created resonances with each other, patterns emerged. These patterns are known as *Binah*-Understanding. We call all these occurrences "God's thoughts." But, according to the Bible, "My thoughts are not your thoughts, says God" (Isaiah 55:8). The form that the Infinite Light takes is not that of ordinary mental operations such as reasoning and calculating. The mind of God—God's will and wisdom, as the mystics often refer to it—is the power behind each new burst of creativity in the universe. Our very words—will, thought, mind—are far too small for us to imagine the entity behind the creation of an entire universe, let alone many universes, as Kabbalah suggests.

The levels we are trying to describe are represented in the system of Kabbalah as *sefirot* of the head. The three aspects of universal mind are portrayed in traditional kabbalistic diagrams as *sefirot* at the crown and the right and left temples. The crown, in Hebrew *keter,* is physically the fontanel, the opening in a newborn baby's skull due to the fact that its bones have not completely grown together. We come to earth still open to our heavenly connection. The right and left temples hint at the other two *sefirot* of the head, *Chochmah*-Wisdom and *Binah*-Understanding. A fourth quasi-*sefirah* of the head known as *Da'at*-Knowledge also appears in modern mysticism.

Kabbalah reminds us that these three (or four) energies are so intimately interrelated that they are really one. "Mind" truly refers to the unifying aspect of consciousness. The greatest affirmation in Judaism is the statement, *Shema Yisrael Adonai Elohienu, Adonai Echad*—Hear, O Israel! The Lord is our God, the Lord is One! Rabbi Abraham Isaac Kook, chief rabbi of Palestine from 1920 until his death in 1935, wrote that this sentence contains the most powerful thought a person can think. If we want to relate to the mind of God, our first act must be to affirm God's unity—that God is one and the only One, the Source of all unity:

> The affirmation of the unity of God aspires to reveal the unity in the world, in man, among nations, and in the entire content of existence. . . . This is the most august thought among the great thoughts that man's intellectual capacity can conceive. It is revealed to him through his receptivity to spiritual illumination. It may take him to the height of a revelation of the Divine, by the way of reason, the knowledge called "face to face."[1]

Our yearnings toward universality, our intuition that we are all one, our knowledge that God is One—all are messages from the great mind. As the famous physicist David Bohm wrote, "The universe is one seamless, unbroken whole."[2]

The term for "head" in Hebrew, *rosh,* has the same root as the term "beginning." These *sefirot* of the head connect to and undergird all creative developments in the entire universe, reaching down to all conscious mental activity on this planet. But, like the bulk of an iceberg, their activity is beyond our conscious awareness. The activity of the mind of God is not unconscious in the sense of a lower-level, physical activity, but rather "transconscious," going beyond the awareness of our normal waking state. These *sefirot* of the head are called "the hidden things" because they are completely invisible until they express themselves at a more accessible level.[3] As we try to explicate and make them "visible" in the next few sections, remember that we are always straining to express the inexpressible, using the best metaphors we can find.

The Beginnings of Desire: *Keter*-Crown

The realm or power that brings forth the universe . . . is not simply located there at that point of time [in the beginning], but is rather a condition of every moment of the universe, past, present, and to come.

—Brian Swimme and Thomas Berry

The highest *sefirah* on the Tree of Life is known as *Keter*-Crown, or will. The Hebrew term for will, *ratzon,* also means desire. The first thing that had to happen for a universe to appear is that it had to be willed. Or, a desire arose. In retrospect, we say that God wanted to create a world. But already the words define what was as yet undefined—most simply, a will that resulted in some change from what was. Will is the origin of creativity.

The metaphor of crown tells us something else about will. We find that not only in Judaism but also in Hinduism's yogic tradition the highest energy point of a person is called crown—the crown chakra. A crown is a physical metaphor or symbol for a higher energy that, for people who can perceive it, hovers above the head. In medieval paintings it was represented as a halo. Kings, priests, and other officials were supposed to have this energy, and perhaps began wearing gold crowns studded with jewels to make sure that their subjects recognized that their authority derived from a "higher power"—whether they deserved it or not. On a spiritual level, the energy above the head is a kind of light that emanates from the soul.

The most advanced theories in biology suggest that some conceptual construct, similar to the idea of a crown, is necessary to explain the amazing capacity of organisms to grow in a certain direction and regenerate themselves. There seems to be something—some biologists call it a "morphogenetic field"—that organizes the action and direction of an organism.[4] The Jewish mystics say that everything, even a blade of grass, has an angel that says to it, "Grow! Grow!" Similarly, we often speak of the "will to live" as a powerful force in life. In Kabbalah, this power of will is an energy that points to a goal.

Keter is expressed in a particular name of God found in the Bible, the name revealed to Moses at the burning bush: *Ehyeh asher Ehyeh,* "I will be what I will be." This means that because everything is the unfolding of the Divine will to "be," all of creation is connected to God's ultimate Oneness. Biologically, the human species came from one genetic source; on a spiritual level, humanity also has only one source. In Kabbalah, this is referred to as the Primordial Human (*Adam Kadmon* in Hebrew). This Adam was, as we saw earlier, made precisely "in the image of God." Ancient sources portray *Adam Kadmon* as a gigantic person shining with light who could see from one end of the world to the other. Every human being that exists or has ever existed is connected to that original Adam; collectively we are that Adam. On the personal level, Judaism teaches that the soul is completely pure because of its connection to the Divine essence represented in the Crown. No matter what happens while the soul is in a physical incarnation on earth, nothing can harm the soul or disrupt its connection to God. Moreover, our soul is always trying to express its true essence through our lives.

Because we are given free will, we have the possibility of tuning out, so to speak, from our soul connection. Over time, blockages can develop, a kind of hardening of the spiritual arteries, in the mental, emotional, and physical channels through which the soul is trying to express itself. But the soul remains—disappointed perhaps, in not being able to do its work completely, but without changing its unique essence. This means that it is always possible for a person to return to the Source, to return to God, for there is an ultimate Divine anchor in the soul of each one of us. Think of times when you have awakened to life again, when you had a renewed sense of wonder at the possibilities open to you. This absolute ability to return—in Hebrew *teshuva*—is built into the structure of the universe itself. This is one of the meanings of ultimate Oneness.

Wisdom and Wildness: *Chochmah*-Wisdom

For the Nothingness (Ayin) *that is God's blessed* Chochmah
is the source of life, welfare, and delight.
—Rabbi Schneur Zalman of Liadi[5]

Energy from the Crown emanates forth a "supernal luminescence" that is called *Chochmah*-Wisdom.[6] We cannot say what direction it goes, because it is before direction and indeed generates the possibility of direction itself. It is an experiment, an exploration, the emergence of the possibility of "something" even though it is "nothing" yet. This *sefirah* is the channel for creative force in the entire cosmos. In the natural world, the result is amazing and totally unpredictable diversity. In the human world, the results are inspiration and revelation, including what is called "illumination" in mysticism. These experiences are the foundations of all the world's religious traditions and the origin of multitudes of great creative endeavors.

On the cosmic level, we know now that the universe cannot be accidental, the result of random collisions of atoms.[7] There has to be some source of form or organization—what we would colloquially call "purpose"—in the universe as we know it. If the universe is in some sense aimed at, *Chochmah*-Wisdom is the bow that shoots the arrow toward its target. We cannot see this bow, just as we cannot see the elementary particles hypothesized by physicists. But just as scientists track the movements of particles with sophisticated instruments and find their imprints scattered on a screen, so we infer the *sefirah* of *Chochmah* from its results—creativity and diversity.

The mystics turned to a passage from the biblical Book of Proverbs to extol *Chochmah*'s role in creation, in a way that expresses the joy of this Divine energy:

> The Lord created me the beginning of his works,
> Before all else that he made, long ago . . .
> When there was yet no ocean I was born, . . .
> When he set the heavens in their place I was there . . .
> And knit together earth's foundations.
> Then I was at his side each day, his darling and delight,
> Playing in his presence continually,
> Playing on the earth, when he had finished it,
> While my delight was in humankind. (Proverbs 8:22–31)

This kind of wisdom is not expressed directly in words—what could express the "playing" of God? We can take a hint from Brian Swimme's description of the wildness in natural evolution. Speaking of the conscious choice of animals as they moved into new territory, he writes:

> Their movement into their future evolution began with commitment to a vision—a vision strongly felt but seen as

> if fleetingly and in darkness. Perhaps it was just the sheer thrill of the gallop that captivated the first horse's consciousness and convinced it to make that species-determining decision: "We will run, come what may." No vision of itself in the future, and yet the future pressed into its experience of the moment: "Here is a way to live. Here is a path worth risking everything for."[8]

The Divine wisdom, called by kabbalists *Atzilut,* or the world of Emanation, comes from a place beyond stasis and stability, an act "worth risking everything for." With such an act, God created the universe.

Chochmah is often referred to as being like a flash of lightning, probably because of its extraordinary brilliance and ability to illuminate everything simultaneously. The phrase "flash of inspiration" carries some of the same meaning.[9] The thunderbolt appears as a symbol in many cultures, often expressing the impact of the Divine world on the human, as in the thunderbolts of Zeus. The same image appears in Tibetan Buddhist mysticism as the *vajra* or diamond, which stands for a profound level of illumination. In its more archaic formulation the *vajra* symbol was also a lightning bolt.

Lightning is one of the experiences recorded of the ancient Israelites at Mount Sinai, the core revelation of Judaism. The accounts of that experience suggest profound levels of transformation—for example, the Torah comments that they "saw the voices." This statement hints at a much larger experience than simply hearing words spoken, as Rabbi Schneur Zalman of Liadi explains:

> "It was *shown,*" actually with physical vision, as it is written, "And all the people saw the voices" (Exodus 20:15)—"they *saw* what is [normally] heard." And the Rabbis of blessed memory explained, "They looked eastward and heard the speech issuing forth, 'I am,' etc., and so toward

> the four points of the compass, and upward and downward," as is explained . . . that "There was no place from which God did not speak to them. . . ." Therefore the Israelites repeatedly fainted out of existence, as the Rabbis taught, "At each utterance their soul took flight, . . . but the Blessed-Holy-One restored it to them with the dew with which He will revive the dead."[10]

These descriptions allude to time/space dissolution, synesthesia (crossover of types of sensory perception) and altered states of consciousness. Similar experiences of illumination and insight in many mystical traditions are unusually intense in their clarity and bodily effects, and potentially transformative in their results.

Kabbalists say that the *sefirah* of *Chochmah*-Wisdom manifests in the first word of the Ten Commandments: *Anochi,* meaning "I Am." Absolute Oneness expresses itself as "I," what we usually call a personal deity, that is, the Divine expressing itself in the metaphor of "person." Divinity that was beyond all categories willingly enters a category that we can understand, an entity that wills and acts: "I am the Lord your God who took you out of Egypt." This is the most concrete expression of the act worth risking everything for—to choose human beings to join God in creating a better world.

The creative powers of this *sefirah* include the creation of the roots of entities called "souls."[11] Just as one root of a plant can diversify above the surface of the ground into many stems, so there are soul roots in *Chochmah* that later diversify into many individual souls. Thus Rabbi Aryeh Kaplan comments, on the famous rabbinic saying "Who is wise? He who learns from every man" (Avot 4.1): "It is on the level of Wisdom that all men are one."[12] Significantly, this idea broadens our concept of soul. A soul is not limited to being a personal essence, but also, on a deeper and more hidden level, is connected to other souls across time and space. Like stars and constellations and galaxies, some souls seem to be closer than others, forming systems or clusters. Their original light is *Keter*-Crown; the different frequencies beginning to emerge come from *Chochmah*. Whether we are aware of it or not, *Chochmah* means that each of us is an audacious experiment of God. Like the first shoot that ever sprouted from the earth, like the first horse about to gallop, we are each a new creation.

Like light streaming from its source, new possibilities emanate from the Divine all the time. We are unaware of most of them. The bow shoots forth energy at every moment, a ripple or vibration arising out of the darkness, to which creation listens. Recent scientists describe this listening even in the emergence of the universe as we know it:

> Hydrogen listens to voices of the galaxy and responds by creating stars. . . . "Listening" then refers to that quantum sensitivity within the cloud that enables it to initiate an entirely new adventure within the galaxy . . . The vibrations and fluctuations in the universe are the music that drew forth the galaxies and stars and their powers of weaving elements into life.[13]

Rabbi Abraham Isaac Kook wrote of the human spirit in similar words:

> Waves from the higher realm act on our souls ceaselessly. The stirrings of our inner spiritual sensibilities are the result of the sounds released by the violin of our souls, as it listens to the echo of the sound emanating from the Divine realm.[14]

Have you experienced moments when you felt your soul was stirred, that perhaps there was a purpose in life waiting for you? Such moments are real. They are the call from your essential nature.

The next step in the unfolding is that the streams of light and ripples of sound from *Chochmah* embed themselves in the sea of consciousness called *Binah*.

Pattern and Imagination: *Binah*-Understanding

In the beginning of the King's authority
The Lamp of Darkness
Engraved a hollow in the Supernal Luminescence.
—THE *ZOHAR*[15]

If *Chochmah*-Wisdom is waves of energy, *Binah*-Understanding is form.[16] At the level of Divinity, God "understands" and upholds the forms that creation can take. From the perspective of our world, *Binah,* like *Chochmah,* is still only potential—indeed, Rabbi Nachman of Breslov called this *sefirah* the World to Come. This means that it contains Divine Light and supreme knowledge, which cannot be revealed completely now, but only in a future state.[17] Still, *Binah* has more structure and is closer to our world than *Chochmah*. Symbolically, *Binah* represents the mother-matrix; in more modern terms, *Binah* is the Divine template or pattern of existence.

The description of *Binah* as *Ima* or Mother and *Chochmah* as *Abba,* Father, comes from ancient teachings and is very prominent in the *Zohar.* We must recognize that at the level of the upper *sefirot* there is really no gender, for all such distinctions belong to the lower world of duality. But as metaphors, father and mother express a fundamental aspect of the creative process in terms that we can immediately grasp. Father brings forth a seed, which cannot grow on its own; it needs the nourishment of the mother's womb. "The *potentia* of the world (the seed of *Chochmah*) is externalized and individuated in the womb of *Binah* but remains concealed like a foetus. Therefore *Binah* is called the concealed world."[18] Many seeds come forth, but only a few come to fruition.

Binah-Understanding as Mother is reminiscent of the Great Mother of archetypal mythology and psychology, the matrix out of which differences and relationships come forth. The kabbalists described her as the "Vacated Space," the hollow carved out of Infinity so that a finite universe could exist.[19] In that sense, *Binah* represents the beginning of separation, the world created through *tzimtzum,* Divine contraction. Still, at her level differences do not create opposition but only harmony. As the mystics put it, "Lovingkindness alone manifests" in the upper three *sefirot,* and, quoting the Book of Psalms, "The world is built [the Hebrew word for "build" is related to *binah*] on lovingkindness" (89:3).[20] *Binah* is like a sea of Divine consciousness in which our personal minds swim.

Because the upper *sefirot* are deeply united, the triangle shape in which the first three *sefirot* are traditionally represented may be somewhat misleading. It suggests that the Father and Mother are dualistic opposites, set across from one another as the base of a triangle. We can also see their relationships in the following form, recalling a seed in the womb:

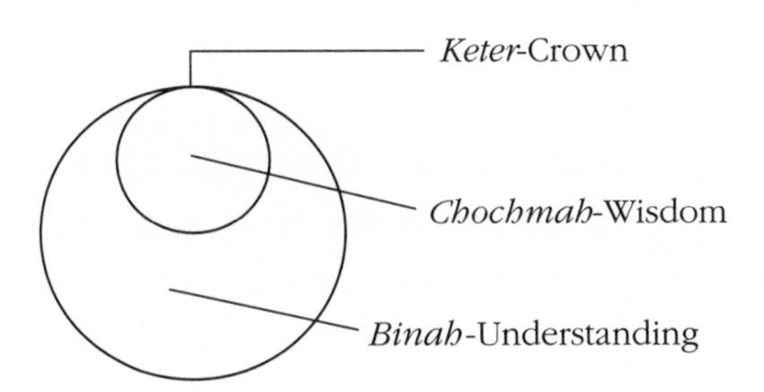

Another approach is suggested by the way the kabbalists placed these three energies in the human body. *Keter*-Crown is at the fontanel, *Chochmah* is in the space between the skull and the membrane of the brain, and *Binah* is connected to both the center of the brain and to the right side of the heart.

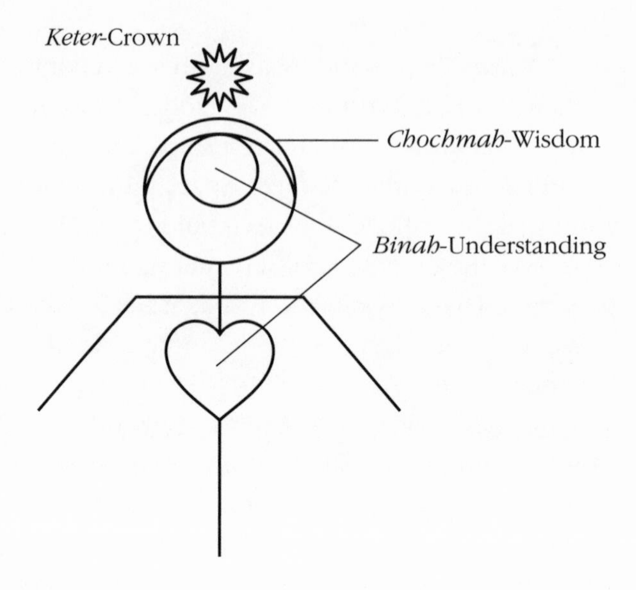

How does *Binah* operate? As Divine/soul energy moves from *Chochmah* to *Binah,* it enters into the mother-matrix. While this is still a hidden world, it nevertheless gives a certain level of formation and expression to the abstract vibrations of *Chochmah*. Some force draws sparks of energy toward one another so that they bond and become what we might be able to recognize as thoughts, or even more fundamentally, images or metaphors.[21] Like gravity in the physical cosmos, *Binah* makes it possible for ideas and patterns to have stability.

Since *Binah* is in the center of the brain, it is probably related to what some mystics have called the "third eye." Telepathic events, dreams, and prophecies emerge from this overarching consciousness. *Binah*-Understanding represents information—in-FORM-ation—that belongs to anyone. My ten-year-old daughter once told me, quoting a teaching from her *rebbe,* "When you have an idea, remember that it is just part of what's floating around out there, and you happened to be the one to pluck it out of the air." Of course, it is quite possible that some people are more attuned to the various forms of inspiration. For example, the great Russian composer Tchaikovsky experienced his creativity as being like that of the sudden and energetic growth of a plant:

> Generally speaking, the germ of a future composition comes suddenly and unexpectedly. . . . It takes root with extraordinary force and rapidity, shoots up through the earth, puts forth branches and leaves, and finally blossoms. . . . I forget everything and behave like a mad man; everything within me starts pulsing and quivering; hardly have I begun the sketch, ere one thought follows another.[22]

The "extraordinary force" of the experience is like *Chochmah,* while the branches, leaves, and blossoms are images of *Binah.*

More commonly, information coming from *Binah* is encoded in images, as in dreams. As we decode it by remembering dream symbols, we bring it down to the level of ordinary intellect, then into the emotional realm by our feelings about it, and finally into the realm of action by telling the dream's story. Kabbalah expresses this multileveled processing of information by connecting *Binah* directly with certain *sefirot. Binah* is connected to *Tiferet*-Splendor and the feeling of deep joy because the Talmud says, quoting a verse from Psalms, "the heart *understands* [Hebrew *binah*]."[23] *Binah* also has an intimate connection with the tenth *sefirah, Malkhut*-Manifestation, for one is "mother" and the other is "daughter."[24] In other words, the world of action is informed by *Binah.*

This multileveled characteristic of *Binah* suggests that it pervades many aspects of our unconscious as well as our conscious selves. Most fundamentally, it provides the templates to which all the other *sefirot* relate. As we indicated when discussing *Chochmah,* religions are usually rooted in fundamental revelations from some spiritual source that provides a unique way of accessing higher realms. The "flash" or seed of the revelation is *Chochmah,* and its elaboration into a basic pattern is *Binah.* In Judaism, with the revelation known as the giving of the Torah, we saw that the experience of *Chochmah* is embedded in the word *Anochi.* The form-creating qualities of *Binah* are represented in the Ten Commandments—ten principles that became a template for all of Jewish life for millennia to come. In other ways, the revelation of the Koran in Islam, the enlightenment of the Buddha, and the crucifixion of Jesus in Christianity formed a basic pattern for each religion.

To say this *sefirah* provides for the formation of a template or matrix means that it yields a pattern that can be filled with different contents. In other words, *Binah* tells us that, prior to our ordinary thinking, there exists a pattern that governs our thinking. Every society imprints its unconscious patterns on its members through language and customary behavior. Every religious and spiritual tradition seeks to imprint a different and higher template than society's, urging us to live on another level. We spoke of the will of the soul, coming from *Keter,* as an angel that says to the blade of grass, "Grow!" Here, on a more concrete level, the template of a tradition is like an angelic model that offers a focus for aspiration: "Grow toward this ideal!"

The idea of a template is configured physically in a temple. Architecturally, a physical temple creates a sacred space that conveys the underlying patterns of a tradition. The original temple of Judaism was a portable sanctuary or tabernacle *(mishkan),* which incorporated cosmic symbolism in its components and structures.[25] In a parallel fashion, the medieval cathedral, with its great sculptural programs and stained glass, told the stories that informed European Christianity's basic template. In Tibetan Buddhism, monks create temporary sand paintings that portray the palaces of Buddhas and Bodhisattvas through an exercise that is both meditative and aesthetic.

People on spiritual journeys often encounter temples, palaces, or great places of learning in other dimensions. One of my teachers frequently visits in her dreams a "Universe-City," where spiritual teachings are disseminated. Other dreamers I have known find themselves in retreat centers or ancient temples with similar functions. These are usually revelations of *Binah*-Understanding. Here is a remarkable excerpt from an account of a near-death experience, where the soul of the dying person was brought by a Being of Light to a place of spiritual teaching:

> Like wingless birds, we swept into a city of cathedrals. These cathedrals were made entirely of a crystalline substance that glowed with a light that shone powerfully from within. We stood before one. . . . It had spires as high and pointed as those of the great cathedrals of France, and walls as massive and powerful as those of the Mormon Tabernacle in Salt Lake City. The walls were made of large glass bricks that glowed from within. These structures were not related to a specific religion of any kind. They were a monument to the glory of God.
>
> I was awestruck. This place had a power that seemed to pulsate through the air. I knew that I was in a place of learning. . . . We moved forward, up a splendid walk and through glowing portals of crystal.
>
> . . . Rows of benches were lined up across the room, and that radiant light made everything glow and feel like love. . . . There was no one to be seen, yet I had a strong feeling that the benches were filled with people just like me. . . .
>
> The place reminded me of a magnificent lecture hall. The benches were positioned in such a way that whoever was sitting on them would face a long podium that glowed like white quartz. The wall behind this podium was a spectacular carousel of colors, ranging from pastels to bright neons. Its beauty was hypnotic. I watched the colors blend and merge, surging and pulsing the way the ocean does when you are far out at sea and look into its depths.[26]

This extraordinarily vivid description is a *Binah* experience because it portrays architectural pattern suggesting a temple/template, together with an emphasis on learning.

The method by which *Binah* enters human consciousness is what we call "contemplation"—literally, con-template-ing. Most traditions have some form of contemplative meditation that helps a disciple internalize the template of the tradition. Christian mystics meditated on the sufferings of Christ, and Buddhists meditated on a mental image of a decomposing body. Psalms or hymns, chants or dances entrain images and metaphors with rhythm and melody to help practitioners internalize the basic elements of faith. The point of all such meditations was, and is, to remake the mind—and ultimately the body—as the "temple of the soul," meaning, in the image of the religious ideal.

Judaism has several interrelated templates, all expressing the will of God *(Keter)*. First is the Ten Commandments, whose words brought God's will down to earth in discursive form. The remainder of the Torah, including Judaism's "Oral Torah" (discussions of laws, at first transmitted orally but later written down), amplifies and clarifies the ten basic principles. Another template is the image of the *mishkan* or sanctuary, which was revealed to Moses in a vision. It expressed the Divine will to manifest on earth, as "God's house." Being in God's house became an important metaphor for connection to God: "Happy are those who sit in Your house!" (Psalm 145); "Only one thing I seek: to stay in the House of the Lord all the days of my life" (Psalm 27). Yet another version of the template is the Tree of Life that emerged in kabbalistic thought, unfolding in another way the fundamental understanding that God wants to be manifest in this world: *Keter*-Crown seeks to evolve into *Malkhut*-Manifestation.

All these images involve mind, imagination, and heart engaged with the basic template, which is intended to be internalized in each individual's body, mind, and soul. The template of *Binah* seeks to unfold itself on all levels.[27] From the perspective of Kabbalah, *the entire organism suffers when it has no deeper template*. Thus the *sefirah* of *Binah* is one of the keys to our crucial task as human beings: to restore wholeness to life. In fact, the study of Kabbalah itself is one of *Binah*'s methods because it asks us to reflect on the basic template of creation.

But we must remember that such reflection is not merely an esoteric exercise. The goal is depth, internalizing what we learn into our entire manner of thinking, feeling, and acting. The fragments we learn in any intellectual endeavor can ultimately be enfolded in a unified understanding by relating them to the basic template of *Binah*. As one of the great ethical writers in modern Judaism explains, "Only through contemplation, the concentrated tracing of experience back through effect and cause to the first Cause of all, can man attain wholeness and unity within himself."[28]

In your own life, if you experience vivid positive images in dreams or meditation, or if certain passages of sacred scripture "speak" to you, spend time contemplating them.

Unification and Intellect: *Da'at*-Knowledge

This is precisely the true nature of reality: No spiritual phenomenon can stand independently; each is interpenetrated by all. Only the limitations of our mental capacities impede us. . . . When man rises in his spiritual development his eyes will open to see properly: "Then the blind will see and the deaf will hear, and the earth will be full of the knowledge of the Lord as the waters cover the sea" (Isaiah 35:5, 11:9).

—RABBI ABRAHAM ISAAC KOOK[29]

How do we achieve that unification? On the one hand, it must be a gift, since it comes from a world beyond human reality. Yet, as with everything in the higher worlds, we have reflections of unity within ourselves. These reflections appear as the *sefirot* that stand on the central column of the Tree, at the levels of intellect, character attributes, and action. Here we will consider a quality called *Da'at*-Knowledge, an "eleventh *sefirah*" emphasized by mystics since the time of Luria. *Da'at*-Knowledge is actually not an independent energy of its own, but is formed by the confluence of *Chochmah* and *Binah*, and is also regarded as the externalization of the hidden *Keter*-Crown.[30] The term *da'at* appears early in the Bible, for the forbidden tree is called the Tree of *Da'at,* Knowledge (of good and evil). Also, when the Torah speaks of the union of Adam and Chava, it uses the same term—Adam "knew" his wife. This tells us that the energy that is called "knowledge" has a particular role in the human world.

Rabbi Nachman describes *Da'at*-Knowledge as something that can be acquired: "Acquiring *Da'at*-Knowledge is comparable to the building of the Holy Temple, while an absence of *Da'at*-Knowledge corresponds to its destruction."[31] The Temple is correlated to the template, *Binah,* so *Da'at* represents our connection to *Binah* and the upper *sefirot.* Moreover, since *Da'at* is considered to be an external manifestation of the crown *sefirah,* the epitome of oneness, it also has to be a unified knowledge. Finally, when Adam was intimate with Chava, it was called "knowing," so *Da'at* is also an intimate or internalized knowledge.

Thus while *Keter* is beyond human comprehension, *Da'at* is oneness, unification, in the mirror of human intellect. It is what we usually call the process of internalization. When we study a subject so thoroughly that we internalize it, where something we learn becomes second nature, we have a sense of unity with that knowledge. An artist who studies the great masters, then incorporates what she has learned in her own paintings, is using *Da'at.* Their inspiration and their kinds of artistic vision become hers, so that *Da'at* is receiving from *Chochmah* and *Binah* and transmitting them to the lower *sefirot. Da'at* is represented in the body by the brain stem and spinal cord, which are the messengers of neural impulses from the brain throughout the rest of the body.[32]

Da'at-Knowledge implies "the limitation and finiteness of a knower, a known and a knowing."[33] Yet despite the finitude of a human being, kabbalists hold that we can glimpse oneness through our minds. Rational intelligence, artistic awareness, and meditative contemplation are methods that have been used in all religions. We will discuss some of these methods further in a later section on basic spiritual practices. *Da'at*-Knowledge is the mental work we do when it serves our higher desire to seek unity rather than our lower urges to satisfy egotistical needs. This *sefirah* is the human intellectual and contemplative reflection of *Keter.* While its manifestations are diverse, its aim is one.

As we gaze toward the higher *sefirot,* we glimpse a realm of open, free creativity, with the emergence of profound and magical forms. These forms speak to us from levels beyond our ordinary existence, of a world of majesty and glory, of the Source of all that is. To move from this higher level to the reality in which we normally live and breathe—the everyday world rather than the sacred space of prayer and contemplation—is a leap across a great divide. Metaphorically, it means crossing the "firmament" between the upper worlds and the lower worlds (Genesis 1:7).

A *midrash* says that when God created the firmament to split the lower from the upper waters, the lower waters complained. God comforted them, saying, *you will be the source of salt, and no offering will be made on My altar without salt.* The salty oceans are, of course, the source of life as we know it. Life in the lower worlds is an offering on the altar, a service to God.

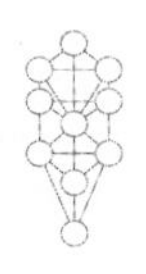

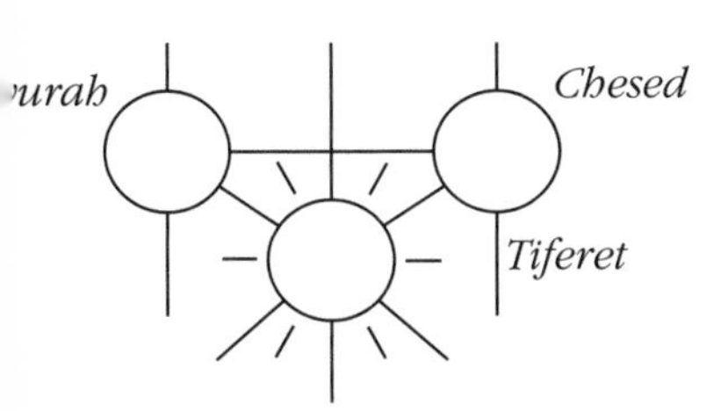

4 Divine Energies

A World of Multiplicity

In the biblical creation story, there is a moment when the upper and lower waters are separated by a great expanse usually called in English a "firmament." We can imagine the firmament as that thin line—not really a physical line—between the ocean and the sky on a clear day. On the upper side of the line is *Binah,* leading to heavenly levels of consciousness. *Da'at* sits immediately below the line, connecting to the world of finite human experience. The regions further beneath the line are worlds of separation: instead of oneness, multiplicity.

Yet they are also worlds of dynamism—flowing, surging, holding back—a world of almost constant movement. Here, it is as if God were saying, "I have created opposites, upper and lower, black and white, left and right. Now bring them together. Live in the lower world from the higher perspective of the world of unity."

On the Tree of Life, the world of multiplicity is represented by the seven lower *sefirot*. The *sefirot* of the left and right pillars represent opposites, while those of the middle pillar are a centering force, each with its own distinctive quality.

The first six of these seven lower *sefirot* are referred to as those of "building" because of their dynamic energy, which comes to rest at the last *sefirah* of *Malkhut*-Manifestation. The six

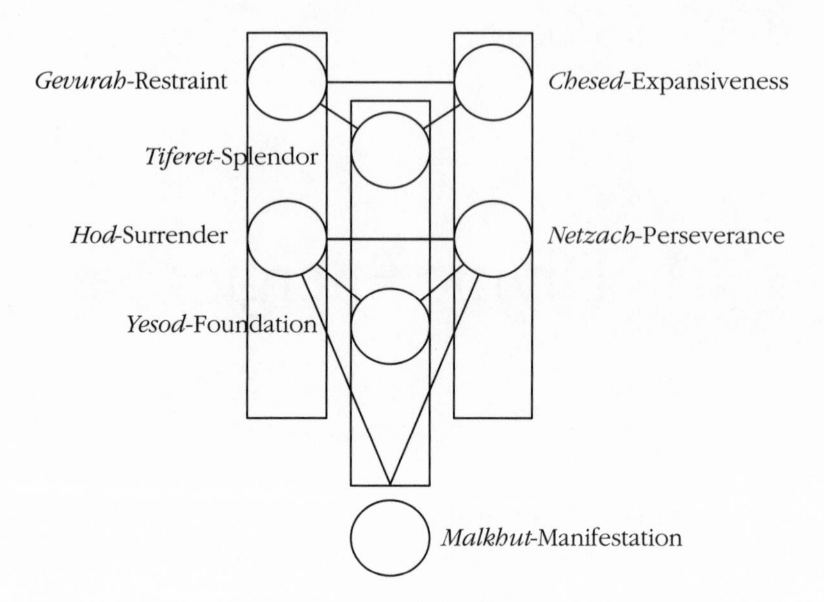

The Seven Lower *Sefirot*

sefirot are also called the *midot,* which literally means "measures." Unlike the first three *sefirot* of the head, which are essentially one or unmeasured, these principles have limits—indeed, as we will see, they limit one another. Like the measurements of an architect in designing the form of a building, they create the frame of life. They also create the frame of the human body. While the first three *sefirot* are those of the head, the next six are frequently portrayed as two triads, represented on the body as the upper and lower torso—the heart and abdominal cavities. The last *sefirah* is at the feet.

The word *midot* also means "attributes." They are qualities that can be discerned in the world, something like character traits in a person. They are qualities of God-in-the-world, and qualities we can see in people. We will discuss personal aspects of all the attributes in Part III. Here we will focus on their larger significance.

We will begin with the two uppermost *sefirot, Chesed*-Expansiveness and *Gevurah*-Restraint, which constitute the basic expression of duality in the universe.

Dynamics of Duality

All that the Holy One created in the world
was created male and female.
—TALMUD, BAVA BATRA 74B

If you have read books on Kabbalah before, you have probably seen these two *sefirot* called by other names—Lovingkindness and Strength, Love and Power, Compassion and Discipline. I use a more impersonal terminology, Expansiveness and Restraint, to emphasize that these *sefirot* do not represent merely human qualities, but are basic to the entire universe as we know it. The reason we can easily find parallels to them in the details of our emotions and relationships is that these qualities can be found in everything. Indeed, they are sometimes used to describe the two sides of the entire Tree of Life.

Chesed-Expansiveness and *Gevurah*-Restraint are the foundation of the known universe because they are principles of duality, opposites, counterforces. Their primal dynamic is captured in the following description of the conditions of the universe's emerging:

> In the primeval fireball, which quickly billowed in every direction, we see a metaphor for the infinite striving of the sentient being. An unbridled playing out of this cosmic tendency would lead to ultimate dispersion. But the fireball discovered a basic obstacle to its movements, the gravitational attraction. Only because expansion met the obstacle of gravitation did the galaxies come forth. . . . Many of the inventions of the natural world arose out of beings meeting the constraints of the universe with creative response. Only by dealing with the difficulty does the creativity come forth. . . . The beauty of the response arises from an inherently difficult situation.[1]

The billowing out of the fireball is an expression of *Chesed*, while the obstacle of gravitational attraction, a fundamental constraint of the universe, is *Gevurah*. The difficulty leads to beauty, which happens to be one of the names of the central *sefirah, Tiferet*-Splendor.

Everywhere we encounter fundamental dualities: light and darkness, movement and rest, male and female, fire and water, positive and negative poles of electromagnetism.[2] "Twoness" is also the dynamic of creator and creation. In this sense, *Chesed* and *Gevurah* are intimately involved in the creation of the universe. When God only was present—when Divinity was totally expanded, we might say—no world was possible. The Ari explained that God contracted himself—an act known as *tzimtzum*—bringing into being a hollow space, which we saw was compared to *Binah,* inside the fullness. This was an act of restraint. Into this space, God emanated a beam of light, known as the *Or Ein Sof,* or Light of the Infinite. From this all creation emerged—expansiveness again.

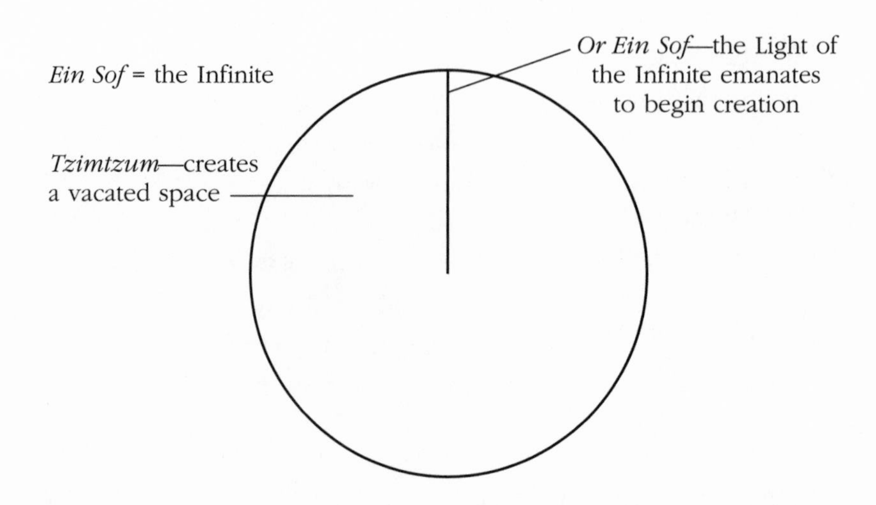

Through that Divine self-restraint, another reality was made possible, a universe unfolding in the vacated space, a world that appears to be sustained by its own laws.[3] After the first expansion of the universe, its elements cooled—they were "restrained," and stars could form. The forces of Expansiveness and Restraint are elegantly presented in the picture of the solar system, where planets circle the sun at massive speeds, with enough energy to hurl themselves out into the universe, except that the bond of gravity or restraint keeps turning them slightly toward the sun, creating ellipses as their trail.

Religions have been based on the dual principle—for example, the battle of Light with Darkness, or God versus Satan. Yin and Yang are opposites understood as fundamental to the universe in the traditional Chinese worldview. Our biblical creation story distinguishes upper from lower waters, water from dry land, vegetation from animals, and so on. Spirit energizes the waters *(Chesed)*. The waters are gathered *(Gevurah)* so that dry land can appear. The earth produces growth *(Chesed)* and each produces seed "according to its kind" *(Gevurah)*.

Making distinctions and recognizing opposites is also a basic human task. One of the blessings in the Jewish prayer book, said daily in the morning, thanks God for our power to make distinctions: "Blessed are You, Lord our God, Ruler of the Universe, who gives the mind the power to distinguish day from night." Making distinctions is not a bad thing; neither are what we call "opposites." Judaism also has a blessing specifically for appreciating distinctions, the *Havdalah* blessing said at the end of Shabbat on Saturday night:

> Blessed are You, Lord our God, Ruler of the Universe, Who distinguishes between the sacred and the profane, between light and darkness, between Israel and the peoples, between the seventh day and the six days of creation. Blessed are You, Lord, Who distinguishes between the holy and the ordinary.

Indeed, making appropriate distinctions is one of the ways that the original mistake of Adam and Chava can be corrected. The forbidden tree was the Tree of Union of Good and Evil. When they ate of the fruit, good and evil became mixed and confused in the world. The human task is to clarify the difference between them and choose the good.

Love Is the Source: *Chesed*-Expansiveness

Chesed creates the possibility of existence as we know it. That is why it is traditionally called Lovingkindness. It is the force of giving and going-out-toward, an energy that wants an "other" to exist and flourish. *Chesed* is the root of the concept of a loving Creator, which is deeply embedded in Western religions. The Source of the universe has the desire to bestow existence, goodness, and blessing on another entity. The rabbinic tradition says that God's mercy sustains the universe—if it were not so, the world would not stand.[4]

On the human level, the Torah's essential message is lovingkindness. In many Jewish prayers, and in Islam as well, God is called "the Compassionate One." In Christianity, the expansiveness of Divine love has been a part of its theology since its earliest beginnings: "God so loved the world"; "Love never ends" (John 3:16; 1 Corinthians 13:8). While Eastern religions do not focus so much on the personality of a deity, still we see the attribute of outgoing love in the Buddha, who is sometimes called the Heart of Compassion, and the Bodhisattvas, who desire to free all beings from enslavement to desire.

In Judaism, the essence of *Chesed* appears in the figure of Abraham, the first patriarch of Judaism and thus of all the Western religions, who with his wife Sarah set out to an unknown land at the command of God. Abraham is the archetype of *Chesed* because of his hospitality. He opened his tent to every passerby, putting forth the message that "My house is a place of support for you." This generosity was a Divine quality, a *midah,* for all to emulate. Other figures also represent *Chesed* in Jewish tradition.[5]

The beloved prophet Miriam, according to tradition, helped save the Hebrew babies from death at the hands of Pharaoh in Egypt. As a reward for her compassionate leadership, God gave the Jewish people water throughout their forty years of travel in the desert. In the biblical Book of Ruth, Ruth herself, her future husband Boaz, and her mother-in-law Naomi are all commended as caring for others beyond the call of duty. Interestingly, this story makes a particular point of noting that they cared for the deceased—Naomi's husband and sons—and for the deceased's honor. *Chesed* has no concern for whether the favor will be returned. Just as God sustains the universe without being guaranteed anything in return, so the earth supports us, and parents give of themselves endlessly for the sake of their children.

Chesed is experienced as unconditional love, as blessing beyond our wildest dreams, as beauty and delight that take our breath away. Andrew Harvey, a modern mystic, writes of his childhood experience of India in a way that vividly conveys his experience of Divine blessing and support:

> India also revealed to me that God was present in the sometimes savage glory of nature. Just behind our Delhi house there was a wilderness full of snakes and tangled brambles that was haunted by what seemed like thousands of peacocks. Almost every evening, as dusk started to fall, I would badger my ayah to take me for a walk there because I knew that this was the time when the peacocks would start to dance, fanning out the turquoise-blue-gold splendor of their tails. I still dream of those peacocks, appearing suddenly in the doorway of a ruined tomb or from behind a darkening bush; the rapture their outrageous beauty filled me with as a child has come for me to be a sign of how the Divine threads all of the creation with its secret splendor. . . .
>
> India initiated me also into what Keats called "the holiness of the heart's affections." For me as a child, God was

> as much in the sweetness of familial and friendly relationship as in the glory of the Himalayas or of the Taj Mahal or in the Sanskrit chanting of the temple priests.
>
> I remember how easy it was to talk to anyone in my childhood world, how accessible everyone, from servants and wandering holy men to politicians and plump, silver-haired maharinis, always was despite my endless questions. For all its terrible inequalities and religious restrictions, the India of my childhood was for me a place where I felt utterly at home with others. . . .[6]

That sense of being "utterly at home," of being supported, cherished, and connected to the world around is the manifestation of *Chesed*. See this in your own life—think of times and places when you have felt surrounded by blessing—whether in the beauty of nature, in some activity, or among people who were special to you.

Separation and the Reality of Pain: *Gevurah*-Restraint

The other side of the duality is *Gevurah*-Restraint. This *sefirah* embodies the possibility that something independent can exist, something that is not entirely dependent on its creator. If God had never contracted, there would be no universe. Out of God's restraint, the universe can evolve. With gravity, the universe can attain stability. On the human level, restraint is justice. The desires of individual beings are restrained by laws and courts on behalf of the larger community, which would otherwise dissipate into chaos.

Understand that *Gevurah* is the opposite of *Chesed*—but also that these two *sefirot* are opposite poles of one whole. Both come from the wholeness of love. Love as *Chesed* expresses itself in total support of being, saying "yes!" to every movement of freedom and self-expression. Love identifies with growth, well-being, and happiness and puts itself behind entities acting for the good. Parental love is a good example—think of a parent who takes the hands of an infant who is struggling to stand, helping the child find his balance. On the other hand, *Gevurah* is also an act of love. If we really love others, we know that we cannot overwhelm them with our support, in effect doing everything for them. Thus the parent will also sometimes exercise restraint, standing back and letting the child struggle to stand on his own and develop independence.

Once specific identities emerge, the conditions of life change. In a universe of entities that have different identities—the world of not only duality but multiplicity—every time one entity expresses *Chesed,* others will of necessity have to experience *Gevurah.* Your self-expression is a boundary to mine, and mine a boundary to yours. Out of mutual respect, we allow this to be the case—I restrain myself from invading your boundaries, and you do the same. We wish that such balance and respect would operate harmoniously, out of the love that embraces all beings. Such a world would be like living among the angels—as the Jewish liturgy says, each company of angels gives permission to the other to take its turn at praising God. No pushing and shoving in heaven![7]

Here, it doesn't work that way. This brings us to the second important aspect of the duality of *Chesed* and *Gevurah:* On a practical level, it is impossible to have a world of different, unique, individual entities where suffering does not occur. When a volcano expresses *Chesed*-Expansiveness, the heat and force that produce molten lava can cause severe limitations to the plant, animal, and human beings around it. From an objective viewpoint, nature is simply taking its course. But if we take account of the experience of the beings affected, we must recognize that they experience pain. At the moment of the restriction imposed by the molten lava, the animals must experience loss of support and a blockade of the fulfillment of their potential. These experiences are possible outcomes of limitation, of *Gevurah.*

From the interactive, inter-inclusive duality of *Chesed* and *Gevurah*—loving support and independence—arises a universe of interdependent beings, including the whole range from subatomic particles to human beings, angelic forces, and God. Because God chose to create in this way, God, too, is interdependent with us. This fact lies behind a mysterious statement in the *Zohar,* that the "arousal from above" depends on the "arousal from below." The arousal from above is God's action; the arousal from below is human action. God depends on us, and we on God. Abraham Heschel, drawing on Hasidic tradition, stated it explicitly: "God is in need of man." We are in need of one another, and of plants, animals, and minerals. Reciprocity is built into the structure of the universe. Expansiveness and Restraint are the poles of that reciprocity.

Moreover, *Gevurah* has traditionally been referred to as punishment or judgment. To borrow a metaphor from galactic experience, it is like the consuming fire of a star dying, becoming a black hole, pulling all matter into its intense gravitational field. On the human level, the effect can range from confusion to overwhelming loneliness to fear of death. The kabbalists called it the experience of chaos and dread. As the ancient text known as the *Bahir* says about the attribute of *Gevurah,*

> It is Chaos. It emanates from evil and astounds people. And what is that? It is that regarding which it is written, "And fire came down and it consumed the burnt offering, and the stones, and the earth, and it evaporated the water that was in the trench" (1 Kings 18:38). It is also written, "The Lord your God is a consuming fire, a jealous God" (Deuteronomy 4:24).[8]

When God expresses *Gevurah,* some of the ordering force of the universe is removed, and that is why it is experienced as chaos.

Isaac is the biblical figure associated with the *sefirah* of *Gevurah*. One reason is that he was very nearly sacrificed to God;

only at the last moment did God stop Abraham from killing his son. The demand that God placed on Abraham to sacrifice Isaac has been considered, in Western tradition, a test of faith, and *Gevurah* is the source of tests and obstacles. In addition, Isaac was less outgoing and expansive than his father Abraham. He never left the land of Israel, and the Torah mentions that he redug the wells of his father that the Philistines had plugged up. Kabbalistically, Isaac "dug deeper" into spiritual life rather than expanding outward into worldly life.

The female prophet who represents *Gevurah* is Hulda. In the reign of King Josiah, a time when the Torah had been nearly forgotten, a scroll of the law was found hidden in the Temple. Josiah sought Hulda's advice as to what to do, and she informed him that the scroll was indeed God's law, and should be followed to the letter. This is the aspect of *Gevurah* that embodies strictness and discipline. It may be surprising to us to find a female prophet advocating strict obedience to the law, since we tend to assume that women are softer and more compassionate. Traditional Kabbalah, however, associates *Gevurah* with the feminine and *Chesed* with the masculine. And historically, spiritually inclined women in many traditions have often been known to take on more than was required of them as a way of deepening and protecting their connection to the Divine.[9]

Some theologians have spoken of *Gevurah* as the absence of God. Yet, as the Hasidic masters teach, we cannot say God is absent from the world. If God really abandoned a relationship with the universe, everything would cease to exist. We can't even say that *Gevurah* has to do with "bad things" happening, while *Chesed* is about "good things." Unlimited blessings can also have negative effects. Rain is a blessing for crops, but too much rain—too much Expansiveness—is not good either. (The traditional Jewish prayers for rain ask that the rain come "for a blessing and not for a curse."[10]) The stories of people who win the lottery and then find their lives much too complicated are another example. On the other hand, what first appears to be a negative thing may turn out to be for the good.

We tend to see the aspects of *Chesed* and *Gevurah* through the lenses of linear time, rather than through the more comprehensive space-time of higher levels. Since we cannot see future good results that come from something we experience as evil, or the future evil from something that looks great to us, we seesaw our way through life. In the biographies of some of the world's great leaders, we see this dynamic. When the great medieval Sufi scholar, Rumi, lost the teacher and companion that he had loved, his grief knew no end. But out of that experience he produced beautiful religious poetry that still inspires us today. Another example is Malcolm X, a leader among African-Americans in the 1960s. His early life as a criminal landed him in prison—certainly not the result he would have planned. But from that experience, he began learning and acquiring new perspectives on life that enabled him to become a leader of his people. We usually don't realize that both dimensions of the duality are always present, but we can see only part of the picture at any given time. Do you recall events in your own life that you thought were disasters, but then it turned out that something better was waiting around the corner?

Kabbalah offers us a unique perspective here. In the big picture, on the level of unification, God's sustenance of the universe is itself a tremendous act of ongoing love. This love indeed never ends, nor stops even for a moment. But, on the lower level where we live, God appears to be dealing out judgment and punishment. The lower dualistic level is understood as the "revealed," while the higher unified reality is the "concealed." The great seventeenth-century kabbalist Rabbi Moshe Chaim Luzzatto describes these levels:

> In all of God's dealings with us we can posit two dimensions, the revealed and the concealed. The revealed is reward and punishment (to the recipient of one or the other, good or bad). The concealed is the deep design inhering always in all of His deeds, to guide the creation to

> the universal perfection. For this is certainly the case: there is no deed, small or great, whose ultimate end is not the universal perfection, as stated by our sages, "All that is done by Heaven is for the good" (*Berachot* 60b), and by the prophet: "Your wrath will turn back and You will console me" (Isaiah 12:1).[11]

From this point of view, what we call evil is a withdrawal by God into a greater concealment.

A PERSONAL GOD

However, the idea of balancing good and evil does not tell the whole story. We have a long tradition in the West, beginning with the Bible, of God responding to some kinds of human actions with a sharp, punishing response, while providing reward for other actions. The ancient prophets described the punishing response as God's anger or zeal. God's "consuming fire" was a direct response to human sins. Near the end of Deuteronomy, the last book of the written Torah, this Divine response is described as a hiding of the Divine face. "Then My anger will be roused against them and I will abandon them and hide My face from them. . . . On that day I will hide my face because of all the evil they have done in turning to other gods" (Deuteronomy 31:17, 18). Divine favor was a direct response to repentance and good deeds.

Often, people have interpreted the stories of Divine punishment as if God had an angry personality. It is important to recognize that the Bible uses many anthropomorphic expressions, both physical and psychological, to illustrate how God's actions and feelings are like those of humans. Judaism has always insisted on understanding God in a personal way. It does *not* mean that every time something bad happens, God is punishing someone. Rather, we have two perspectives on God and Divine action in the world: a more impersonal one, as described above in discussing the relationship between cosmic *Chesed* and cosmic

Gevurah, and a more personal one, which the biblical stories often portray in terms of God's love and punishment. The question is, how can the two perspectives be reconciled?

The sages tell us that the Torah itself shows two different ways God manifests in our world. Two different names are frequently used for God in the Bible—the four letter name Y-H-V-H, which cannot be pronounced but is usually replaced by *Adonai,* and the name *Elohim.* These are usually translated in English Bibles as "Lord" and "God" respectively. *Adonai* is the personal aspect of God that intervenes in history and our lives, while *Elohim* is God as manifest in nature and law, balancing everything in accord with cosmic justice. Y-H-V-H is *Chesed, Elohim* is *Gevurah.*

When we address God personally, we evoke that aspect of the Divine that emanates mercy and lovingkindness. Without the personal aspect, the world would become an empty shell, a mechanical object working according to laws of nature. Our lives would be subject to an automatic kind of karma, in which the fruits of our actions would weigh heavily upon us and progress would be very difficult. Judaism has a concept similar to karma in the metaphor of the scales upon which each person's deeds are weighed every year at Rosh Hashanah (the Jewish New Year). But Judaism also insists that because of God's mercy, we can ask forgiveness and wipe the slate clean. The natural balancing of *Chesed* and *Gevurah* might lead to an equilibrium, but the Divine Creator wants more than just equilibrium. By adding an extra measure of love and mercy, God ensures that the balance will come out toward the good.

This approach has some interesting implications. If God has experiences and feelings, is it true that, as the medieval philosophers said, God never changes? (In the philosophies of the Middle Ages, inherited from the ancient Greek philosophers Plato and Aristotle, change was associated with physical form and its imperfections. God, being non-corporeal, must not change.[12]) The biblical view seems to be that God is not an objective entity or an impervious cosmic mind; rather, God responds—God has an inner life, and we can interpret God's life in terms analogous to ours as sad, pleased, regretful, angry, and, of course, loving. God's "anger," then, is the way the Bible speaks of the human experience that we are calling *Gevurah,* while God's "love" is the way it describes what we are calling *Chesed.* Both are God. They are two sides of one coin just as in physics, wave and particle are two forms in which light can be perceived and described.

Kabbalah encourages us to think of God's relationship to us in human terms. The terms "Father" and "Mother" for two of the *sefirot* are one example. Another is the description of God's relationship with the Jewish people as being analogous to that between husband and wife. The mystics also speak of an aspect of God—the *Shekhinah,* the feminine Divine Presence *(Malkhut)*—that is "in exile" with us, exile being the condition in which we experience separation from God. We can imagine God experiencing the sphere of human activity as a chaotic and even painful part of the universe God created.

This brings out another implication, namely that God has built into the structure of the universe ways for us to call forth the positive and diminish the negative. Human beings have the responsibility to act in ways that enhance the side of love and support. When the Bible promises rewards for certain actions such as honoring one's parents, it is prescribing modes of behavior that evoke positive responses in Divine consciousness. God will respond to us in ways similar to the way we respond to one another. When we cause pain to one another, God may respond by "concealing the Divine Countenance," as a way of urging us to call forth God's love once again. The ancient writers understood this relationship, even if their metaphors were not the same as ours. For the ancient Jewish people and their spokesmen, the experience of God's closeness was very intense, and the experience of God's distance was in the form of plague and fire. They understood that God cries out when we are neglecting our fellow human beings and when we are neglecting our spiritual lives.

One of the great teachers of the twentieth century, Abraham Joshua Heschel, wrote in this vein about the Holocaust, and it is worth pondering his words to consider how we have objectified and distanced God:

> Through centuries His voice cried in the wilderness. How skillfully it was trapped and imprisoned in the temples! How often it was drowned or distorted! Now we behold how it gradually withdraws, abandoning one people after another, departing from their souls, despising their wisdom. The taste for the good has all but gone from the earth. Men heap spite upon cruelty, malice upon atrocity.
>
> . . . "Where is God? Why didst Thou not halt the trains loaded with Jews being led to slaughter?" . . . Indeed, where were we when men learned to hate in the days of starvation? When raving madmen were sowing wrath in the hearts of the unemployed?
>
> . . . Our world seems not unlike a pit of snakes. We did not sink into the pit in 1939, or even in 1933. We had descended into it generations ago, and the snakes have sent their venom into the bloodstream of humanity.
>
> . . . God will return to us when we shall be willing to let Him in.[13]

When we abandon our Divine purpose, there are likely to be consequences. *Gevurah* means that God is leaving room for human freedom, but if we misuse it, God becomes even more concealed, and on the level of the revealed world the results are bitter, as Heschel suggested.

Still, we must also remember that not all suffering is the result of a flawed relationship to God. Viruses have a drive to exist, even at the expense of their human hosts. Humans and their machines make mistakes. Above all, we should never suggest to other people that their pain and suffering is Divine punishment. Introspectively, it may sometimes be appropriate to ask whether a misalignment with Divine intent is adding to our problems. *Gevurah* asks us to go in all humility (which does not mean self-abasement or excessive self-criticism) into a deeper relationship with God—to "dig deeper," like Isaac.

Vision and Higher Purpose: *Tiferet*-Splendor

Man is composed of all the spiritual entities, and he is perfect in all attributes, and he was created with great wisdom . . . for he comprises all the secrets of the Chariot and his soul is linked therein, even though man is in this world. Know that, unless man would be perfect in all the forces of the Blessed-Holy-One, he would be unable to do as he does . . . There is a great supernal power in men, which cannot be described.

—*SEFER HA-NE'ELAM*[14]

All our questions about pain and suffering are themselves a hint to the next level, the *sefirah* of *Tiferet*-Splendor. Our questions arise out of our inner sense of purpose, our deep belief that things ought to make sense, and our visions of ideals that could be realized. The amazing thing about the human species is that, despite all the apparently senseless sufferings, most people still believe in a larger purpose to life. That is because we possess the energy of *Tiferet*-Splendor. We see patterns, growth, and development. The patterns are no more than a dim reflection of the glowing template of the world of unity, but they give us hope. The vessel of that hope crystallizes our organizing purpose, and human energies organize themselves around it, like filings around a magnet.

The *sefirah* of *Tiferet* represents the emergence of conscious purpose. While purpose exists at every level of creation, it does not become fully conscious until creation arrives at the first human being. In the biblical story, dualities alternate: light and dark, water and dry land, sun and moon, plants and trees, birds of the air and fish of the sea, and finally, on the sixth day, animals and humanity. Only here does God say that creation is "in

His image" (Genesis 1:27), and only here does the Divine breath enter a creature (Genesis 2:3). Image means the possibility of likeness: Just as God has a purpose, now creation includes a being that can embody purpose. Breath is like spirit, a force that hovered over the waters of chaos in order to begin bringing it into form. Most of all, just as God is One, so this human being is one—not dual, not divided.

As we saw earlier, the first person, Adam, contains both male and female, and is the perfect image of God the Creator. Moreover, just as the metaphor of "King" is used for God, so Adam is given "dominion" over the earth. With the emergence of Adam, purpose could be made apparent. A king can have perspective over the entire kingdom, and can decree in light of this great range of perception. Humanity, God's ambassador on earth, could carry forward God's project—to reveal what God intended but heretofore concealed. As one of the Hasidic masters put it, "Man is a microcosm, a miniature universe, a complete structure."[15] Similarly, philosopher David Ray Griffin states, "The human person incorporates all levels from subatomic particles to self-conscious mind."[16] Since God put all the created powers into human beings, the human species alone could execute the Divine will completely.

The idea of human dominion has become suspect in recent times because we have become more aware of how human rulership over the world has led to corruption and destruction of what once was truly a paradise. In less than 200 years since the beginning of the Industrial Revolution, we have changed the face of a unique planet where life evolved into amazingly diverse, beautiful, and intelligent forms, into one where thousands of species, and the quality of life itself, are being threatened by our chemicals and concrete. People concerned about the health of the earth have questioned whether human existence should be given the pre-eminent value that biblical tradition has assigned it—perhaps we have forfeited our right to dominion?

We must acknowledge the force of this criticism. The biblical tradition itself affirms that human beings long ago began corrupting the earth, in the "generation of the flood" and the "generation of the dispersion" (who built the Tower of Babel). God declared, after saving Noah and his family from the flood, that "the imagination of man's heart is evil from his youth" (Genesis 8:21). But God did not despair of humankind, and continued to respond to those who sought to live a higher and truer way, like Abraham and Sarah, ancestors of the Jewish people. The task for human beings today is to live up to the higher ideals that humans also represent, and to continually seek a higher and more inclusive vision—the perspective of a king saving his kingdom, rather than a narrow and ego-centered point of view.

The emphasis on the visionary powers of human beings comes in an ancient *midrash,* which says that Adam could "see from one end of the world to the other." Adam is compared to the lights of heaven, "to give light on earth" (Genesis 1:14). In other words, Adam, male-and-female, had a complete vision of the Divine work and its ultimate purpose. Then Adam was divided into a gendered being, expressing in bodies (but not, Kabbalah tells us, the same kind of bodies we have now) the duality that inheres in this level of creation. When these two beings were expelled from the Garden, their holistic vision was lost.

But we still use the word "vision" to express an awareness of higher purpose. The person who can see wondrous possibilities that have not yet been actualized is called a "visionary." Even our concept of the universe as an evolving, magnificent organism depends on the vision of human beings, extended through the scientific instruments that reveal billions of years of space-time or the intricacies of molecular genetic structures. Humans have always sought to expand their capacity to see the purpose of things, seeking wisdom from ancient astrologers, who tried to discern meanings in the movements of stars, or from the speech of prophets and oracles. Today, the subject of cosmology (literally, knowledge of the whole cosmos) is an exciting area for physicists and mathematicians as well as philosophers and theologians, once again in search of the complete vision.

Tiferet-Splendor is the *sefirah* of vision, purpose, and capacity for high-level organization in light of that purpose. Its name suggests the beauty and magnificence of the created being who possesses the vision of creation's purpose. This *sefirah* is also called Truth, because it is the place where human perception can meet Divine revelation.

According to Kabbalah, the figure who represents *Tiferet* is Jacob, third in the lineage of biblical ancestors of the Jews. When Jacob first left the land of Israel, he dreamed of angels going up and down on a ladder to heaven, and he proclaimed the place of the dream the gate of heaven. He promised that if God returned him home in safety, he would honor God there. His challenge was to remain true to the vision through many trials, including more than twenty years outside the land, working for an uncle who cheated him, the death of Rachel his beloved, and the loss of his favorite son, Joseph. Jacob returned and built the altar—traditionally believed to be the site of the Temple in Jerusalem. Thus the *Zohar* calls Jacob the "bolt" that holds the entire creation together. His vision of angels on the ladder tells us that he saw the connection between earth and heaven. The central rung on the ladder is *Tiferet*. Also, the mystics tell us that Jacob's face is engraved on the Throne of God, which also is represented by *Tiferet*.[17]

Among the female prophets, Sarah represents *Tiferet*. The biblical commentaries tell us that Sarah's tent was the model for the holy sanctuary, and that her life represented a confluence of innocence, beauty, and wisdom. Thus she is aligned with the Divine template and manifests the central pillar—like Jacob, she is the bolt of creation.

These symbolic references reveal the honor and splendor given to human beings who identify themselves with God's ultimate purposes on earth. This is our task as well. But this high place in the scheme of things means also that the fate of the world lies in our hands. We, too, must make sure that all the rungs on the ladder are in place, that our connection to the heavenly template is secure so that we can live a truly good life on earth.

THE HEART CONNECTION

What makes it possible for humans, among all animals, to carry the vision? How is it that we have the potential to make the right choices, to energize what will support and magnify the best of life? Kabbalah teaches that it is the human heart.

On the diagram of *sefirot, Tiferet,* at the center of the upper torso, is usually associated with the heart and corresponds to the heart chakra in the yogic traditions.[18] It also is a center into which all the upper *sefirot* flow and from which the lower *sefirot* emanate. Furthermore, this heart center in traditional Kabbalah is directly connected to the uppermost *sefirah, Keter*-Crown, which points to the essential soul. This tells us that the heart can become a direct expression of the soul. On a personal level, the heart can overflow with soulfulness into the *sefirot* immediately below it, until it is expressed in the human personality and energizes behavior on an everyday basis. On the collective level, human passion, rightly directed, can change the world.

By passion, however, we do not mean emotions. Kabbalah teaches that our ordinary emotions are a function of the lower torso. The heart sustains a higher level: an overriding passion connected to what is meaningful, something great enough to motivate one's entire life. The Edmund Hillary who longs to conquer Mount Everest, and the Mother Teresa drawn to comfort the poor and sick are heroic examples from history. But so is the daughter of one of my friends, whose love for animals led her to volunteer for the SPCA, spending her time caressing abused and abandoned pets. Or my student at the university whose passion for soccer drove him so hard that he failed my class.

Yet even these examples of Splendor, our most powerful passions and motivations, are only hints to the larger vision: the ultimate purpose for which everything was created. In the heart is also our deepest understanding—as we saw earlier, *Binah*-Understanding resides in the right side of the heart as well as in the brain. We think our deep thoughts in the heart. Thus when the Bible wants to express an important idea forming in the mind of God or of a person, it uses the expression, "he said in his heart."

Rabbi Nachman offers us a beautiful parable of the heart in one of the stories included in his multileveled story "The Seven Beggars":

> There is a mountain. On the peak of the mountain there is a stone. From this stone, there flows a Spring.
>
> Everything has a heart. Therefore the world as a whole also has a heart. . . .
>
> The mountain with the stone and the Spring stands at one end of the world. The Heart of the World stands at the opposite end of the world. The Heart of the World faces the Spring and constantly longs and yearns to come to the Spring. It has a very, very great longing, and it cries out very much that it should be able to come to the Spring. The Spring also yearns for it.
>
> The Heart has two things that make it weak. First, the sun pursues it and burns it. The second thing that weakens the Heart is the great longing and yearning that it constantly has toward the Spring. It longs and yearns so much that its soul goes out, and it cries out.
>
> When it wants to rest a bit and catch its breath, a great bird comes and spreads its wings over it, protecting it from the sun. It can then relax a bit. However, even when it is resting, it looks toward the Spring and yearns for it.
>
> One may wonder, since it yearns for it so much, why does it not go to the Spring? However, if it were to come close to the mountain, then it would no longer see the mountain's peak. It then could not gaze at the Spring, and

> if it stopped looking at the Spring, it would die, since its main source of life is the Spring. . . .
>
> If the Heart died, then the entire world would cease to exist. The Heart is the life force of all things, and nothing can exist without a heart.[19]

The Spring is the flowing forth of the Divine, represented by the *sefirah* of *Chochmah*-Wisdom. The Heart, *Tiferet,* has two aspects, both of which take its energy—its yearning for the Spring and the effects of the sun. The yearning is the aspect of the heart connected to *Binah,* the Mother, who yearns for *Chochmah,* the Father. It is also the indescribable yearning of the human soul for God.

The aspect of the sun in *Tiferet* is the pull of waking consciousness—life under the sun, so to speak—with all its daily tasks, physical needs, and material desires. This is the world in which we all live. Through the energy of *Tiferet,* we carry the sense of purpose that demands we take responsibility for that world. But that responsibility takes its toll on the Heart. Rabbi Nachman is telling us that the human heart is stretched between the longing for God on the one hand, and the pull of responsibility for, and responsiveness to, the world on the other. Yet exactly that tension is where we must live. If the Heart tried to go to the Spring, it would no longer be able to "see the mountain's peak" and "gaze at the Spring." The Heart would lose its visionary capacity, its sense of purpose for life, and it would die.

On the other hand, the Heart becomes exhausted by the world in which it lives. To live under the sun is its true purpose, but it needs the "great bird" to give it respite. The Hasidic commentaries explain that the wings of the bird are like the lungs on both sides of the human heart. Rabbi Nachman taught that the heart produces such internal heat (like a sun) that the lungs are needed right next to the heart to cool it with breathing. The heart is nourished by the breath.

In the Unfolding of Creation, Adam-Humanity represents the Heart of the World, positioned at *Tiferet*-Splendor among the *sefirot*. With its connection to *Binah*-Understanding, the human heart longs for a higher world. But at the same time it knows that it can only gaze at that world. Gazing is a code word in Hasidic writings for meditation, and it reminds us here of "con-templat-ion"—renewing our connection to the basic template of existence. Meditation and contemplation of the vision regenerate the passion the Heart needs to continue beating, maintaining the flow of life.

But the Heart of the World beats not for itself, but for the world as a whole. Indeed, it is so connected to the world that it can be drawn into it too much, and "burned" by its desires, as we will see in the next chapter. Still, the Heart must beat—and humans must work for the good of the entire world. To have respite from its work, the lungs offer shade and coolness. This means not only doing spiritual practices like breathing and meditation, which Rabbi Nachman recommends, but also seeing ourselves in a magnificent system of reciprocity, represented by the lungs, which exchange carbon dioxide for oxygen, moment by moment. When we recognize our place in the cosmic story, the grandness of God's creation and the multitude of details, like the amazing mechanics of breathing, that sustain our life, we can appreciate more fully the profound honor we have been given of sustaining life on this planet in return.

In order to become more aware of the heart *sefirah* in your life, try the meditation called "Breath Is the Signature of Spirit" in Part IV (page 183). It can help you develop a heartfelt connection to the vision of higher life on the one hand, and gratitude for planetary life on the other. These qualities are what we need in order to become truly a manifestation of beauty and splendor.

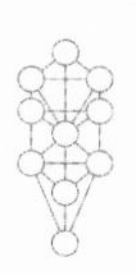

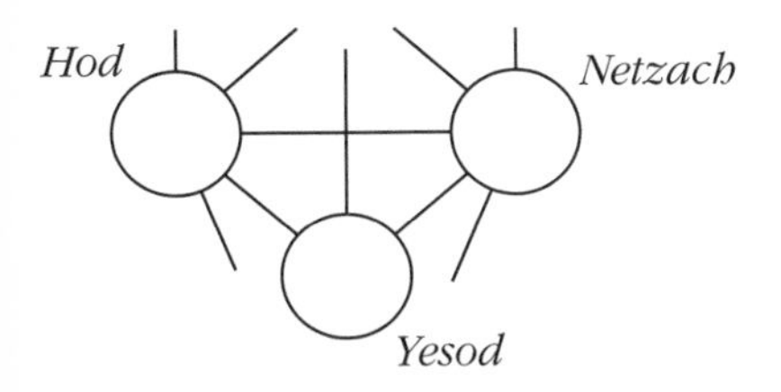

5 Divine Actualization

Contemplate the wonders of creation, the Divine dimension of their being, not as a dim configuration that is presented to you from a distance, but as the reality in which you live.
—Rabbi Abraham Isaac Kook[1]

Harnessing Life Force: *Netzach*-Perseverance and *Hod*-Surrender

The level of *Tiferet*-Splendor has the potential to mirror Divinity in this world. From the viewpoint of Kabbalah, from *Tiferet* upward, humans interact with God and with other forces greater than humanity. From *Tiferet* downward, humans strive to direct the world as ambassadors of God, intertwining human and Divine will. Out of the human potential to co-create, each generation faces the task to sustain and care for the world. By bestowing kindness on all creation, humanity can actually imitate God.

This task requires harnessing the energies of *Netzach*-Perseverance and *Hod*-Surrender. These are the *sefirot* of life force, the energies of survival and procreation. They manifest as desires for food, sex, and the means to ensure those necessities, such as power and wealth. They also run parallel to *Chesed*-Expansiveness and *Gevurah*-Restraint as a basic duality.

The expansive energy is called *Netzach,* corresponding to *Chesed*. On the level of human civilization, it becomes the drive to achieve and continue, imitating Divine expansiveness. Its energy appears in the drive of life to emerge everywhere—tiny plants that peek out between desert rocks, penguins that adapt to the frigid climate of Antarctica. In the human being, perseverance is symbolized by the will to live and to express oneself in relation to one's environment. Some have called it domination because of its emphasis on expansive self-expression. We see *Netzach* in the desire to make a mark on the world, to leave behind memorials and monuments testifying to one's existence. Our tendency is to fall in love with our own creations, like the story of Pygmalion where a sculptor created the form of a beautiful woman and fell in love with his own statue. This is the negative side of *Netzach*. It can become exploitative or manipulative, but we should also remember that it usually contains inherent qualities of love and good will because it is from the side of *Chesed*.

According to the kabbalists, *Netzach* was a primary quality of Moses, the greatest prophet and first chosen leader of the Jewish people. He persevered not only through all the battles with external enemies—from Egypt and Amalek to the tribes that wanted to prevent the Hebrew slaves fleeing Egypt from going into the Holy Land—but also through all the challenges raised by the people, ranging from laziness and stubbornness to questioning of his leadership. Among women, *Netzach* is represented by the prophet and judge Deborah, whose spiritual leadership enabled the Jewish people to prevail in their struggle for the land of Israel. In individual human beings, *Netzach* is also expressed in the strength of the body, the way the organs and muscles of the body respond to a person's will and put forth effort to carry out his or her wishes.

Its companion *sefirah, Hod*-Surrender, parallels the energy of *Gevurah*-Restraint, expressed now as the inclination to yield and withdraw. As complex organisms develop, the specialization of cells means also that each type of cell is willing to become dependent on others. The symbiosis of plants manifests the ability of life to yield and share resources. In both the animal and plant worlds, each species is able to respond to the presence of others in the same environment.

In the human being, *Hod* has many dimensions. In relation to God and the larger collectivity, it is expressed as the impulse to sacrifice, imitating the Divine *tzimtzum* in "sacrificing" space for the sake of creating a world. As mentioned earlier, in our most ancient stories—Cain and Abel, Noah—and in the most ancient levels of civilization we find the mysterious practice of sacrificing what is valuable to the Divine.[2] *Hod* also includes willingness to sacrifice oneself for the larger whole, as in martyrdom or war. In Kabbalah, Aaron the first High Priest, brother of Moses, is said to represent *Hod*. Chief of sacrifices, he was also known as a peacemaker who made harmony and cooperation come into being in place of conflict and strife. Thus *Hod* includes the ability to cooperate and create networks. Among women, *Hod* is represented by Chanah, whose prayer, the sages say, is the epitome of how a person can come close to God. She is also a model of sacrifice, for she dedicated her only son, Samuel, to the priesthood.

In the individual human being, *Hod* means the ability to yield or step back, removing one's ego from a situation. It involves the capacity to feel inwardly and process that information in order to sense how things fit together. *Hod* also enables us to access information not available to normal consciousness, as when our cells "remember" injury by replicating scar tissue. In its more negative formations, however, this *sefirah* can express itself as negativity, feelings of victimization, or withdrawal from creative interaction with the world.

Out of these powerful energies of *Netzach* and *Hod* many things emerge that are beautiful and amazing, for humans are creative in their own right. Families become clans, tribes, societies, civilizations. Prophets and seers bring forth rich visions that guide ritual ceremonies, dances, and martial arts as well as music and visual arts.[3] Technologists invent tools to make life more comfortable and to enhance our experience of creation: a fire pit, a furnace, a hammer and anvil, cast bronze; polished stones, carved stones, jewelry and ornaments; clay pots, porcelain, glass and crystal. The cooperative effort of humankind indeed leads to dominion over nature.

Yet these creations are also things to which human beings can become deeply attached, rather than using them to honor God and the larger creative process. Human civilization is a tale of how the effort to build a world of splendor became mostly an effort to accumulate material goods, fame, progeny, wives, sex, food, or money. Christians called this tendency the sin of pride. Buddhists called it ignorant craving. Jews called it *yetzer hara,* the evil inclination, or misdirected desire. Even secular reconstructions of human prehistory point to a crisis as humans passed from gathering to hunting to agricultural societies, inventing war and empire, and later racism, nationalism, and even genocide.[4]

Why? What is common to all these interpretations is that somehow, in the human psyche, anxiety and fear arose—fear of not being good enough, or of not having enough. Self-doubt and insecurity seem inherent in the human psyche. Recall that the Eden story tells us of the serpent who enticed human beings with the thought of being like God—they doubted their own self-worth even though they were already created in God's image. Existentialist philosophers of the mid-twentieth century captured some of the depth of human fear by calling it "ontological anxiety"—fear of not being. Psychologists sometimes have suggested that this anxiety arises out of the experience of independence itself, as a fear of loss of parental love.

Whatever the origin of the problem, the reality was that natural energies of survival, or instincts, became entwined with what psychology later would call ego. Beautiful physical productions became wealth, bodily strength and vitality became power, and the intimate exchanges of man and woman became merely sex or marriage exchanges in economic and political systems. Shoring themselves up against doubt, humans sought reassurance from the external world. Group identity became a powerful source of security, filling an inner void. But the emphasis on group identification nourished exclusiveness and fragmentation in human society, until finally fear ran the world instead of love. *Netzach* and *Hod,* the creative energies at our immediate disposal, became the locus of a new problem—not the general problem of pain in the world of duality, but how human beings create their own suffering.

The energies of the *sefirot* of the lower torso, designed for the concrete and practical application of Divine love and discipline using the tools of survival and procreation, became corrupt. Some Jewish mystics say that the lowest *sefirot* are the location not merely of the lowest level of soul, but of a specifically different soul called the "animal soul." Acting primarily from animal instincts of survival and defense, the animal soul battles the Divine soul, which seeks to live in accordance with a higher vision. This interpretation is a way of telling us how powerful our egotistical desires have been. Down to the present, *Netzach* and *Hod* in the human realm are still given over to competitive and

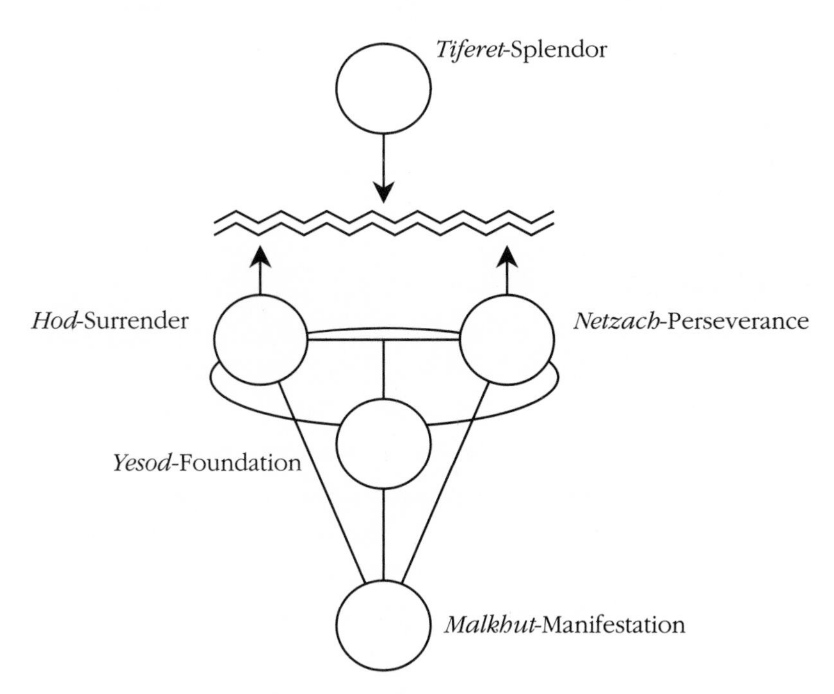

Without connection to the vision of *Tiferet,*
human energy circles around itself.

ultimately self-devouring processes. In Western culture, which now affects the entire world, *Netzach*-Perseverance became predominantly a masculine characteristic, *Hod*-Surrender a feminine one. Instead of being a gracious flow of exchange between heaven and earth, up and down the entire range of the *sefirot,* human energy circles around itself. The whole earth—and, Kabbalah tells us, the heavens too—suffer from our narcissistic fear, which severs our connection to Divine vision.

A new unification is needed. Not only do we need to maintain our vision, keeping *Tiferet*-Splendor connected to the higher worlds, but we also need to manage the world in accord with that vision. *Netzach* and *Hod* have the tendency to separate from their Divine source, becoming materialistic and self-worshiping. It is as if the serpent won his point: Now humans think they are like gods. These energies must be organized through the *sefirah* called *Yesod*-Foundation in a way that keeps the connection open to higher levels.

Lineage, History, Karma: *Yesod*-Foundation

A proton and a neutron joined together. Two protons and two neutrons, two protons and one neutron. Such primal enduring partnerships entered existence for the first time. The first stable ground of the universe made its appearance. All future ground—whether that of stars or of planets or of continents—would find its strength from this, the world's first foundation.

—Brian Swimme and Thomas Berry[5]

Yesod-Foundation is usually portrayed as the *sefirah* of reproduction or, more broadly, generativity and transmission. In the larger animal and plant world, the process through which this occurs is primarily genetic. The species drive to live and expand one's reach *(Netzach)* combines with the need to draw back and respond to others *(Hod),* creating an ecosystem. The ecosystem in turn encourages the development of new forms. Within each, effective strategies for this eventually become part of the genetic pool, the "Foundation" for the future. In the human realm, *Yesod* is represented as the genitals and womb.[6]

But the idea of transmission must embrace far more than sexuality and genetics. Humans transmit information from their families and their entire lineage, from society and culture. *Yesod* is the place where all that is collectively experienced is merged and passed on to the next generation. Like the birth canal, it channels into specific and unique form the multitude of experiences that any given society has accumulated. Essentially, it is the Divine quality of memory. In some kabbalistic sources, *Yesod* is called "All," signifying its comprehensiveness.[7]

Yesod then will also include what is popularly called the karmic history of an individual. The term "karma," which I borrow from Hindu and Buddhist philosophy, means the results of actions that have been performed in all lifetimes. The tradition of Kabbalah also holds that souls usually incarnate many times and carry the residue of previous lives into each succeeding one.[8] Unfortunately, the concept of karma is often interpreted negatively and deterministically, as though karma is a burden to be carried, dragging us down.[9] From a Jewish point of view, however, we have to say that this is absolutely not true. First of all, Hindu, Buddhist, and Jewish mystical thought would agree that the very fact that we have been born in a human incarnation means that we have accomplished a great deal in our previous lives. In addition, Judaism holds that God counts good as weighing more than evil: "God remembers kindness for a thousand generations" (Exodus 33:6–7). God is not only *Elohim,* but also *Adonai,* a personal deity characterized above all by love and mercy. The condensation of the accumulated deeds of one's past lives will be heavily weighted with good qualities.

Since our parental and cultural heritage is also available through *Yesod,* we can access the merit of the good deeds of our ancestors. Other traditions, such as Buddhism and Christianity, also speak of a store of merit accumulated by the great acts of figures of the past. We stand, the rabbis have said, "on the shoulders of giants." The Jewish prayers each day include thanks to God, "Who remembers the devoted acts of our ancestors, and Who brings a redeemer to their children's children." Remembering is also re-member-ing, reuniting the broken pieces. Divine remembrance infuses the *sefirah* of *Yesod,* because God pieces together and holds the memory of past goodness for us. *Yesod* thus enables us to bring into this lifetime a mastery of many good qualities, from all that has been learned and accomplished by our ancestors and ourselves in the past.

The Kabbalah associates *Yesod* historically with a special master—Joseph, the favored son of Jacob. Jewish tradition tells us that Joseph was a holy master of power, wealth, and sexuality because he had withstood the temptations presented to him during his years in Egypt. He developed the means to sustain and nourish the whole nation during the years of famine and, in addition, saved his father and brothers, and their families, the beginnings of all the Twelve Holy Tribes, and established them in safety.

Joseph represents the *sefirah* of *Yesod* because he forged powerful links between past and future. He did not add new insights or revelations to the Jewish heritage, but he preserved the lineage, the moral power, and the faith of his ancestors through trials and tribulations. When he faced a crisis, he used the faculty of remembrance of his ancestors; the commentaries say that when he was tempted by his master's wife, he saw his father Jacob's face, and this enabled him to resist. He was also a seer—Joseph the Dreamer—and an interpreter who could discern what the future would hold. He stood at the doorway between past and future, master of history. At the same time, he never forgot the dependence of every person and event on God.

The ability to be totally immersed in the world of history, politics, and economics, and yet remember God is the way of the most holy masters. Thus Joseph is called in Kabbalah the *tzaddik* or "righteous one." *Tzaddik* is a term for a holy person, but in Judaism a person is also required to sanctify the world. It is far easier to deal with one's desires for fame, wealth, and physical pleasure if one can simply avoid them by becoming a hermit. Joseph was a *tzaddik* because he lived in the midst of all these—a person of fame and power, tempted by beauty and pleasure, and with access to the wealth of all of Egypt—and still remained deeply connected to God.

The female prophet associated with *Yesod* is Abigail, who eventually became one of King David's wives. She was originally married to a wealthy man who refused to help David when he and his supporters were hiding out in the back country, gathering strength to fight King Saul, who opposed David's inheriting the kingship. Abigail secretly gathered food and supplies and, on her own, took them to David, prophesying that he would soon be king. Shortly afterward, her husband died, leaving her free to marry David. From a kabbalistic point of view, Abigail was the channel through which God sustained the Divinely chosen king, just as Joseph had sustained the ancestors of the Jewish people. Like Joseph, Abigail belonged to the ordinary world of wealth and political wheeling and dealing, but she was able to see God's hand in the events of the world.

REWRITING THE PAST

He who by reanimating the Old can gain knowledge of the New is fit to be a teacher.
—ANALECTS OF CONFUCIUS 1:11[10]

All humans manifest the *sefirah* of *Yesod*-Foundation when we pass on a heritage, whether to the next generation or to our contemporaries. We do this in the initiation rites of the generation, but also in the casual stories we tell of our ancestors and our past. The rites of transmission begin in childhood with schooling and continue throughout every passage in adulthood. Such stories and ceremonies are literally the "Foundation" for a world that is about to be born with each new generation. They express both the creative spark that is our sense of identity, and our cooperation with others, our sense of being part of a larger whole that is created by the collective, reciprocal work of *Netzach* and *Hod*.

Today, for the first time ever, the entire world can hear the stories we tell. Through worldwide mass communication and massive interaction of people from different countries and traditions, we do have the possibility of something new emerging. But what most often happens is that we revert to the archetypes of dominance. In a multicultural age, the most common international symbol seems to be that of the superhero who conquers aliens of one sort or another. Should we not be trying to teach instead that no sentient being is alien to us? Further, the public channels of tradition have most often been created and maintained exclusively by males. Surely we must insist that women's perspectives be included, publicly as well as privately, as we formulate our teachings for the next generation.

Most of all, the heritage we pass on through *Yesod* must be inclusive, connected to wholeness. It must be connected to prophetic vision, which takes history and forges it in accord with a vision of the future. This is the spark that enlivens the passing on of tradition, the continuance of society, the renewal of the past. Some traditions, notably the Hindu and Buddhist, place a great value on what is called "direct transmission." The direct current that runs from *Keter* through *Yesod* is the means by which the energies circling through our social world are purified and refined in light of a higher vision.

In Jewish tradition, prophetic vision and history are intimately related. The history books in the Bible, like Joshua, Judges, Samuel, and Kings, are part of the collection of the Prophets, or *Nevi'im,* just as much as Amos, Hosea, Isaiah, and Jeremiah. Both history and prophecy involve the ability to see the big picture of processes going on in a temporal framework. The prophet is nourished by the fact that his heart is attached to the ideal, "gazing at the Spring," to use Rabbi Nachman's metaphor. Yet there is a difference between what happens in the upper triangle, around *Tiferet*-Splendor, and what happens in the lower triangle focused at *Yesod*-Foundation. Whereas the energy of the heart is characterized by yearning, that of the lower torso is processing and clarifying. Its guardians are the kidneys, whose main job is refining. Our refining is a re-envisioning of not only our current society but also our traditions, remnants of the visions of previous generations.

Sometimes, our sense of discomfort with the past makes us want to throw out symbols, practices, and beliefs that don't agree with us at the moment. This is not the kind of purification I am suggesting here. What must be refined, in order for the heart's love and the prophet's vision to be passed down to the next generation, is the residue of collective emotion—especially the negative emotions of fear, resentment, humiliation, and desire for domination or revenge—that swirls through the *sefirot* of *Netzach* and *Hod*. We will learn in Chapter 7 ways of dealing with these emotions on an individual level. Collectively, however, we must recognize that these emotions shape the symbolic frameworks through which we usually interpret everything. All our religions, however elevated and creative their visions, are also clouded by residues of ancient wounds.

In Chapter 1 we spoke of cleaning the sediment out of a glass lamp. The process is nowhere more intense than here. As we become more articulate about what we are striving for—as our gaze into the future and toward the ideal becomes clearer—we work even more assiduously at examining and refining our concepts of the past, which means redefining ourselves.

History shows that human beings do this redefining continually. When a country goes through a political revolution and a new government takes over, suddenly the heroes of the country change. When the Russian Revolution overthrew the czars, city names were changed and statues of revolutionary heroes replaced portraits of emperors; even history textbooks were rewritten. Similarly, when we decide to apply for a different kind of job, we rewrite our resumes to emphasize different relevant experience and background. We remake our past, including all the components of our self-concept, in light of a new vision of the future. This happens not only in an intellectually articulate way, as with resume-writing and school textbooks, but also with ritual, art, and music.

The urgent task now is to reformulate our future and past not in accordance with political needs but by attuning ourselves to spiritual realities: God alive in the world, creativity afoot, with the long-sought unity of the planet, and a desire for the health and well-being of all beings guiding our every move. The model can be taken from Joseph, who reinterpreted what happened to his family. When his brothers were afraid that he might take revenge on them for what they had done to him, he reassured them: God planned all this:

> Now do not be distressed or take it amiss that you sold me into slavery here; it was God who sent me ahead of you to save people's lives . . . God sent me ahead of you to ensure that you will have descendants on earth, and to preserve you all, a great band of survivors. So it was not you who sent me here, but God, and He has made me an adviser to Pharaoh and lord over all his household and ruler of all Egypt. (Genesis 45:5–8)

We need to reconnect to the grand design, as Joseph urged his brothers to do. He told the story with an eye to the future and the betterment of humanity—"to save people's lives . . . to ensure that you will have descendants." We must retell the story of our planet and the natural world, and the story of humankind. In our stories of nature, we must reinstate God and spirit, while at the same time incorporating insights from ecology, seeing ourselves in relation to a diverse and sentient world rather than as dominating nature. Historically, the great stories that have inspired the world must be retold. Jewish tradition, with its great Exodus story, the story of Divine redemption from slavery, has inspired liberation movements all over the world. In the past two centuries, women and oppressed minorities have been contributing their own stories to this stream of collective memory. Our stories must "re-member" humanity by speaking of those who have been denied their voice and their access to avenues of influence.

We need to incorporate into our stories and communal rituals more of the *sefirah* of *Hod* rather than only the heroic stories of *Netzach*. Many heroes did not conquer but gave of themselves, working endlessly on behalf of others. These are sacrificial stories—Mahatma Gandhi, Martin Luther King, Jr., Mother Teresa, and Nelson Mandela, people who must be part of everyone's new international cultural heritage. Along with these heroes are the exiles—people driven from their homes and disconnected from their roots. Judaism is a paradigm because Jews have been in exile for two millennia already. Many other communities and individuals are in "exile" from their homelands—African-Americans disconnected from Africa, Tibetan Buddhists whose lands were conquered by China. With the dislocations of war and with ever-increasing worldwide immigration, these are only a few examples among dozens. How do people reconnect to their destiny when they are strangers in a strange land?

We must tell our own tradition's unique stories with these issues in mind. We must tell stories of creativity, of struggling against odds, of refusing to oppress others, of love and compassion and forgiveness, of people placing Divine wholeness and connection to other beings above all else.

And we must tell stories of miracles. We can only break through the vise grip that mechanistic science has on our consciousness by recognizing the role of God in everything. The Baal Shem Tov, founder of Hasidism, taught that no leaf falls without God's willing it. Each of us experiences amazing events—from coincidences to clear miracles—in our lives. We must see the Divine acting in all these and have the courage to tell those stories. When we do, we will see that the billiard-ball causation of the old mechanistic science is not the only force in the universe. God is in our midst, with the force of cohesion rather than mere causation, bringing people and events together for an ultimate good. "God sent me before you."

The above epigraph of Joseph was so fitting because it put events in the right perspective: Each person has done his part; the end result is up to God. All that we have done, all that we have attempted, all that we have learned is not ours but God's. Whatever we thought or hoped or expected might happen from our individual and social efforts, the ultimate result is out of our hands.

Like the belly of a woman in her last few weeks of pregnancy, *Yesod*-Foundation is heavy with potential and difficult to carry. At this point, we recognize the enormous responsibility we have to be channels for a reformulation of perspective. We must take the "All"—everything in heaven and earth—and add our own creative spark to transmit to the world. When we are aware that *Yesod* is the transmission of Divine will that began at *Keter,* we can express our gratitude and move forward with freedom.

The work of this *sefirah* will be easier for you to internalize if you practice the meditation called "Contemplating Your Place in History" in Part IV, page 185.

Bringing Energy into Form: *Malkhut*-Manifestation

Divine energy has constellated itself in many transformations, through each of the *sefirot.* This energy now results in something: what exists (*yesh* or "isness" in Hebrew). Present existence is *Malkhut*-Manifestation. Normally it is all that we see and hear and touch. All the other levels are invisible. They are, as Kabbalah says, hidden worlds.

Malkhut is our ordinary life, lived on the thin skin of a world while great events surge beneath. The empty feeling of "What am I doing here?" comes up when we have skimmed along the surface for too long. The human being is meant to explore, to go beyond mere appearances. From the time that ancient astronomers asked why the moon appears at a different time every night and contemplative souls delved into the darkness of the human psyche, we have been trying to decipher the mysteries. Judaism insists, however, that mere contemplation of mysteries, or even personal experience of them, is not enough. The insights and knowledge we receive must be used to transform the world. This happens in the *sefirah* of *Malkhut*.

Only in the arena of *Malkhut* can we complete the circuit of thought, emotion, speech, and action. When we consciously act, we make changes in the physical world through actual contact with it, or we set vibrations in motion with our speech. In this way, truly new things come into being. We think, we organize, and finally we speak and act. Our "decrees" become reality. The capacity to initiate decrees and have them carried out—to introduce a new will into the world—is kingship, the literal meaning of the Hebrew word *malkhut*. In Kabbalah, *Malkhut* means that one's true intent, whether unconscious or conscious, reaches completion. In Rabbi Nachman's story of the turkey prince, *Malkhut* is restoring ourselves to our true noble essence, like the prince once again sitting at the banquet table.

The truth of the realm of *Malkhut* is that we will bring everything we know and feel into actualized reality in some form. We as humans have the gift of being able to be conscious of the depths of being and experience them. One of the amazing adventures of humanity in the last two hundred years is the discovery of undreamed levels of existence: the mysteries of the genetic code, the forces within the atom, distant stars and black holes. Will we exercise conscious, ethical control over our knowledge of other dimensions of existence? Will we ask what God wants us to do with it? Will we consider the larger implications of our actions? Or will we follow the most enjoyable or profitable path and leave the results to chance?

Problems arise when, at this final point of action, we have separated ourselves off from the whole. For example, we know we have a responsibility to vote in elections. The template on which democratic societies are based is expressed in the will of the people and the equality of all citizens. In the United States, these principles are seen as Divinely sanctioned in their origins. Social institutions are set up to regulate our interactions, in accord with that original high intent, but the correspondence between the original Divine will and the society we live in depends on, among other things, our vote.

We will, hopefully, prepare ourselves by studying the candidates' past records and their positions on important issues. Through this effort, and then casting our votes, we issue our "decrees" to be considered with all the others who vote. Normally, we just accept the results. But sometimes we suddenly become attached to the outcome. For example, in the American presidential contest in 2000, apparently rational people became intensely partisan. They stopped listening to others and stopped being self-critical. Instead of thinking about the process as a whole, they got stuck in one particular version of reality, fixed in their own ego's perception of themselves and their place in the universe. This is a temptation that occurs all the time at the level of *Malkhut:* We are tempted to build ourselves a rigid little universe in which we insist on being the star players.

How do we correct this rigidity? One way is to remember that responsibility is not something that can belong to a person ("it's *my* responsibility"). Responsibility is the ability to respond, which implies a larger context, a community, a world of other actors and thinkers, and God as a major player too, with intricate processes linking heaven to earth. This is the Jewish concept of covenant. We are all responsible for one another and to one another. You may be a prince or princess, given dominion over your part of the world, but you live in a larger world of nobility, including a Divine King who is intimately involved.

It is also important to respect processes for decision-making that are designed to include many different factors and arrive at a balanced decision. This is the final guidance of the arrow to its exact place on the target. Judicial and legislative procedures are the most common such processes in secular society. In religious traditions, values and principles (such as are enshrined in law) are usually combined with the insight and compassion of spiritual leaders. In Judaism, for example, there is a process by which one decides every action: *halacha,* literally "the walking," the general term for applied Jewish law. Built on the deliberations of sages over three thousand years, and in many historical eras and cultures, *halacha* defines how a person can walk rightly in the world.[11] Not every Jew today accepts traditional *halacha* as binding authority, but the concept of a way to walk with integrity and responsibility runs throughout Judaism and similar ideas appear in every truly spiritual path. A way of responsibility must mark *Malkhut*—a way of responding collectively as well as individually to the Divine intent. Then *Malkhut*-Manifestation becomes the mirror of *Keter*-Crown not only in vision but in reality.

Following the Rule

The path of responsibility is reflected in the fact that every lasting religious community has its rule. The Eightfold Noble Path of Buddhism insists on right ways to act, speak, and earn a living, as well as how to follow a spiritual intent and meditate. In medieval European monasteries, such guidelines were called the *regula* (Latin for "rule"), as in "the Rule of Saint Benedict." Interestingly, this word probably comes from the Hebrew word *regel,* which means foot—the part of the body that walks (as in *halacha*). Although every general rule has many specific rules, each tradition conveys the sense that the details relate to an overarching concept of how to live the best possible life. In the Western religions, the concept of a rule is related to the concept of a God who reveals Divinity to the world. The rule is the manifestation of Divine will, to the extent that human beings can understand it. In many Native American traditions, there is the concept of a Way, close to the Hebrew concept *derech.* Judaism says, "*Derech eretz* is the foundation of Torah," meaning that the way of the earth accepted by humanity—the ethical rules and codes of civility recognized by all—are basic rules for Jews as well. On those general ethical principles is built the further, more detailed path of *halacha.* The rule in each religion usually urges people to a higher path than is prescribed by society at large. In each religion there is also another, still more demanding kind of path, called in Hebrew *nativ,* meaning a personal path that must be blazed by each individual.[12]

Today we live in a time when people often reject rules and laws, in Judaism and elsewhere. Living according to a rule passed down by tradition seems superficial. *Malkhut* has lost its connection to the processes that gave rise to it. In the villages and towns of traditional societies, the rule was alive. People were able to feel connected to the process of setting specific rules through their social networks and their leaders. From the point of view of the *sefirot,* we can say that the families, clans, and respected teachers of the community's heritage embodied *Yesod*. The *tzaddik* in Judaism, the saint in Christianity, or the guru in Hinduism embodied *Tiferet,* and the mystic represented the possibility of access to yet higher realms. Their guidance, decision-making, and examples of personal discipline ensured that *Malkhut* with its rules was intimately connected to all the levels of Divine creation and revelation. But to modern individuals, living without a vibrant religious society, organized religion may seem to consist only of alien rules and empty rituals. Living by the rules alone feels like going into a museum that has been looted of its treasures. Entire galleries are empty, paintings have been ripped out of their frames.

Our concern about superficiality and rote practice is not only a result of modernity. Mystics in all traditions preached to people about spiritual emptiness. They knew that human society, including its religion, sometimes lost its connection to the upper worlds. They wanted desperately for people to live from inside—not to break the rules, but to reach the heart of the tradition within the rules, where the life and the spirit are. Even in a very religious society, people could become dependent on others for their connection to God, and that society could forget who God really was. Sufis criticized Islamic legalism, Martin Luther fulminated against a church that defined salvation in terms of "works," the Taoists of China criticized the sterility of Confucian society. In

Judaism, the prophets, the rabbis of the Talmud, and all the mystics urged that we put our heart into our observances. The message of the mystics is: Find your own connection to *Tiferet* and beyond. Learn from society and your teachers, and at the same time know that you will not be merely an imitation of them. Know that you, too, can be an agent of transmission, of *Yesod*; you, too, are a prince, an ambassador of God in the world of *Malkhut*. But a prince does not set out to overthrow the rules; rather, he or she *exemplifies them in their noblest form*.

Perhaps we can turn around an ancient Zen parable that says that if you see someone pointing at the moon, you shouldn't mistake the finger for the moon. In the case of religion, this meant don't mistake the rules of religion for ultimate reality or God. On the other hand, if you are looking for the moon—or, to use a better analogy, trying to find a constellation in the sky—you would be a fool to ignore the finger pointing you in the right direction. The finger that points is the rule, with all its implications.

The rule is, in short, a measure by which we live. Its specifics are the result of the cooperation of Divine and human intent, down through the ages, filtered through all the conditions of nature and human society. This perspective assumes that the vast majority of the rules and laws in modern societies are good and life-enhancing. Like laws of nature (which we also now understand have evolved over time[13]), the greater the diversity of situations in which they have survived, providing for both continuity and creativity, the more fundamental they are to the human project. That is one reason why Judaism, like most traditions, has changed its rules very slowly over time.[14]

It is possible within Judaism to have what is called "an argument for the sake of Heaven"—differences of opinion based not on our own desires, but on the sincere conviction, based on deep knowledge of tradition, that a certain course of action is or is not in accord with the Divine will. Yet Jewish mystics have always insisted that we can't break the laws and still achieve spiritual freedom. We may feel that we have risen above the need to

He who, having cast aside the ordinances of the holy writings, follows the promptings of desire, does not attain perfection, nor happiness, nor the highest goal.
—THE BHAGAVAD GITA[15]

do exactly as the laws of society or religion dictate, but that feeling usually comes from egotistical perception, not spiritual insight. Most importantly, any consideration of revising the rules must come from a place of unification and compassion, not an "us-versus-them" perspective. Otherwise, we will generate yet more conflict and suffering.

Interestingly, in Judaism the rules themselves—the *mitzvot*—often have mystical significance. Kabbalah teaches that if one focuses intensely on a Divine commandment—one of the given rules—one can achieve higher levels of spirituality. When the *Sefer Yetzirah* comments, "They rush to His saying like a whirlwind" (1:6), Aryeh Kaplan adds, "The fact that [the mystic] is pursuing a Divine 'saying' allows him to have access to much higher states of consciousness than he normally can attain. It is for this reason that many mystics would engage in meditations related to the observances of various commandments."[16] Similarly, the *Tanya* teaches that performing a commandment is a way to unite directly with the Divine will—it is, in essence, a mystical act.[17] By putting our will at the service of the Divine, we reduce the scope of the ego, which typically asks us to rationalize our actions in service of our self-interest.

There are two general rules on which, so far as I know, all spiritual teachers agree. One is doing good and giving to one's fellow human beings, especially to those in need. The work of serving others is the most universal way to eliminate ego. Moreover, in Jewish mysticism, acts of goodness are the basis of what is called the "arousal from below"—human action that will in turn stimulate God to shower Divine love on earth. As Rabbi Schneur Zalman of Liadi wrote near the turn of the nineteenth century, on the eve of the technological and ideological revolutions that were to transform world culture, compassionate action is the crucial thing:

> After the creation of "man to work on it" [the earth], every arousal from above, to arouse the attribute of the Supreme Expansiveness, depends on an arousal from below, that is, *the charity and kindness that we do in this world* . . . in these times . . . the principal service of God is the service of charity.[18]

The other virtually universal rule is to set aside time for your relationship to God. In Judaism, this essential aspect of spirituality has been instituted through insistence on the collective and personal observance of Shabbat (the Sabbath), which has been admired and sometimes adapted by many in other spiritual traditions.[19] The rules surrounding the observance of the seventh day as a rest day have helped guarantee that its holiness will be preserved. But whether or not you take on a Sabbath, a substantial amount of sacred time is a crucial part of spiritual practice.

The realm of rule-governed action, "kingship" or *Malkhut,* is expressed symbolically in the figure of King David, who is said to be the ancestor of the Messiah. The Hebrew letters of the name David signify "empty and empty"—holding nothing for himself. David, says the tradition of Kabbalah, comes to teach the utter destruction of ego. The opponent of the Messiah is known as Gog, whose letters mean "full and full"—that is, full of himself even after having been shown the reality of God.[20] The prophetess who represents *Malkhut* is Esther, who also sought nothing for herself even though she was chosen queen over a great Persian empire. She won her people's salvation from an enemy through prayer and fasting, not physical conflict. Both figures suggest that the ultimate "war" is the battle between the ego and the infinite. When that war is over, the ultimate manifestation—known in the ancient sources as the Kingdom of God—will be complete.

We will now turn to exploring how we can implement a kabbalistic understanding of the world from a more personal perspective. But first, here are the *sefirot* as we have described them in the Unfolding of Creation, for your review:

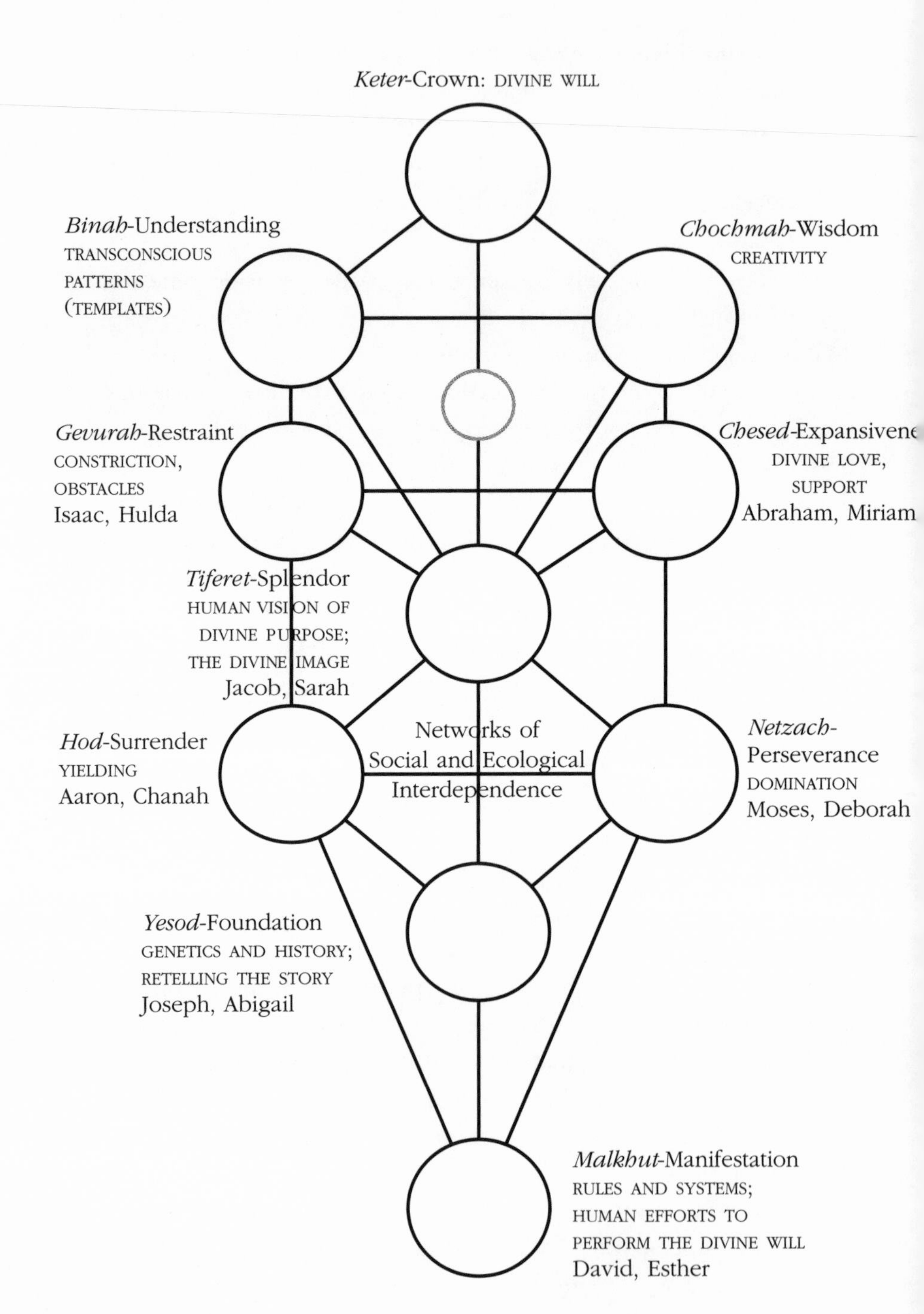
Keter-Crown: DIVINE WILL
Binah-Understanding
TRANSCONSCIOUS PATTERNS (TEMPLATES)
Chochmah-Wisdom
CREATIVITY
Gevurah-Restraint
CONSTRICTION, OBSTACLES
Isaac, Hulda
Chesed-Expansivene
DIVINE LOVE, SUPPORT
Abraham, Miriam
Tiferet-Splendor
HUMAN VISION OF DIVINE PURPOSE; THE DIVINE IMAGE
Jacob, Sarah
Hod-Surrender
YIELDING
Aaron, Chanah
Networks of Social and Ecological Interdependence
Netzach-Perseverance
DOMINATION
Moses, Deborah
Yesod-Foundation
GENETICS AND HISTORY; RETELLING THE STORY
Joseph, Abigail
Malkhut-Manifestation
RULES AND SYSTEMS; HUMAN EFFORTS TO PERFORM THE DIVINE WILL
David, Esther

PART III

THE PATH OF REMEMBERING

6 Clearing the Path

Beware! Say not: "He is All Beautiful
And we His lovers." You are but the glass
And He the face confronting it, which casts
Its image in the mirror. He alone is manifest
And you in truth are hid.
Pure love, like beauty, coming but from Him,
Reveals itself in you. If you can steadfastly look,
You will at length perceive He is the mirror also.

. . .

Your world-captivating beauty, to display its perfections
Appears in thousands of mirrors, yet is One . . .
The unique, the incomparable
Heart-enslaver is One. All this turmoil and strife
In the world is from love of Him.

—Jāmī of Persia[1]

Examining Our Personal History

Kabbalah says, along with the Sufi poet, that we are the thousands of mirrors of the One God. How can we realize this awareness in our lives? How can we know, through all the world's turmoil and strife, the love and beauty that God wants to manifest within us? We do it by filling *Malkhut*—ordinary existence—with Divine reality, clearing all the sediment from the lamp so that light can shine all the way through from *Keter*-Crown.

Understanding and contemplating the *sefirot,* as we have begun to do in Part II, is the first step. We now have a map of Divine reality seen from a cosmic perspective, from the process of creation to the way that humans try to manifest the Divine will in society. Now we can use that information to begin our own personal kabbalistic journey, from *Malkhut* to *Keter.*

We must begin by addressing our personal history as it manifests in the lower sefirot—*Malkhut, Yesod, Netzach,* and *Hod.* I would like to say that we will erase our personal history, but that sounds too extreme. We must make our personal history simply an interesting adventure of the soul, not the center of life. Unfortunately, we have usually been induced to think of our life histories as tales of failures and wrong turns interspersed with accomplishments of which society approves. Then we agonize over the past and wonder why we don't feel connected to our achievements. This is another variation on the serpent's old admonition: "Doubt yourself!"

The spiritual process I suggest takes a different direction. We want to discover the largest and greatest sense of ourselves—our connection back to our original Source. And then we want to let the Light of that Source flow through us completely, as though we were empty vessels.

As we are growing up, we rarely see ourselves as vessels of Divinity. In the world of the turkey prince "under the table," we experience ourselves as dependent on the good will of others. Unlike most animals, we do not have the abilities we need to sustain our own lives. We need a long period to become full human beings. During that period, we are involved in innumerable exchanges with the other beings in our lives, exchanges that offer us opportunities to define our lives. But we don't really know enough to make conscious choices for most of that time. We reach adulthood still entangled in the energies of childhood and adolescence—the social energies that, as we saw in Chapter 5, are embedded in the four lowest *sefirot.*

We must disentangle ourselves in order to live our soul's mission effectively. The most important aspects of that disentanglement are to recognize how our identities have come into being, and how our ties to the past hinder us.

Ego and Naming

We begin by identifying our attachments to our egos. The ego is connected to the roles we play in life, and to our current version of our personal identity. This attachment begins very early in life, when the society we live in gives us a name.

Recall that the lowest of the ten *sefirot, Malkhut,* is the world just as we ordinarily see it. Divine energy is present but normally concealed. This world is physically organized according to natural laws and socially constructed by our culturally determined perceptions. These natural and social constraints constitute "the rule," as we described it in Chapter 5. When children are born, they are immediately given a place in this world—a role. The action by which this is done is the naming of the baby.

Names are the signature of the *sefirah* of *Malkhut.* The first act of Adam in the Bible, really the act that completed creation, was to name the animals. Rabbi Yitzchak Ginzburgh observes that "Adam . . . drew the full experience of life into 'every living creature' by calling it by name."[2] Our names are a gift of the world to us, usually from our parents and close relatives, who thereby assign us a place in the world. We soon learn to respond to our names differently from any other word we hear. We become identified with the name: I *am* David, I *am* Sarah. This identification is the external formation that is associated with the personality we call the ego.

By choosing a particular name, those who named us already created an image of who we were. Perhaps we were named after ancestors, to place us in a lineage. Many cultures have rules (remember that *Malkhut* is about the application of rules) that dictate what names can and cannot be given. Ashkenazi (European) Jews do not usually name after a living relative, but frequently after a deceased one (Sephardi, or Mediterranean, Jews follow different customs). Other cultures have restrictions about certain names, for example names of people who died in unusual ways. In some societies, it is considered a good thing to name after the parent, so that we find "John Sr." and "John Jr.," or even Richard I, II, and III. Sometimes, parents are creative with names, inventing new ones or taking rarely used ones for their new baby. Sometimes parents say that they saw something about this baby that led them to give it a particular name. Often in American culture, it's just "I always liked that name."

The importance that we attach to the name becomes clear if we observe how often children struggle with the name they are given—usually during late childhood or adolescence. If they've been called by their Hebrew name, they will switch to the English version—and vice versa. They will cherish nicknames given by their friends—or hate them. They will play with their signatures, trying to get exactly the right style. It is as if the ego that manifested in the world when they were born can no longer hold their energy; it has to be adapted and enlarged in some way.

Even as adults, we sometimes change our names. Women have traditionally taken on their husband's last name, signifying that they will take on the task of caring for his lineage as well. Frequently, married women will sign documents with both their maiden and married names: Jane Smith Jones, for example, rather than Jane Louise Jones. They are saying (perhaps unconsciously) that they are bearers of both lineages. A change in religion frequently brings a change in name, or an additional or "secret" name. Moving into a new society often initiates a name change, usually to be more acceptable among one's new associates. Immigrants to the United States often changed their original names to make them easier for English speakers to pronounce. Equally often, the customs officers changed the name for them, and the new arrivals decided to accept it.

All this working and playing with names are symptoms of the process of trying to fit a soul into an ego, which is a cultural construct. But this world-stage reality is only one level—what Kabbalah alludes to as the *sefirah* of *Malkhut.* On this level, we are like actors on a stage, each with a part to play, and the entire system of education in every culture is to teach us what that part is. Each of us may be incredibly creative and undoubtedly unique, but at the level of *Malkhut,* people will always see us in roles. Different people will perceive different roles—parent, child, teacher, friend, businessman, artist—but this reflects the fact that the rules or social structures are about roles.

Seeing the discrepancy between one's assigned role and one's inner sense of self is the first step in maturity. Young children don't question their place; they respond to their names, imitate their elders, and diligently acquire social skills. Sometimes they are still fairly young when they begin to feel uncomfortable about who they are. They may say, as one of my children did when she was five, "I'm the worst kid in the world." This is an expression of an intuitive sense that their ego-persona is not their true self, and it can come out as a wild scream: "I don't fit in! I'm a terrible person!" Later, children may withdraw or become socially disruptive. They flit from one group to the next, or hold desperately to their small clique of friends. They are discovering that the ego is not all there is. By the time of adolescence or early adulthood, they are often ready to shake up the world, or at least their corner of it, to let us know about this discrepancy—what they often call hypocrisy.

Yet as we mature, we may find that it is not necessary to change our roles radically or overthrow all the rules. Our light can shine from where we are. From time to time, we read stories in the newspaper about amazing people hidden away in various corners of the globe who have lived a long, contented, and admirable life without ever going more than ten miles from where they were born. While this is almost unimaginable to those of us who take airplane journeys of thousands of miles just for a week's vacation, such lives speak a profound truth. We feel we have to travel the world to achieve self-fulfillment. Really, the desire to travel is a metaphor for a deeper desire—the inner desire to expand the reach of our soul.

The first thing to ask, then, is what were we given—what was our "given" name? Perhaps our soul engineered the choice. Jewish mysticism holds that when a person is given a Hebrew name, that name contains a secret of the person's true identity. Sometimes a rabbi will recommend that a person take a new name for a certain reason, for example when he or she becomes seriously ill. The names given in these holy circumstances hold special importance.

If you have a Hebrew name, it is a good idea to study it carefully. If you were named for an ancestor, find out as much about that person as possible. List the names you have had since birth. Besides your obvious names, include nicknames, pet names used by certain relatives, tags you didn't like, fantasy names that you thought you might adopt. If you could choose a new name today, what would it be? Ask yourself what each of these names represents to you. Coming to awareness of your name(s) and the whole naming process will help you understand where you have been and where you are going. It is a good place to begin the examination of your own personal history in the light of Kabbalah.

The Past and Its Presence

What else were we given? Scientifically, we now recognize that the DNA in each cell encodes the physical information necessary for growing an entire human being with a unique physical constitution, emotional temperament, and even its own typical styles of intelligence. The source of the DNA is the combination of genes from our two biological parents. Since these genes come from their union, the genetic heritage is appropriately represented by the *sefirah* connected with procreation and transmission of tradition, the *sefirah* of *Yesod*.

Genetics is not the only resource, however. Science can show us which parent a gene came from, but it remains a mystery why the genes combine in the particular way they do—why one child in a family gets the "tall" genes and another the "short," one the brown eyes and another the blue. Judaism teaches that God is behind this process. God is the third party in the creation of every child, and the Divine design appears in the unique combinations that individuals receive.

Now, according to Jewish mystical teaching, people reincarnate until they have accomplished their soul's mission. The soul's mission is to reveal itself. The challenges that were not met, the work that was not accomplished in one life, will be offered to the person again, in another form and through different sets of circumstances. According to Kabbalah, the results of past lives—our accomplishments and our failings—are encoded in our bodies. The great eighteenth-century thinker known as the Vilna Gaon (R. Eliyahu Kramer, 1720–1797) held that the unique possibilities and limitations of one's physical body derived from one's previous lives. The "selection" from the genes of parents to create each unique self, the combinations of genes affecting one's physical constitution and related temperamental qualities and mental abilities, are related to the way one lived previously. In Jewish teachings, the process of transmitting those qualities is not merely a mechanical process but the design of a loving God. If indeed the challenges we must face are imprinted in our bodies—our physical body, our emotional temperament, and our mental abilities—these gifts provide a key to what we have to do in this life.

No wonder the *sefirah* related to this process is called *Yesod*-Foundation—it is the "foundation" built in previous lives. Think of all the things we now know are given, or heavily influenced, by inherited characteristics—channeled through our parents, "selected" by our past-life actions. Our characteristic voice and walk. Tendencies to strength on the one hand, or weakness on the other, in various areas of body and mind. Talents in art, music, physical activity. Extroversion and introversion. Each of these, and many more, represent gifts to us, through which we will in turn transmit our spiritual gifts to the world.[3] Despite the appearance that infants are totally passive, they already have the material from which they will create. The *sefirah Yesod,* on the personal level, is the creative channel through which the Divine Light enters and transforms the physically based genetic heritage.

This perspective helps us to understand our mission in life more deeply. We must never think of our spiritual purpose as something external to us. Achieving our highest purpose is not a matter of accumulating quantities of good deeds, any more than it is accumulating quantities of money. Nor is it that we have to become something or someone else. It is a matter of working with what is immediately before us, with us, and in us, and thus revealing the Divine Light hidden within our own being, this particular and unique form.

Even more importantly, the encoding from past lives includes the positive qualities we have previously mastered. The Bible teaches that God remembers goodness for a thousand generations, while God recompenses evil for only three or four (Exodus 33:6–7). The Hebrew word for generations, *toledot,* shares the same root as the word for birth, *ledah*. We can understand this as meaning that all the good we have done accumulates and is preserved from a huge number of lifetimes. The "bad" is, perhaps, what we are continuing to work on in the most recent lifetimes. The "thousand generations" of goodness crystallizes in the endowment we are given at birth, and becomes a source of strength, something to fall back on.

At the same time, we know that this endowment must be refined and cultivated so that it becomes a useful instrument in our hands, not a wild energy. The Talmud says of King David that he was destined to shed blood, but it was up to him whether he would become a murderer, a warrior, a ritual slaughterer of meat, or a *mohel* (ritual expert in circumcision). He became a warrior on behalf of his people. With all of us, certain qualities will be encouraged by society; our religious heritage can offer a higher vision and a good personal discipline to help us refine our talents. But the crucial work has to be done on our own.

Choosing Companions

The realm of mystery tells us: You live in a world full of light and life. . . . Be attached to the legions of living beings who are constantly bringing forth everything beautiful. In every corner where you turn, you are dealing with realities that have life; you always perform consequential acts, abounding with meaning and with the preciousness of vibrant life. In everything you do, you encounter sparks full of life and light, aspiring to rise toward the heights. You help them and they help you.

—Rabbi Abraham Isaac Kook[4]

The next set of energies we must transform on the personal level are the dynamic pair of *sefirot* known as *Netzach*-Perseverance and *Hod*-Surrender. Kabbalah calls them the Companions, with the specific mystical connotation meaning those who accompany us on our spiritual path. However, we have many companions long before we realize we are on a spiritual path—all the other people we encounter in our society. We are affected in subtle or gross ways by all of them.

When the kabbalistic Tree of Life is portrayed on the body, these *sefirot* are the legs, from the hips to the knees and heels. As such, they are our support systems. Socially, they represent the way our families, tribes, and communities serve us as we are growing up—guiding us, giving advice, and protecting us. *Netzach* and *Hod* also represent ways of giving and receiving, the reciprocal relations that constitute society, community, and family. The system of relationships we learn when we are young also includes a connection to the larger natural environment. Depending on the type of society we grow up in, we may learn to love, avoid, or dominate nature.

While the legs and heels are peripheral to the body, and indeed a person can survive physically without them, the energy of *Netzach* and *Hod* is truly Divine. We know this from the fact that the Hebrew word for heel, *ekev,* has a numerological value of two times a name of God *(Elohim).* This tells us that the Divine energy is acting here, too, bringing in the influences we need to carve out our particular destiny. Indeed, the two times suggests a doubling of significance, while the name *Elohim* symbolizes

Divinity expressing itself through the structures of nature and society. Thus the heel may allude to the very important social and genetic influences that we bring from our father's and mother's sides.

Still, it is important to remember that while social influences are powerful, they are not determinative. They are interacting with us. We have choices. Our relation to *Netzach* and *Hod* is, therefore, different from our relation to *Malkhut,* which, as discussed above, represents the social context in its givenness. As the kabbalists often repeat, "*Malkhut* has nothing of its own." Infants have no control over who their parents are, whether they will be raised by their birth parents or not, whether they will live in a stable home or a dysfunctional one, whether they will live in one place or move frequently, who will be their caretakers, teachers, and peers. In the modern West, these influences are largely determined by parents, guardians, and social institutions for fifteen to twenty years.

Yet *how* we respond to these influences, how we select and attract, or resist and repel aspects of society is crucial. Those responses are the individual's work with the forces of *Netzach* and *Hod.* That work colors and enriches our dominant emotional energies. For example, even young children can resist and protest their circumstances; they can choose a small group of friends from the dozens of other children they meet; they can cling to a special teacher or an aunt or uncle more than their parents. Their options seem limited from an adult perspective, but they are real and significant. As a child, I identified with one particular aunt out of about thirty aunts, uncles, and older cousins. At that time, my favorite aunt was a kind of black sheep in the family (or so I thought from a child's perspective), living a more adventurous life than anyone else. Since she moved frequently and had settled in exotic California by the time I was a teenager, I rarely saw her, but I resonated with her energy. I allowed and embraced her influence on my life, integrating it into my own inner self-formation.

Netzach has the quality of expansiveness—it stands on the same side of the Tree of Life as the *sefirah* of *Chesed*—because it is our active embracing of alternatives. We say an internal "yes" to the situation or person presenting itself. Sometimes our choice is even more active, taking initiative and exerting our will, trying to control a situation—thus this *sefirah* is traditionally called "Victory." The clubs we join, and the sports we play all nurture the emerging self.

The other side, *Hod,* is that of withdrawal and restraint. A child has to accept certain social forms as part of one's life. Family and cultural customs, tribal heritage, styles and fashions—in everything from clothing and home decoration to how we manage relationships—surround us daily. Yet, we can perform our own small *tzimtzum* (contraction), saying an internal "no," withdrawing our energy from the activities and relationships we dislike. We surrender externally and restrain ourselves internally. This restraint teaches us, in the larger world, not to be swept away by the crowd.

Depending on our temperament and our stage in development, one or the other side may be easier for us. At the college I attended decades ago, ninety percent of the student body joined fraternities or sororities. I found it offensive that during "rush," so many girls were being hurt by the judgments of others, and I refused to join even though I was offered membership in a number of sororities. I found it more in accordance with my inner truth to say "no." One of my sweetest friends, however, was a sorority girl through and through—she had thrown herself into the current of the society and taken a part in shaping it. Neither of us was wrong, but she was playing *Netzach* in relation to the given social structure, while I was adopting the position of *Hod.*

The dynamic of these two *sefirot* is to be in constant alternation and mutual interaction. Like the two legs when we walk, they work in tandem to go in a certain direction. The child who insists on staying in his room to read while the parents worry about his social development is withdrawing, but at the same time he is persevering in nurturing an aspect of self that feels right to him. When the toddler begins shouting "No!" at every outfit her mother takes out of her closet, she is asserting herself at the same time she rejects what is being expected of her.

As we grow older and find our way through more complex social dynamics, we not only have more choice in these areas—how individualistic we will be, how much we will conform—we also have more choice of associates. We choose as friends individuals who share our sense of identity, with whom we feel most comfortable. These groups—and they may frequently change as we go through different phases of life—are the people we bond with and grow with. From the cliques of early adolescence to the social circles we form as we establish our independent lives, these become new support systems at each stage in life. We are always developing the "legs" we need to walk.

Through our friends, *Netzach* and *Hod* shape us in new ways, particularly from adolescence onward. The crucial importance of companions is suggested by a story I heard from a rabbi who works with troubled teens. He always asked the teens he counseled, "How would you react to this if you were a parent? What do you think your parents should do?" Usually the boys or girls would respond with excellent answers, and often thought their parents should exercise discipline and set more boundaries. However, whenever he asked how parents should respond if their son or daughter was running around with a friend who was a negative influence, they just shrugged and had no suggestions. The message was, "Don't mess with my friends." Or, as the rabbi put it, "If your child has to choose between you and his friends, you're toast."

Similarly, choosing one's companions becomes increasingly important as one develops spiritually. Judaism advises people to make one's home a place for Torah scholars to come and teach, and never to sit among "scoffers" who ridicule such higher pursuits.[5] Great masters in all traditions describe how they had to leave behind the companions of their youth in order to have the right support for their higher endeavors. Kabbalah speaks often of secrets shared among the Companions. The Sufi masters traditionally went wandering, not for sights of this world but to find kindred souls. The teaching that comes from these examples is that your Companions should be those who can mirror to you the true Divinity of your nature.

You can probably see in your own life how your friendships have tended to change as you focused more on spiritual matters. Are there people you know who are on a spiritual path with whom you would like to associate more often? If so, seek them out. If not, pray that God will bring such people to you.

Transforming Emotional Ties

Now let's go one level deeper. The choices we made, the people we felt attracted to or withdrew from gave form to our unique emotional and physical being. These networks of reciprocity left an imprint on the various levels of our soul, but particularly on the vital life force that is most deeply connected to the *sefirot* of *Netzach* and *Hod*.

We are, as we say, *emotionally tied* to the important events and people of our past. It is as if we have spun energy fibers out of the core of our emotional selves that attach us to people, groups, and events.[6] Some of these energy connections are helpful; some will impede us as we try to move further. All of them will have to be transformed and elevated—and in some cases disconnected.

To understand why releasing these ties is an important part of spiritual development, we must understand those odd phenomena that we call emotions. There seems to be no parallel in the animal world to the wide range and subtlety of emotions experienced and described by humans. In addition to the variety of words we have for emotions, art and music elicit and, in a sense, "paint" our emotional range. As we enter any new situation, or even imagine ourselves in a different context, energy runs through the body to inform us of our multilayered response to various possibilities. For example, if we think of going shopping for gifts, different emotions will be aroused than if we imagine going to the dentist. All the past experiences we have of gift shopping and dentistry will feed information into our nervous system. The channels through which we process this information are what we call emotions.

Our body stores a vast range of emotional responses, as modern therapies have discovered. We often find that certain kinds of physical treatments (acupuncture, movement therapy, hands-on body work) sometimes release old memories. In 1998, I went to my doctor, a movement therapist, for one of a series of treatments for a shoulder injury. We were also exploring some chronic back pain. To release some of the tension in my back, he asked me to stand on a small rocking platform and practice keeping my balance. After a little practice, I stepped off the platform and felt a great relaxation and lightness in my knees. Suddenly, a memory of a kind of sweet sadness washed over me. My mind then flipped back to 1964, when a beloved friend told me goodbye on the steps of my college dormitory. I was amazed. I had not entirely forgotten my friend's leaving school. But I had completely erased the memory of those feelings until this simple exercise unlocked the emotion buried in my knees.

Conversely, emotional experiences have physical results. For example, fear with its instinctive fight-or-flight response is sometimes translated in the human system as anxiety. Sustained anxiety then affects the heart, circulation, and hormonal levels. On the other hand, when we can evoke loving feelings, they in turn produce greater physical relaxation. This connects to the powerful effects that people experience in biofeedback or certain forms of meditation.

Hod is the way we experience the currents of feeling that run through our bodies in response to our external environment and/or our own thoughts. It is also the energy that enables us to feel acceptance and gratitude (*hoda'ah* in Hebrew is related to "thanksgiving") and to let go of attachments. *Netzach* is the energy of building. It is "motional" and motivational, energizing us to create the enduring structures of our bodies and initiating external responses. As we mature, our capacity to observe both of these energies develops more fully, and we can see our impulses and emotions without judging them.

The patterns of *Netzach* and *Hod* are formed throughout our lives and are geared to helping us survive and succeed in society. They can become habitual response patterns that influence our present action and our ability to imagine the future, often inhibiting our ability to imagine and act on our full potential. People who undergo deep trauma as children may carry a set of physical and emotional responses that dominate their entire lives. For example, over the years I have met many people who had survived the Nazi Holocaust as children in hiding. Many of them had learned that the best way to deal with any threat is to disappear—to close down all reactions and go into complete silence. As a result, in difficult situations their normal personalities can change, unexpectedly, into stony withdrawal. All of us have such survival strategies, though not usually to such extremes. The only kind of tie that does not inhibit us is pure, unconditional love—a rare phenomenon to say the least.

An important corollary to this is that emotions are not something that "happen to" us. We cannot blame our emotions on our circumstances. Emotions are "e-motions," movements out of our core self. Because they develop in interaction with the environment, we may tend to blame our upbringing or our society for our reactions. But Judaism, along with many spiritual traditions, teaches us that we can attain a perspective from which we can master them.

Who knows others is perceptive;
who knows himself is wise.
Who conquers others is forceful;
who conquers himself is strong.
Who knows contentment is wealthy; who strives hard succeeds.
Who doesn't lose his place endures; who dies but doesn't perish lives on.
—Tao Te Ching[7]

Ben Zoma says, Who is wise? He who learns from every person, as it is said, "From all my teachers I grew wise" (Psalms 119:99).

Who is strong? He who subdues his personal inclination, as it is said, "He who is slow to anger is better than the strong man, and a master of his passions is better than a conqueror of a city" (Proverbs 16:32).

Who is rich? He who is happy with his lot, as it is said, "When you eat of the labor of your hands, you are praiseworthy and all is well with you" (Psalms 128:2) . . .

Who is honored? He who honors others, as it is said, "For those who honor Me I will honor, and those who scorn Me shall be degraded" (1 Samuel 2:30).

—Pirke Avot 4:1

If all the therapies and healing movements of the last two centuries have accomplished anything, it is to demonstrate beyond doubt that some of the patterned physical and emotional responses we accumulate are counterproductive, self-contradictory, and damaging to health and relationships. This is not a big surprise: Jewish mysticism, along with many other spiritual traditions, recognized the danger of carrying negative emotions. Scholarly rabbis, Zen masters, and Christian monks all agree that passions such as anger, lust, and melancholy (what we call depression) are hindrances on the spiritual path. The question is, how can we overcome our negative tendencies and create a satisfying, emotionally healthy life? We can work in two complementary ways, corresponding to the *sefirot* of *Netzach* and *Hod.*

Netzach builds experiences that are conducive to good emotional habits. This *sefirah* enables us to do things that help create positive emotions and a spiritually oriented emotional life. For example, we can decide to do things that will generate positive emotions: call a friend, go for a walk, change into clothes we really like, make order in a messy room. By choosing spiritual reading material, going to places that inspire us, and being around people we admire for their depth and sensitivity, we can add spirituality to our emotional life. We can make time to study, or to meditate. All these are active practices. Judaism has always taught that by *doing,* one eventually integrates the characteristics of *being*—that is, of becoming the kind of person one wants to be.[8] This is the beginning of every deeper phase of spiritual work:

building an external framework, a stronger vessel that can receive and hold inspiration.

Hod, on the other hand, enables us to observe, learn about, and disconnect ourselves from emotional ties. The first step is to restrain our expression of emotions—say, outbursts of anger or anxiety—or, if we cannot restrain ourselves in the moment, remind ourselves to go back and look at them later. Further, we must begin to see that the original energy of an emotion is essentially a piece of information. Imagine that when you were a small child, a guest in your house made a face that your child's brain translated into fear. That energetic information was sent to your brain as first-impression information about the encounter—something to fear. Then your thought processes went into action and decided how to respond—for example, you cried.

Such pieces of information are often correct. We call them intuitive, and we often say, "I should have gone with my first impression." Sometimes, however, our first impressions are incorrect. I might look back at an encounter with a teacher and say, "I reacted to him as if he were my father." It is as if some cue in the teacher's behavior triggered an old memory, and the energy of the information traveled down a well-worn emotional track, a familiar neural circuit. (This happens all the time in male/female relations, where one's partner triggers responses that were created in relationship to one's opposite-sex parent.)

But, correct or incorrect, the emotional track is there, and every time we meet someone that reminds us of a significant experience, we experience energy along that track. If we ever want to be able to meet people without experiencing the same old energy, we have to stop the flow of energy along that track. This means disconnecting from the old webs of connection so that every response we make comes from a place of freedom, spontaneous and unburdened by expectations and patterns of the past. What more could we want in our social relationships? However, this work is not easy, and it usually takes a long time. We must reconsider all our relationships in a more objective light, and gradually reduce their effects on us. You can do this by practicing the exercise called "Releasing Your Past" in Part IV (page 187).

The two *sefirot* of *Netzach* and *Hod* work in tandem. Remember, they represent your support system, like your two legs. Just as your legs work alternately to keep you on track and in balance, the external changes that you make in your life will work along with the internally oriented practices. Usually you won't even need to monitor this balance actively—they require each other, and you won't be able to move far ahead with only one leg. It is certainly the case that if you work with the *sefirot* in the ways I suggest, your life will change. Whatever your physical age, you will now enter spiritual adulthood.

Collective Demons and Their Victims

Although the patterns examined here are largely personal, it is important to add a word or two about the collective dimensions of the *sefirot* of *Netzach* and *Hod,* because they often impact our personal lives. You probably have noticed that some people carry wounds that are so deep that it seems impossible for them to heal. Some people seem "possessed" by rage, by grief, or by a grandiose self-image. All too frequently these states lead to violence against self or others, or to extreme exploitation of others. If you have read this far in this book, you are probably not possessed in this way yourself, although you may recognize some part of this tendency in your past. Most individuals who struggle with this level of inner pain cannot approach a spiritual life until they have made a major change.

Still, any of us may find ourselves unexpectedly in a relationship with someone like this—an abusive parent, a distraught sibling, a spouse who turns out to have a very "dark" side, or a person to whom we have turned for teaching or guidance but who has become exploitative. When we see mass movements that lead people into grotesque behavior, from the Nazi movement of wartime Germany to late-twentieth-century suicide cults, we can be fairly certain that the leader or leaders are deeply wounded individuals. Those who follow are inescapably affected, though not usually to the same degree.

Such wounds are probably carried from previous lifetimes. Sometimes individuals carry the wounds of a generations-old family system or even an entire nation. As a general rule, if we're part of the wounded system—the family or the intimate social group of a wounded person—we should not try to become healers of the individuals involved. Specially trained outsiders may be able to help. We can be compassionate while at the same time remembering to protect ourselves from any direct harm.

Yet we are also being called to a different response of our own. When we find ourselves in a system containing demonic wounds, we are being asked to examine our connection to the larger collective. Do we have habits of thought and speech, patterns of action and reaction, that maintain dysfunctional families from generation to generation? How does our ethnic heritage or religion perpetuate wounds that families and nations may carry? On Ash Wednesday 2000, the Pope and the Cardinal of the Diocese of Los Angeles at last issued messages apologizing for historic actions of the Roman Catholic Church as well as their personal actions that have hurt or alienated groups and individuals. When an institution that affects a large collective has acted in ways that damage others, the wounds on both sides are deep and lasting. Christian persecution of Jews, wars with Muslims, inquisitions, and witch trials left scars on all members of Western culture. A public apology is not a cure, but it is nevertheless a great and historic act, which can allow people to release attachment to some of their wounds as a beginning of healing.

Another way such wounds develop is when people are robbed of the dignity of their specific identity. While we are all humans and we aim for a love of all humanity, it is crucial to the development of the ego that we be allowed to express our group identity. Normal development requires a sense of distinctness. A child does not go from being an infant, with no sense of separate identity from the parents, directly into being a developed individual. The stages of later childhood and adolescence are full of opportunities to create group identity. Another way of saying this is that a child must experience herself as part of a "We" distinct from other groups ("They"), before she can become an individual.

The nature of those intermediate identities can be enormously varied. Ethnicity and religion are two examples of identity markers in modern society. Sometimes geography provides a major marker—"I'm a Texan" or "I'm a New Yorker." Lineage can be significant too—"I'm a *sabra* [born in Israel]" or "My grandfather was a rabbi." In some societies, gender provides a major marker, when for example men and women are initiated into very different roles. Being a gang member or participating in a political movement may give a person a special identity, especially in late adolescence. Even though we may see these as partial and separatist identities, and ultimately not spiritual in content, we must recognize that they are important as part of a developmental stage.

A person whose identity is denied, or who suffers humiliation around a crucial identity marker, is likely to suffer deep wounds. Most third-world peoples suffered in this way from the actions of colonial powers, as have African-Americans and Native Americans in the United States from the acts of Anglo-American governments and individuals. A natural response, when the oppressive circumstances have lifted slightly, is to lash out at the perceived oppressor. If solutions are not readily available to remedy past injustice, an individual or group can create an entire ideology around its past oppression. This response is what some modern analysts have called "victimology."[9] It limits the opportunities for healing and perpetuates the wounds.

Alternatives exist. Once, when discussing the difficulties of the Palestinian Arabs in Israel, I asked a rabbi his opinion of what was happening. Clearly, I said, the Palestinians have suffered a great humiliation both in the wars with Israel and in their treatment since. What is the remedy for this? He answered simply, "Pride in accomplishment."

We have seen this approach in many situations. Mahatma Gandhi was known for his programs of nonviolent resistance to British oppression in India and South Africa in the first half of the twentieth century. What is not often remembered is that Gandhi insisted that a crucial part of the effort was self-help programs—people spinning their own wool and wearing homemade cloth—to build self-esteem. Without this, he believed, the people could not be strong enough to practice nonviolence.

Spiritual practice has been proven to be part of such efforts as well. Dr. Martin Luther King, Jr. accomplished work similar to Gandhi in emphasizing "strength to love" rather than reaction against the dominant society. He drew on the spiritual riches of Afro-American Christianity, including a spirit of deep faith and willingness to forgive, to create a nonviolent movement that would begin to heal the wounds of racism. In parallel ways, Nelson Mandela led a peaceful revolution in South Africa, after years in jail under the apartheid system, and created what has been called a "politics of reconciliation."

The same strategies can work against our own demons. On the personal level, an individual afflicted with demons of rage or grief needs spiritual and psychotherapeutic help. On other levels, however, we all carry a collective responsibility. The less wounded have to help those who carry more of the pain by standing beside them and providing strength to love through their own love. We can model, each in our own ways, taking full responsibility for our lives and refusing to be victims or to justify our lives by appealing to our pain. We can dip into the resources of our spiritual traditions to find the ways to broaden our perspectives, to forgive, heal, and reconcile.

Finally, we must all become aware of the damage we have done by using our unique, separate identities as an excuse for separatism. Indeed, one of the motivations for this book came from my deep feeling that within my own tradition, Judaism, and in the relationship of Judaism to other religions, many wounds need to be healed. We must all develop a perspective on life that has its source in ultimate oneness. In building our personal and social structures through speech and action, we must at all times attend to how they affect others and how they ripple out into the larger world. When we tread on others' toes, we must be willing to yield and make corrections. The *sefirot* of *Netzach* and *Hod* can help balance our collective world as well.

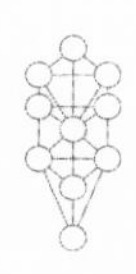

7 Realizing Your Intent

Each life converges to some centre
Expressed or still;
Exists in every human nature
A goal,

Admitted scarcely to itself, it may be,
Too fair
For credibility's temerity
To dare.

Adored with caution, as a brittle heaven,
To reach
Were hopeless as the rainbow's raiment
To touch,

Yet persevered toward, surer for the distance;
How high
Unto the saints' slow diligence
The sky!

Ungained, it may be, by a life's low venture,
But then,
Eternity enables the endeavoring
Again.

—EMILY DICKINSON, "THE GOAL"

Spiritual Awakening

The energy of the next *sefirah* on the Path of Remembering, *Tiferet*-Splendor, is always calling to us. It is our purpose in life, our personal connection to Divine vision. But we spend many years—at least twenty, and often twice that long—just growing up and establishing ourselves in life. Most people are not ready to answer the call of *Tiferet* until sometime in early to middle adulthood, and many of us not until we are elders. We have to first go through the phase of becoming socially responsible individuals, contributing to society, caring for our loved ones, raising a new generation. In this process we learn to support others emotionally and receive love in return. We learn what enriches us and what drains us. We have confronted problems and solved some of them. We have created the basic structures of "normal" human life.

Usually by this time we also have some sense of where our personal configuration emerged. We may be able to see our place in the dynamics of our family of origin, how we have left it behind or how we are still enmeshed in it. We can observe our stumbling blocks in social relations—"I'm too shy" or "I get too aggressive in arguments." We have a sense of ourselves—although we are usually far too self-critical! We are beginning at least to steer our emotional course through the pitfalls that everyone encounters, whether it be financial issues, the death of loved ones, career choices, or the joy and struggle of raising children. Hopefully, we are also able to see something of our society's place in history. At the end of the last chapter, we noticed that it is possible to take responsibility in such a way that we allow the wounds that society creates to begin to be healed. We can even see ourselves as part of a larger "family," how we have been enmeshed in the limited views of our society and how we can transcend them.

All this means that we have begun to master the four lowest *sefirot*. Yet we still may not be clear about our appropriate role in the larger cosmic drama. If we are turkeys under the table, we can now stick our heads out from under the tablecloth and see that there's a bigger picture. But our appetites and insecurities often make us quickly go back under again. Especially in our society, our basic physical needs have been amplified so that, despite all our labor-saving and time-saving devices, we still spend an enormous amount of time satisfying our needs. The basic need for safety that is provided for a lion by his den, or in medieval times by the walls and moat of a castle, may be amplified into needing a high-security apartment and several bolts on the door. We can spend hours comparative shopping for the best alarm system, and still waste time arousing our worries again by reading newspaper stories about burglars. We're also greatly concerned about the opinions of other turkeys, so we are subject to social pressure as well.

A spiritual awakening usually begins when we recognize the futility of the life of a turkey under the table. Even if we are not able to articulate the problem clearly, we see that many of the ways we spend our time, many of our daily activities, are simply different ways of doing the same old thing—providing ourselves and our families with food, safety, continuity, and some pleasure. We see that our lives are not so much different from others around us, or even from animals who do the same things on instinctive programming. Then we ask, "Is this all that human life is about? What does it matter if I do this or not—billions of others live such lives. I'm trying to be a good person and manage what I've been given to manage. But what for? Why am I here?"

These questions arise out of a higher level of our being than our emotional and social selves. They represent an igniting of the spark of the soul, coming through the *sefirah* of *Tiferet,* whose energy radiates from the center of our being. Once the energy of this *sefirah* is awakened, we have to listen to it. If we try to shut it off or ignore it, we will damage ourselves and short-circuit the higher development of our lives. At this point in life, these questions have to do with our inner truth—indeed, Truth is another word for this *sefirah*.

As the great first-century rabbi Hillel said, "If I am not for myself, who will be?" Society, however much it supports our development, will always set limits on personal development because social institutions are created with their own demands for conformity. Even our friends and spouses may feel uncomfortable if we change too much because it rocks the boat. The *sefirah* of *Tiferet*-Splendor, which now begins to shine with Divine Light, insists that we go on a personal search.

We look upward now, not backward to our past or horizontally to our current companions who are in our emotional and spiritual comfort zone. Imagine that the four lower *sefirot* form a goblet, looking upward to be filled by the reality of our awakened soul.

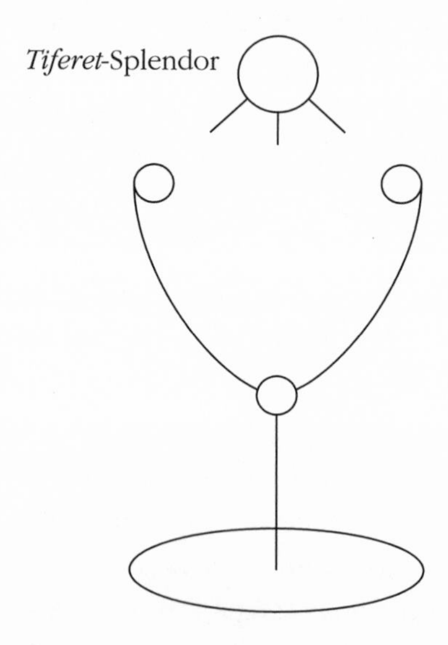

Our search can take many forms. Frequently, it involves turning to religious or spiritual teachers or organizations. This is quite appropriate because they are the bearers of the deepest wisdom of spiritual seekers of all the ages. Although we may intuit that the truth lies within us, we are usually not so arrogant as to think that we can answer all the deep and important questions without listening to the voices of those who have preceded us. Every accomplished spiritual person has spent time learning from the "elders," from people in their own tradition, or other traditions, who give over their wisdom.

At the beginning, you may find your teacher by going to the religious group of your choice and meeting all the "experts" (priests, ministers, rabbis, etc). Frequently, the person you choose turns out to be simply the person who introduces you to the workings of the tradition. He or she is a gatekeeper. As you move on, the teachers you need will often appear in a more indirect way, and may not even be professional "teachers." Sometimes they will be in your life for a long time, sometimes for only brief encounters. It is almost as if they can't be consciously sought. As the old saying goes, "When the student is ready, the teacher will appear."

Most of us receive great benefit from attaching ourselves, for a time, to a specific teacher. This person not only imparts knowledge but is a model of action, someone to emulate in many ways. Learning happens at a much deeper level when we see another person living the teaching. When we look for a teacher, we want someone who not only knows the information but also has been able to make it meaningful in his or her life.

This kind of relationship has its dangers. The intense personal relationship to a teacher is a little like having a new parent or elder sibling. Precisely because of that intensity, the relationship often awakens early emotional attachments and wounds. As a result, one can sometimes be blinded by the wonderful things that happen in the relationship, to the point that one forgets the original purpose—to find one's own truth. We can be dragged back into the emotional dynamics of the lower *sefirot* and, until we untangle them, we move forward only very slowly. Remember that the teacher is only a channel, the one you happen to have at this particular time. Review meetings with your teachers and fellow students on an ongoing basis to release the emotional energy that you sometimes attach to them. (See "Releasing Your Past" in Part IV, page 187.)

Creating a Practice

Most importantly, a good teacher will introduce you to a practice. The practice guarantees that ultimately you will not be a mere imitation of your teacher. The practice will also be something that has been passed down in an authentic tradition. The various traditions usually suggest methods of self-examination and self-transformation: charitable acts, physical discipline, prayer, confession, meditation, ritual, and ceremony. We will look briefly at these approaches.

First, however, it is important to note that spiritual practice is not on the same level as rules. We talked about rules and roles as part of the *sefirah* of *Malkhut,* part of being in society. For example, your religion may have as one of its rules that you should donate one-tenth of your income to charity. However, taking on charity as a spiritual practice is a different matter. You are being asked to become a person who *embodies* justice and compassion and giving, rather than just obediently following a rule. Similarly, you may have grown up with certain traditional prayers or the ritual of confession. Now, however, you are asked to *become* your prayer and to continually examine how you are practicing your spiritual values. In truth, the rules of a spiritual tradition are intended to be part of a practice. If you grow up with them, you probably will see them as merely rules. If you come to them later in life, it may be clearer that they point to a spiritual practice. Either way you will, at this stage, revolutionize all your ideas about rules.

In Judaism, the path of Jewish law, known as *halacha,* is intended to refine the human being. The word that means to "refine" (*tzaref,* as in removing impurities) can also mean to "join," as when a metal worker joins two pieces with a soldering iron. When we have a practice, we begin the process of refining our human selves and joining ourselves firmly to God. The study of different religious traditions reveals that most of them offer similar recommendations as to how to improve your spiritual life. They all teach a moral framework for life, the discipline and enhancement of one's mind, body, and emotions, and self-examination as one proceeds on the path. These are all the work of the *sefirah* of *Tiferet*.

The practices I describe below are, in my view, virtually universal, although the forms they take are unique to each religion. Look in your own tradition for practices that fall into these categories.

1. *Study and reflection.*
Since you're reading this book, this form of practice is probably an easy one for you. Go to lectures or classes by people who aim to challenge and not merely excite their audiences. Study the foundational religious texts—in the Jewish tradition, there is a truly outstanding and fascinating tradition of Torah study. Find out who are considered truly great deep thinkers and inspiring personalities in your tradition. Even if you can tackle only small pieces of their writings, remember that mastering a paragraph or a few pages written by a real thinker is worth far more than secondhand information. You can join the inquiry into the great questions that have occupied human beings for millennia: How can we understand the goal of human life? How do we make decisions in a way that promotes goodness? What is the origin of evil and how do we address it in our lives?

Posing and answering questions is an enormously valuable discipline of mind, which cannot help but result in greater clarity and intellectual awareness. Hopefully, it also enables us to think critically and recognize when we are hearing truth and when we are being taught only dogma. Some people will be drawn more to this type of study than others, but it can be at least one component of everyone's spiritual path.

At the same time, if we acquire knowledge but it remains external to us, spiritual growth will not take place. Expertise in theology, philosophy, or religious law, if taken alone, can be just another "trade skill." It can be treated as a mere database of objective knowledge that we trot out on demand, but don't think much about in between. Religious knowledge must be internalized. A teacher who helps us understand our studies is essential here. The word "Kabbalah" means "receive" because the tradition had to be received personally, by one person from another, in direct transmission. This was indeed the method of the entire Jewish tradition: God taught Moses, Moses taught Joshua, Joshua taught the Israelite elders, and so on. The written tradition, inscribed in stone or scrolls or books, was the starting place, but not the whole of learning. A teacher or group studying together can help each of us internalize what we learn and apply it to our lives.

Two other practices work in tandem with study to help us incorporate the concepts and information we learn. These are prayer and meditation.

2. *Prayer.*

Prayer is both a ceremony and a personal address to God. Ideally, in prayer we create our own sacred space, closing off the outside world, and speak from the core of our being to the power that guides the universe. Many prayer traditions, including the Jewish prayer book, follow specific forms that help us move toward that inner core. When we speak in that unique kind of language called prayer, we become channels through which Divinity can flow.

Our personal address to God involves at least two dimensions. One is simply to become comfortable in talking to God. We speak aloud from our hearts about our own needs and problems—our personal needs, family or business problems, ideals, and goals. This approach is such a natural way to relate to Divinity that it is found in every spiritual tradition. In Judaism, it has become a specialized form of meditation among the Breslov Hasidim (followers of the teachings of Rabbi Nachman of Breslov). It is called *hitbodedut,* which literally means "isolating oneself." In this practice, we close ourselves off to everything except our conversation with God.

Another good exercise is to make up your own prayers after learning a specific subject matter in your studies. Rabbi Noson of Nemirov, the chief disciple of Rabbi Nachman, composed prayers after each teaching he received from his master. This enabled him to internalize the teachings more fully. In kabbalistic terms, this is using the energy of the *sefirah Da'at*-Knowledge to "bind" one's mind to the subject at hand. For example, you might compose a prayer about the use of visualization, perhaps along the following lines: *May it be Your will, God, that my imagination be turned to holy things, and that I be able to visualize and internalize the deep and profound concepts I am trying to learn. . . .*

The second dimension of prayer is to focus less on ourselves and more on others. Prayer for the larger collective is instilled in Jewish prayers by the fact that most traditional prayers are worded for "us," the entire Jewish people. Some prayers are even broader in concept, extending to the entire human race. (Many Jews have the custom of praying for themselves only indirectly through allusion, for example by reciting a biblical verse that begins and ends with the same letters as their name.)

Think of yourself as an agent appointed to speak to God on behalf of others. Jews have traditionally taken it as their responsibility to pray for the world, just as the sacrifices in the ancient Temple were intended to maintain the world. Biblical commentators have discovered hints about the importance of prayer in the second chapter of Genesis, which tells the story of the first couple, Adam and Eve. It says that "no rain had yet watered the earth" (Genesis 2:5).

Yet, we just learned in the first chapter that all the components of nature had been created, including vegetation and trees. How could this be? It is explained that all the vegetation existed *in potentia,* beneath the surface of the earth, but it had to wait for the rain to come before it could actually sprout. What caused it to sprout? The prayers of Adam and Eve.[1]

In other words, from the time of human creation, the continued workings of the universe depended on human prayer. The Bible goes on to explain that God eventually recognized that humans had too much evil in their minds to do this work properly and so, after the Flood, God decreed that natural processes would not be dependent on humans. "Seedtime and harvest will not cease" (Genesis 8:22).[2] Still, although God took some of the responsibility off our shoulders for keeping the seasons going, there has still been plenty to pray for. In our time, when our incursions into nature have seriously interfered with the natural cycles, we probably should start praying again for them too.

Prayer demands that we go beyond ego. At the same time, prayer is an emotional and not a physical experience like giving money, nor an intellectual experience like study. One of the great contributions of Hasidism to Jewish practice was a renewed emphasis on prayer, and on putting one's heart into prayer. When we try to speak from the depths of our hearts, we discover the deep pain and the profound joy of human existence, both our own and the pain and joy we feel on behalf of others. This is one of the emphases of the Hasidic masters—to cry from the depths of our hearts.

Remember that emotions are subtle forms of information, energy moving faster than thought. When we "go inside" and ask ourselves how we feel about what is going on in life—in our personal lives, in our communities, in the world we hear about on the national news—we dip into a well of deep connectedness. When we then put words to that connectedness, we are in effect asking that good things come in the world on the wings of our deep feelings.

> *I pray because God, the* Shekhinah, *is an outcast. I pray because God is in exile, because we all conspire to blur all signs of His presence in the present or in the past. I pray because I refuse to despair.*
>
> —ABRAHAM JOSHUA HESCHEL[3]

One way this is done in Jewish prayer is through words of blessing. Blessings are affirmations that God is at present doing what we are asking for. For example, we express the sincere request, "Heal us," and then end the prayer with "Blessed are You, Lord, Who is healing the sick." Willis Harman, a great scholar of mental sciences, suggests in addition that when we pray for or affirm something, we should imagine how we will feel when the event or quality we are praying for is actualized. When that feeling includes the aspect of surrender, "Thy Will be done," we are offering ourselves up to God. In Part IV, I outline an exercise, "Deepening Your Prayer" (p. 178), which will help you to give this kind of form to your prayer.

Many people still ask, "What does our personal prayer have to do with the plans of the Master of the Universe? Does our prayer change God's design? Aren't people really praying just to satisfy their own emotional needs?" Remarkably, scientific studies suggest that prayer is healing, and particularly that prayer for others is effective. Generalized prayer for "the best outcome" or "Thy Will be done" is especially effective, both on those who are praying and those prayed for.[4] Exactly how prayer works is not understood, but these studies suggest we should not be so surprised that every religious tradition in the world has some way of invoking and asking the "higher powers" for protection and assistance.

3. *Meditation.*

Meditation in Judaism is a complement to prayer. To put it colloquially, if prayer "goes up," meditation prepares us to receive what "comes down." Thus an important aspect of meditation is to inculcate awareness and receptivity. Another dimension is contemplation, including visualization, which helps us engage our imagination and feeling so that our connection to the Divine can become richer and more complete.

Kabbalistic meditations have ranged from simple *kavannot*—reciting or thinking an "intention" for a specific prayer—to intricate and complex transmutations of the letters of Divine names. Silent meditation and breathing exercises were quite common among kabbalists just as among Hindu and Buddhist teachers. Such methods of increasing awareness, on the one hand, and ability to concentrate and focus on the other, seem to be nearly universal. Most practitioners of such methods also testify that they help in achieving equanimity, a peaceful and serene attitude in the face of life's difficulties.

The first stage of many Jewish meditation practices is called *yishuv ha-da'at,* or "settling the mind."[5] This settling (the root is the same as "sitting") of one's *"Da'at,"* or knowledge, becomes a platform for the utter holiness of the upper levels. In addition, Jewish tradition teaches a specific kind of meditation that can sometimes enable us to be receptive to what is beyond the boundaries of normal thought: *hitbonenut* (from the same root as *Binah,* Understanding). Literally it means "to cause oneself to understand." This approach involves focusing on a particular symbol or concept and connecting it mentally to related symbols and ideas, as well as Hebrew words and letters, building a rich structure of interrelated ideas and images. A *hitbonenut* meditation on water, for example, might involve contemplating water in the various forms it appears on earth, water as a symbol for Torah, verses in the Bible that mention water, and the Hebrew word *mayim* and the meanings of its letters. All these would be "unfoldings," so to speak, of the symbol water.

Meditative visualizations have long been recognized in Kabbalah as a powerful aid to spiritual understanding. The chief disciple of Rabbi Nachman, Reb Noson of Nemirov, wrote about them as follows:

> The ability to visualize something in the mind comes from the power of imagination. What we visualize might in fact be a physical object, but the visualization of that object in the mind is actually a "spiritual" experience. Imagination can thus be thought of as both the highest point of the physical realm and the lowest point of the spiritual realm. It is the bridge between the material and the ethereal. . . .
>
> For this reason, man was called ADaM. He is formed of ADaMah, the dust, the physical; but he can ascend above the material world through the use of his imagination and can reach a level of prophecy. The Hebrew word for "I will imagine" is ADaMeh. In this sense we can understand the meaning of the verse, "Through the prophets ADaMeh [I will be imagined]" (Hosea 12:11).[6]

In this sort of meditative visualization, we use verbal cues to imagine a certain feature of existence—for example, resting in the presence of God in the Garden of Eden, or standing at Mount Sinai to receive the Torah. We do this almost instinctively when we say, "Imagine yourself in the other person's shoes"—essentially a visualization intended to evoke compassion. The number of possible meditative visualizations is limited only by one's imagination. They need not be only about positive, pleasant things; kabbalists—again, like Buddhists—sometimes contemplated the idea of a decaying corpse to remind themselves of the transitory nature of human existence. In general, however, the custom in Judaism is to use positive visualizations based on holy writings. For millennia, the Book of Psalms in the Bible has provided rich subjects for contemplation.

In addition, certain meditations ask us to "empty the mind" or urge the mind to go beyond what can be contemplated. These are kabbalistic forms of meditation to induce *Chochmah*-consciousness. Thinking about impossible things like "What do you see behind your head?" or "Before one, what do you count?" are examples—not unlike the *koans* of Zen Buddhist tradition.[7] These can be very powerful, in the right circumstances and with the help of a good teacher, in opening us up to higher illuminations. However, as we will see in Chapter 8, they do not ensure an end to the spiritual quest.

4. *Rituals and ceremonies.*

Every spiritual tradition has a round of rituals, including daily and weekly rituals, ceremonies connected with lunar or solar calendars, and rites of passage. These rituals are often rooted in ancient spiritual practices and are maintained simply as traditions. Reforming movements in modern religion often throw them out (e.g., many Protestant traditions vis-à-vis Roman Catholicism, Reform Judaism vis-à-vis the received Orthodoxy). A few generations later, however, they creep back in. Humans need to connect with natural rhythms, with a sense of heritage, and with their own bodies in a sacred way. Rituals enable us to do this.

There is an even deeper dimension to ritual. Recall that in speaking of *Binah,* we said that the patterns or templates of a tradition are laid down mentally in that *sefirah*. Rituals give these patterns physical, bodily form. They are the architecture of energy. They are rich in metaphor, symbol, and allusion because metaphor is the link between ideas (in the mind, in *Binah*) and the physical and emotional (in the body, *Netzach* and *Hod*).

Take, for example, rituals using trees or symbols of trees, which occur in many traditions. Judaism's menorah is the image of a tree, the Tree of Life is a metaphor for the Torah, and, as we have seen, the kabbalists elaborated the structure of a tree to explain the entire cosmos. A procession with a Torah scroll embodies the process of bringing the "Tree of Life" and the hidden Divine light into the world. The Christmas tree, originally from ancient European rituals, is decorated with ornaments suggesting rich fruits as well as illumination. The World Tree was a symbol in Hinduism, and the lotus of Buddhism hints at the same image. These "sacred trees" suggest life, growth, a connection between earth and heaven, and branches extending out to the world and bearing fruit.

Every ritual has its repertoire of metaphors that connect us to untold depths within ourselves, enabling us to embrace the collective reality of humanity. Many of Judaism's *mitzvot* are rituals in that they provide physical connections with the basic template, for example holiday rituals and symbols, a *mezuzzah* on the doorpost, or *tefillin* to wear during prayer. Many of these fall into the category known as *eidot,* or "witnesses," asking us to perceive in our bodies and in the physical world our connection to God.

In connection with ritual, forms of music and dance should be mentioned. While these may not be an essential part of every spiritual practice, many traditions include rhythm, chant, melody, and dance as part of ritual and liturgy. In Judaism, music is regarded as a delicately nuanced form that not only expresses heights of spiritual experience for some people, but also can aid in healing and in expanding consciousness, which can then lead people further on their search for connection with God. The vibrations of music enter the body in a different way than intellectual insights.

Musical creativity has helped fire liturgical renewal in Judaism as in other traditions. If you have musical inclinations, or if you simply enjoy listening to music, do include it in your practice. Discover the types of music that stimulate your inner consciousness. Chants, spiritual melodies with or without words, and songs in the holy tongue (even if you don't understand the language) can be an important support to your ceremonial practice.

5. *Confession.*

The practice of confession is connected to prayer, and also frequently to traditional rituals, but it deserves special mention on its own. It is amazing how long we can go without noticing our mistakes, and even when we do notice them, without truly acknowledging them. At the other extreme, some people are so hard on themselves that they seem to be constantly apologizing, believing that they are the cause of what goes wrong around them.

Many traditions have, therefore, ritualized confession, putting it in a set framework at certain times so that it is sure to get done, but also so that it will not become an unhealthy preoccupation. Judaism focuses on Yom Kippur, the Day of Atonement, which occurs each year in the fall. During the ten days before (and many people start preparing for a month earlier than that), we are supposed to review our lives, make amends for what we have done wrong and not corrected, and confess our sins to God. Yom Kippur is the holiest day of the Jewish calendar because of the intense purification that is accomplished through such confessions, prayers, and fasting. Some Jews take on practices of self-examination and confession throughout the year—for example, the day before the new moon each month, or on Friday afternoons before Shabbat.

In most other traditions some form of self-examination occurs, along with confession or discussion of problems with a more experienced person. In Roman Catholicism, for example, confession to a priest is required before partaking of the Eucharist. However, confession may be much less formal. Protestants rejected confession to a priest, but the American Puritans had long discussions with their ministers to help them assess their spiritual state. Methodists originally used group meetings as a way of sharing problems and clearing up issues, while encouraging one another in the faith. In modern times, twelve-step meetings (Alcoholics Anonymous and related programs) have a practice of "taking inventory," which is then shared with a more experienced member. In monastic traditions, conversations with one's teacher serve a similar purpose.

I mention these examples to indicate how pervasive the idea is, even if it is not called confession, of taking a good hard look at oneself and then speaking about it to another person and/or to God. The speaking is important. And the other person has the responsibility of responding truthfully and with deep respect and kindness, to help you on your path—that is why it has often been a spiritual elder who takes this role.

Remember, as you undertake a practice of self-examination, the main point is fine-tuning, not browbeating yourself. Clear sight is the aim, while accepting that each of us is imperfect. If you cannot seem to make progress in a certain area, take the attitude of not worrying about it for the time being. Recall those times when you lost something and searched fruitlessly for it—the more obsessed you became with finding it, the more frustrated you were and the more difficult it was to find. Then, once you "forgot" about it, the lost item appeared. Many parts of yourself you can "find," with a little effort; some parts are temporarily "lost," and the best approach is to go ahead with positive work and accept the difficulty as one of your life's mysteries, which may in time find healing.

6. *Charity* (in Judaism, *tzedaka*).

Every tradition teaches that people who have not renounced possessions altogether must practice charity, giving a portion of one's possessions to those who have less, or supporting efforts to improve the physical or spiritual condition of others. The point of this practice on a spiritual level is to teach us to give more and more of ourselves, so that we recognize that our life is not ours. As the great nineteenth-century scholar Samson Raphael Hirsch wrote:

> You have nothing so long as you have it only for yourself, . . . you only possess something when you share it with others. When you have experienced the supreme happiness of giving, then will you rejoice in the great task for which God has called you—to be a blessing.[8]

The two main forms of charity are connected to the *sefirot* directly above *Tiferet,* namely *Chesed* and *Gevurah.* When we act with *Chesed* flowing through us, we are giving and supporting others. When we act from *Gevurah,* we are practicing non-injury to others and to our environment. Both of these activities may involve an element of what Judaism calls *mesirat nefesh* or self-sacrifice. Indeed, charity is a natural form of sacrifice—a giving up of things to which the ego might attach itself.

There are three main aspects of acting from *Chesed,* each of which takes a multitude of forms in the unique configurations of our lives: the physical gifts we give to support others, the emotional gifts of caring for others, and the mental gifts of teaching others. The physical realm starts with the most elemental, such as giving life through becoming a parent, and feeding or providing food, clothing, and shelter for children or others who cannot support themselves. It includes caring for plants and animals, whether in one's home or in the larger environment. Healing people (or plants or animals) in the realm of the physical is part of this gift as well. Also, we may provide financial help for those who are accomplishing something for the general good that we cannot do ourselves—this is another aspect of the concept of charity.

Emotional giving means being available to others, giving the gift of your time and a sensitive heart. It also means sharing your feelings so that the sensitivity of others can be naturally awakened. This giving can be at home or in a profession, or simply in the social contexts of which you are normally a part. Even the simple gift of companionship can be an important contribution to someone else's life. In many cases, as in caring for children or in the healing professions, emotional giving overlaps with the physical, but it has its own distinctive value.

Mental giving means sharing your thoughts—not simply the words that fly out of your mouth, but your considered thoughts. When you contribute your thoughts to the world, you are a teacher. Your perspective is unique and valuable. Also, by treating others as your teachers, you will encourage them to develop their thoughts.

The other aspect of charity is non-injury, which is connected to the *sefirah* of *Gevurah*. In some traditions, such as Jainism (an ancient religion of India), this practice involves a great effort to avoid harming even insects. In most traditions, more moderate versions of this idea appear. "Whatever is hateful to you, do not do to others" is the way the first-century rabbi Hillel formulated this principle in Judaism. Jewish law also includes injunctions not to cause anguish to humans or animals, not to destroy fruit-bearing trees, and not to waste things. In a sense, all the "negative precepts"—that is, prohibitions—are means of restraining one's ego so as not to do injury to the world.

All of these practices are comprised in the spiritual gift each of us gives to the world, through being an example. When you are a positive example to others, you are living as close as you can to your soul. This is expressed in a famous prayer:

God, make me an instrument of Your peace.
Where there is hatred, let me sow love.
Where there is injury, pardon
Where there is doubt, faith
Where there is despair, hope
Where there is darkness, light
Where there is sadness, joy.
Master of the Universe, grant that I may seek not so much
To be consoled as to console,
To be understood as to understand,
To be loved as to love.

—ADAPTED FROM ST. FRANCIS OF ASSISI

7. *Physical discipline.*

In earlier times, physical discipline usually meant ascetic practices such as voluntary fasting and often, in non-Jewish traditions, celibacy for part or all of one's adult life. Today, it may mean regular, conscious exercise. Disciplining the body is part of heightening one's awareness.

The enormous complexity of the human being, and the variety of stimulants available in modern Western culture, means that our bodies are doing things they were not constructed to do. We sit a great deal, we are "in our heads," thinking, planning, and talking to ourselves an enormous amount of the time, and we have easy access to an array of food and drink—not to mention drugs and cigarettes—that can throw our bodies off balance. When we try to impose a discipline, we usually have weak support systems (in contrast, say, to monks in a monastery). We bounce back and forth between being lax and overdoing our strictness. The great sage Maimonides, himself a physician, advised moderation in everything, but always living with attention to the health of the body.

Many spiritual practices include a body discipline, such as yoga or *t'ai ch'i*. Although the Jewish prophets of ancient times apparently used physical postures in their efforts to attain prophetic insight,[9] Kabbalah did not develop a distinctive or universal practice. Traditional Jewish prayer involved simple practices such as rhythmic bowing and lifting the hands, and dancing was considered an appropriate expression of spiritual energy in many circumstances, but no prescribed discipline of movement emerged. Rabbis concerned about health advocated ordinary physical exercise like walking for people who were too sedentary—which includes quite a few of us today! From this, one can conclude that any healthful and invigorating practice, together with discipline around food and sexuality, is appropriate for most people. I have benefited enormously from incorporating movement into prayer.[10] As for other physical disciplines, the Kabbalah assumed without question that Jews would eat only kosher food and practice the sexual disciplines prescribed by *halacha*.

8. *Community.*

Last but not least is the practice of being an active supporter of a community. For people blazing their own unique paths, or for those who tend to think globally, this is not always easy. But our responsibility does not end with our own small circles of fellow travelers; it also requires us to contribute to a larger community. Judaism has always been rooted in the concept of a "people" and the concrete reality of a *kehillah* (community), meaning either a synagogue or a neighborhood. At the very least, we must remember that our acts reflect like mirrors of our larger community, either enhancing or detracting from it. We are always representing more than ourselves, and building up others as we grow. This is true at the level of family, community, and general religious identity. Community consciousness needs to be part of our spiritual practice. The rabbis taught: "Do not separate yourself from the community" (Avot 4:5).

Being Wholehearted

While practice is essential, we can sometimes fool ourselves into thinking that the practice is our spirituality. Practice is just that: practice. All experts—the pianist, the runner, the welder—practice in order to acquire the skills that enable them to become masters. We practice our spiritual skills in order to master the art of Godliness. Masters are those who perform their arts with complete integrity and involvement of self, with wholeheartedness. The same is true with religious practice.

The aim is expressed in a biblical phrase: "Be wholehearted *(tamim)* with the Lord your God" (Deuteronomy 18:13). The goal is to become completely at one with one's deepest self and with the Infinite Source. If we think that doing the practice is the same thing as being that Self-united-with-Source, we will end up in great confusion. The great medieval philosopher Maimonides wrote that most of the *mitzvot* of Jewish law, which are largely prescriptions for *doing,* have *being* as their aim—the kind of being that is a channel for the Divine.[11]

For example, some people become very involved in the charitable works of their church, synagogue, or community organization, and see this involvement as their spiritual practice. In reality, their work can serve two important functions: First, it supports the organization; second, it is a discipline in which one can practice lovingkindness. Both are quite appropriate. The first function is giving of one's time in return for what one receives from the organization. This is primarily a form of social reciprocity, on the level of *Netzach* and *Hod.* It supports a good social institution, but it is not necessarily spiritual. The second function of such activities can be the real practice: Work on the self through the spiritual practice of charity. If, when we practice charity, we become conscious of what happens to us and others whom we serve, if we literally "take it to heart" by being aware of our emotions, these actions begin to transform us. When we allow ourselves to feel and think about what we are doing, charitable activities help us become wholeheartedly involved in the

Divine design. The actions are no longer only about *doing* what is necessary to support a social structure, but about *being* a different kind of person.

The same can be said of any aspect of practice. Ritual can become empty form or it can be the architecture of Divine energy. Obeying the rules can become an exercise in robotics or an act of deep love of God. Prayer can become habitual words or a flow from the heart, fired with *kavannah* (pure intent). Even meditation, which can lead toward a deep inward contentment, can become an occasion to fall asleep, literally or metaphorically. Our practice must be examined from time to time, to see whether it is keeping us awake and awakening us to new levels, or becoming a support of our ego, keeping us in our persona. Even if it is a new persona—"Now I'm a more spiritual person!"—it is still a persona. In other words, the practical work we do in order to manifest the level of *Tiferet* can become a crutch. What we really want is for *Tiferet*—our true inner being—to shine through in *Malkhut*. We want our light to be revealed in our practice, so that the two are really one.

If we become attached to some area of practice, we need to look at what that attachment is about. Is it about ego, painting the right face for the outside world? Or is our fascination hinting at something deeper we need to learn about ourselves? If we love external rituals, perhaps it is because we need to develop our own sense of ceremony and the movements of energy. If we throw ourselves into charitable work, it may be because we need to develop our heart-connection with others. If we are attached to a teacher, perhaps that teacher mirrors the wisdom that is hidden within us. The key here is to become aware of what each discipline, each external thing we receive, touches within us. Every element of practice is also our teacher—and is the way we become our own teachers.

Thus, arriving at your true self does not mean that you no longer have to follow rules or do the activities of a practice. On the contrary, you will have found much more meaning in the rule, for you will have internalized it, making the practice your reality.[12] A famous Zen story is told of a monk who, before he began practicing Zen, worked at the monastery, chopping wood and carrying water. Then he gave it all up to meditate until he reached enlightenment. What does he do now? He chops wood and carries water.

The Soul's Mission

Without pride and delusion, victorious over the vice of attachment, dwelling constantly in the Higher Self, desire pacified, liberated from the pairs of opposites known as pleasure and pain, the true seekers tread, undeluded, that indestructible path.

—THE BHAGAVAD GITA[13]

As we take our spiritual life more seriously, we frequently find that we are being given more and more responsibility. For example, we may find that we simply must set aside more time for meditation and prayer—we just don't feel good if we try to skimp or rush through those activities. Or we may find that people are unexpectedly knocking on our door or calling us at odd hours for help or a sympathetic ear. Even if we thought we were partially retiring from our worldly busyness to commit to spirituality, we now have just as much business as before—but it's higher in quality, evoking more of our deeper selves.

These changes in our lives are signs that we are growing in spiritual status, being allowed to do more and more for God. As an analogy, think of an emissary sent out on particular missions. As he proves himself, he is given more and more difficult and exacting missions. He hones his skills, becomes more sure of himself, and eventually comes to the point where he can carry out the will of his superiors in very unusual situations, with an extraordinary degree of faithfulness to their intent.

Similarly, you have a mission on earth, which you are discovering. You are to fulfill the will of God by being here, with your particular talents that you bring to every situation—with

Each person possesses a unique admixture of psychological and intellectual qualities which form the basis of his own particular, unique contribution to the sanctification of God's name.
—RABBI ELIYAHU DESSLER[15]

your unique light to shine. You knew this when you came here. You forgot it in the womb. But you will eventually fulfill everything you were created for, if not in this lifetime then in another. One of my teachers calls this mission your "soul contract" with God. You and God worked this out before you came. You helped decide the contract's terms and conditions. You forgot—but now, when you are fulfilling them, you will know it.[14]

Think of times in your life where you felt "This is really me!" It may have been a brief moment of ecstasy when you accomplished a task or had a few moments to do exactly what you wanted. Or it may have been an extended time when you had really satisfying work, where you got up eagerly each day to do the job because it so suited you. (Of course, there were probably times you lapsed into doing it by rote, but there would be moments of ecstatic identification too.) Perhaps it was a time when you had a compassionate conversation with a friend who needed you, or when you were able to truly express yourself to someone else. Or a period of intense creativity when you simply forgot the world. Or a moment when you stood up to pressure and resisted the expectations of others, knowing that you had to be an example of integrity. You were, for that time, free of self-doubt, regret, or worry, free of demands other than your own inner motivation, and immediately present to whatever was at hand.

This sense of immediate presence is the reality of Truth—your unique Truth. In that moment, you were part of what is called the "Chariot" of God; you were manifesting your Divine image to the fullest extent you could at that point in time. You were connecting with Oneness, not on the abstract level of thought or meditation or dream, but in full waking consciousness.

I have seen this wonderful event occur a few times in other people. I mentioned in the last chapter my acquaintances who survived the Holocaust as children in hiding. One was my husband who, for decades, did not speak about the horrors of his childhood. Only in midlife, as more and more survivors were speaking out, did he begin to attend meetings and share his story with others. Yet he knew that he was telling it with a certain flatness, almost as if it had happened to someone else.

Years went by. Finally, in 1998, he decided to gather friends and relatives together to tell his story more fully. I was fortunate to be there, because it was one of those moments of truth. He had decided to tell the story not around suffering and horror, but around gratitude. With every detail, every excruciating event of running, hiding, escaping from the Gestapo, and more hiding, he had a tale of gratitude to tell. Not only gratitude to the non-Jews who hid him and his parents, but gratitude for every incident and every person who aided them in their journey, and gratitude to God.

The radiance of that evening was unforgettable. Often, the expression of our Truth lasts only a moment for us—our "moment of glory," we sometimes say. But the event is no less radiant and powerful for its short existence in linear time.

As we develop spiritually, such moments can occur more often and last longer. Each time we experience a longer sense of our connection with God and our true purpose, it is as if a veil has lifted. As those veils part, one by one, the light of the true self shines through more and more clearly. On a social level, because we resonate with our own inner truth, we recognize that we are not merely a part of society, but also have a responsibility to create and give to society. We can contribute our own creative energies to the building of a better world in which to live. On the spiritual level, our connection to inner truth enables us to direct our prayers, our meditations, and our entire mental, emotional, and physical orientation toward a larger reality, beyond the personal self.

In order to be a man, a person must be more than a man.
—ABRAHAM JOSHUA HESCHEL[16]

Our moments of connection to the higher self and our Divine Source reveal that we are creative, loving, and giving in our very essence. What we want most of all is to express that fullness of being completely. In our deepest selves, we want to be completely true to our mission. We want to be responsible and responsive, from the very core of our being.

This growth toward full acceptance of responsibility is portrayed in a peculiar story associated with the Jewish holiday of Purim. The *midrash* tells us that at Sinai, when the Jewish people received the Torah, God held the mountain over their heads and said, "Accept the Torah; if not, this mountain will be your grave." In other words, the people were so overwhelmed by their experience that it was as if they had no free will. But this would mean that the acceptance of Torah was equivalent to a forced conversion, which is forbidden in Jewish law! The *midrash* goes on to say, however, that the people did in fact accept the Torah voluntarily, generations later. They were suffering persecution in Persia and, under the leadership of Mordecai and Esther, came to a complete acceptance of God's will as detailed in the laws of the Torah.

The account of these later events appears in the biblical Book of Esther. The main point, however, is that a great deal of work—generations of work—was necessary for the Jewish people to be able to accept, sincerely and at a deep level, their collective responsibility for their relationship with God and their mission in the world as witnesses to God. Similarly, we must work on ourselves to recognize that we have chosen and are fully responsible for our incarnation. We can't blame our situation on God, any more than Adam could blame Chava for his eating the apple or Chava could blame the snake for tempting her. Without this full responsibility, this quasi-Divine responsibility, human life is no more meaningful than animal life.

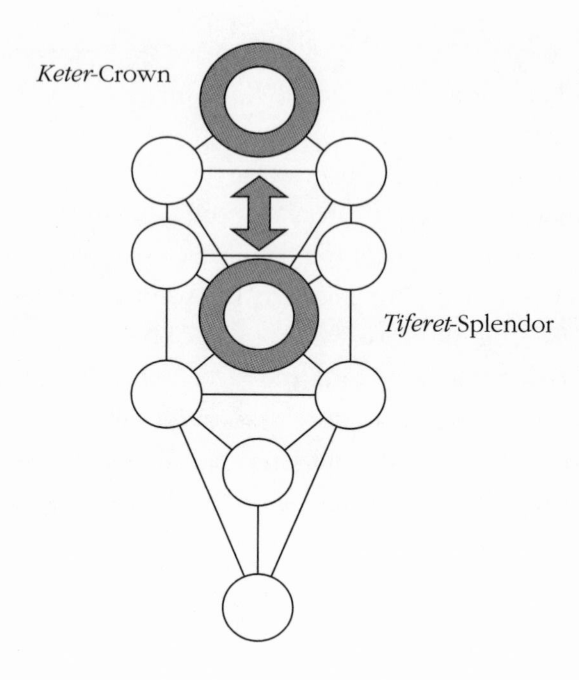

Look again at the Tree of Life. The *sefirah* of *Tiferet* lies on the central pillar, on a line coming directly from *Keter,* the arrow to the soul. Because of this connection, *Tiferet* is a place of oneness, despite the dualities that pull it on either side. We can say that it is the place where we are conscious of truly being ourselves.

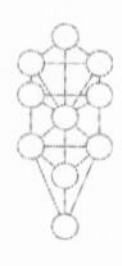

8 Revealing Your Soul

The perception that dawns on a person to see the world not as finished, but as in the process of continued becoming, ascending, developing—this changes him from being "under the sun" to being "above the sun," from the place where there is nothing new to the place where there is nothing old, where everything takes on new form. The joy of heaven and earth abides in him as on the day they were created.
—Rabbi Abraham Isaac Kook[1]

The Light Radiates from Within

The effort of practice opens new doorways. Our increasing willingness to take responsibility for purposeful living—the work of *Tiferet*—expands our horizons and gives us new vision. Since we no longer see ourselves as victims of circumstance, we begin to understand that the experiences of *Gevurah* that used to seem like punishment are actually gifts. Since we are practicing becoming humble and restraining our ego, we begin to recognize experiences of *Chesed* as great blessings, instead of brushing them off as coincidences or taking credit for ourselves. This refined perception of events will attune us more completely to the movements of spirit in the world. Even though we still live in a world of duality, we will be able to function with less resistance and more acceptance. Further, as we develop in prayer and meditation, we will find that visualization, evoking fundamental spiritual patterns, enables us to enter the maternal matrix of *Binah*. As we learn to empty our minds and become more receptive, we may even recognize illuminations from *Chochmah*.

Traditionally, all these developments are portrayed as "ascents" to higher realms. However, as we will see more fully in this chapter, these changes can be better described in a different way. The higher realms are not separate from the lower. As we ascend by becoming more connected to our prayers, we will perceive our personal history—our "lower" life—in different ways. As we meditate more, we will become more compassionate to others and therefore will interact with them in new ways. As we refine each element of our character, our actions will become more in tune with our soul's true purpose. That in turn will enable us to enter into prayer and meditation with greater calm and purity of intent. Gradually, the light of the soul from "above" will illuminate the whole lamp, radiating from our faces with joy, from our hearts with love, and with both gentleness and power from our hands that touch, our mouths that speak, and our feet that take firm steps into the world.

What a promise! How can this happen? The deeper truth is that the fabric of consciousness, from the molecular level up to the Divine, responds to our purposive movement. In other words, when we make choices, our actions set up currents of events that eventually come back to us in one form or another. In Judaism, this is described as *midah k'neged midah,* precisely like the English expression "measure for measure." As we exercise our powers with consciousness, the universe will respond and exercise its powers in return—at all levels, from the hard physical world of the soil we dig in our gardens to the plants and animals, from other human beings we interact with to spiritual entities and ultimately God. The late-twentieth-century physicist David Bohm put it quite clearly:

> . . . If we approach the world through enfolding its wholeness in our consciousness and thus act with love, the world, which enfolds our own being within itself, will respond in a corresponding way. This can obviously happen in the world of society. But even the world of nature will cease to respond with degeneration, due to pollution, destruction of forests, and so on, and will begin to act in a more orderly and favorable way.[2]

We can describe this spiritual development toward love and wholeness not as an ascent but as a spiral. We act from the heart, wholeheartedly, going with prayer and meditation "up" or "in" to the higher levels of consciousness, and moving with compassion "down" and "out" into the world, the lower realms of life. Unless we participate in both directions of movement, our spiritual growth will be stunted. We must become not only mystics pursuing inward transformation, but also prophets bringing the word of healing and transformation to the outside world as well.

We can begin to activate this spiral by recognizing angels.

A Chorus of Angels

Every event is a message from God. You may be riding in a subway, engrossed in your newspaper, when suddenly you notice the conversation of people next to you. A few minutes later, you are buried in the paper again. Why did your consciousness awaken at just that moment? Kabbalah says it was a message you were supposed to hear. Why? A warning from *Gevurah*? A blessing that brings reassurance and comfort from *Chesed*? Your job is to decode the significance of the message in your life.

The word for messenger in Hebrew, *malach,* also means "angel." Angels are encounters with directed energy, sending us messages, often pulling us in a positive direction, sometimes warning us away from danger. I am going to use the word "angel" quite broadly to describe a variety of fairly common experiences that seem to be personal, energetic, and carrying information directly useful to us. We experience these energies around places, people, and the intangible dimensions of life. While this usage of the term may seem strange at first, it is in accord with the mystics' insistence that angels exist at every level of being.[3] To use an analogy from modern physics, different angels exist on different frequencies. As we hear different kinds of music and conversation when we tune into different radio wavelengths, so angels "appear" to us in different ways.

One kind of angelic experience occurs when we lose ourselves, when our felt sense of the boundaries between ourselves and the world dissolves. This is not an intellectual experience, where we detach from the world and go into our minds, but a place where we experience the world, or some aspect of it, so fully that it seems to carry us away. Sometimes this happens in nature, when we feel so much a part of everything around us that we are no longer conscious of being different from the scenery. Aesthetic experience can also bring this sense of disappearing: Hearing certain music exalts you, or you can wander through a museum exhibit so absorbed that time and space seem to dissolve. I still recall a Cézanne exhibit more than twenty years ago at the Museum of Modern Art in New York, where I stood transfixed before a series of studies by the great painter, each of the same scene, each slightly different. I got lost from my tour group and only after a long time, perhaps an hour in that one room, managed to tear myself away.

Such experiences are so overwhelming that we tend to speak of them as passive experiences: "I was drawn into the painting," "I felt uplifted by the music." At that moment, we have been touched and we give ourselves to the world as it has been offered to us just then and there. We feel supported and honored by the universe, and we actively embrace that givingness. This experience signifies that God has sent angels of *Chesed* to carry us upward and envelop us, as if in a cloud of perfection, and we expand in return.

While some *Chesed* experiences are rare, like an encounter with great art, other angels come as regular and tangible sources of support in the form of things we love. The awesome isolation of the desert may delight one person, the intimacy of a forest stream may nourish another. You may prefer sitting quietly with a friend, while your neighbor may be drawn to the busy hum of downtown. These preferences have nothing to do with your talents—what you can *do*. Rather, these are forces that help you *be* the person you truly and deeply are. We could say that if you are a person who loves the desert, the angel of the desert comes to support you when you go there—not only when you travel there physically, but also when you go there in meditation or contemplation.

Still another kind of angel appears as a sense of protection from danger, as when popular religion speaks of guardian angels. I first became aware of angelic protection when I traveled across Arizona and New Mexico in midsummer, only to discover when I stopped for gasoline that I was a thread of rubber away from a blowout in the desert. The gas station attendant looked amazed and said, "You've got Somebody traveling with you." Although at one level I was embarrassed at having paid so little attention to my car, when he said those words I had goosebumps and recognized, in some deep part of myself, that he was right.

Each of these experiences points to higher realms where our souls are nourished, often on a regular and fairly predictable basis. It is important to ask yourself what aspects of your world—what kinds of places, activities, times of day—support and nourish you. Where do you connect with the angels that accompany you? It could be by the tree in your backyard or at your computer (is there an angel dancing on my monitor right now?), on your next airplane trip or at your place of worship, in intellectual work or when you participate in a sports event. When you choose to go to a place or enjoy an activity that feels like one of your pillars of support, think of it as a mirror of your soul's true love—and that God loves you through this experience.

Then there are aspects of experience that go beyond the angels of nature or angelic energies that infuse what is created by human hands. Here is where we find, in traditional contexts, the word "angels" used most often: an experience of the supernal comes with such force and clarity that angelic energy appears to take quasi-human form. Reports of such experiences occur almost universally in religious traditions, including Judaism. Going back to the Bible itself, we find that angels came to Abraham in the guise of travelers on the road; an angel was stationed at the gate of the Garden of Eden holding a sword, and a fearful angel stood in the path of Balaam and his donkey. Jacob wrestled with an angel whom some commentators identify as the angel of Esau, his twin brother. Occasionally, prophets such as Ezekiel and Isaiah have seen in their visions angels that have unusual, nonhuman features—angels with wings, with many faces, angels in the shape of wheels with eyes, angels of fire.

Jewish tradition refers to and even invokes angels at certain times. In the daily prayers, verses from the Bible are recited that describe the angels gathering to praise God at the same time that Jews gather for prayer. At the height of intensity in the daily prayer service, all interruptions cease and each person stands, "imitating the angels," and joins in the *kedushah,* or "sanctification" of God's name. Each community has its chorus of angels, so to speak, that supports and accompanies the community in its prayer endeavor. Also, specific angels are invoked at bedtime to accompany the individual soul on its journey into the world of dreams.[4]

Angels in this sense are real. Their frequent human form may be partly a product of our perception, the only way our minds can make sense of energies that have a quality of personality but are not physically human. The main thing is to recognize them as part of the system of support that comes from the Divine reality in which we are rooted.

Sometimes angelic energies actually coalesce around real humans. We experience a unique energy from someone, of love and guiding support. It's hard to tell whether such an unusual quality is coming from the person's natural personality, or from the nature of the relationship, or is something that transcends human interaction. But it is a special blessing to have such a friend, teacher, or support group. Once in a while, you will find a person or a group that continuously and unequivocally supports you, and allows you to relax your boundaries and transcend your own ego.

My most dramatic personal experience of such a development came after I had been trying to write a novel (an interesting challenge for a scholarly person). Part of the fantasy was a group of people who chose new members according to the inner quality of their souls. After several months of fits and starts, I gave up writing the novel. Then, about a month later, I was introduced to a group of women who were studying their dreams and the inner qualities of their souls! I had, unknowingly, evoked my own retinue of angels. Such gifts are great blessings, all the more because they are surprises. And sometimes the angels we experience in human form are even more amazing than the purely "energetic" angels.

One more experience, related to the angelic realm but involving people who have died, can occur after the death of a loved one. The form of the deceased presents itself to deliver a message—as does an angel—usually to a beloved friend or relative still on earth. Often, people have told me of appearances of loved ones in dreams; sometimes they also appear in waking reality. One woman reported to me that after her sister's death, she went for a walk in the woods behind the house. "Suddenly I heard the sound of beautiful music and saw my sister's form, walking with some people I didn't recognize, right ahead of me. She was very happy." Personally, I was given the gift of knowing my mother was being accompanied by familiar angels—her own sisters—on her death journey. After the convalescent home called me to say that my mother had taken a turn for the worse, I drove there as quickly as I could. As I drove down the freeway, I unexpectedly saw, just above the hood of my car, the form of two of her older sisters whom my mother had loved dearly, and who had passed away many years before. Such experiences tend to be stronger around the time of a death because, as many writers have observed, the veils between the lower and the higher realms become thinner at that time, so we can "see" the angels or the souls that come to support us.[5]

Yet such events do not always occur immediately after death. My husband was astounded to experience the presence of his deceased uncle, Max, in another way. Several years after Max died, my husband said *kaddish* in the synagogue, as he did annually, on the *yahrzeit,* or anniversary, of Max's death. Later that morning, he was cleaning out the garage and came across a box of old audiotapes, some of which were unidentified as to the contents. He popped one into the tape player to see what it was, and immediately heard Max's voice. Max, it turned out, had recorded a greeting to my husband many years before, to send him blessings. The tape had, ever since, been lying among family possessions, waiting for that day when an angel could deliver the message from Max.

Angels and other souls do support us. A *midrash* teaches that before every human being walks a retinue of angels, shouting, "Make way for the image of the Blessed-Holy-One!" Perhaps this is the most delightful group of angels. May we be blessed to see them each time we encounter another person.

Life's Challenges

Chesed experiences can provide us with such a high that sometimes we become frightened when the other side appears. Angels of *Gevurah* are often guardians of the sacred, like the angel at the entrance to the Garden of Eden, and they remind us of where we cannot go. Others are challengers, like Esau's angel in a wrestling match with Jacob. In our ordinary life, we tend to think of these as represented in the lessons we have to learn. Unlike the often painful lessons of lower levels, however, the angels of *Gevurah* come as midcourse corrections or fine-tunings of our direction in life. By the time we reach the level where we are acting from the heart-space of *Tiferet,* we are resonating with our core self most of the time. Here we know that even the "bad" things in life are methods to enhance our ability to accomplish our purpose in the world.

Sometimes *Gevurah* is purely an inner experience. For example, we feel unsuccessful in efforts to accomplish tasks, or to reach out to people, and we begin to wonder whether our life really makes sense. We may be unable to pray, but at the same time we feel needy and anxious. We wonder if we are alone in the universe. The great Rabbi Joseph Soloveitchik, one of the most learned men in both Judaism and secular studies in the twentieth century, wrote of this side of experience in his book *Lonely Man of Faith*. Humanity, he believed, has two dimensions. One is what he called "majestic Adam," the side that leads us to master our environments and create the world. The other side is that of "lonely Adam," a side that feels untouched by our creative accomplishments and unfulfilled no matter how many loving and rewarding personal relationships we have. Among Christian mystics, this experience is often expressed in terms of darkness, as in the expression "dark night of the soul."

The darkness can be frightening, but when we recognize that it is merely a doorway to another dimension of relationship to God, we can walk through it. We are being asked to develop a very private and personal relationship to God. It is as though God is saying, "I am not always to be found in my vast creation. Come and meet me in secret." The messenger calling us to inwardness—like Isaac who "dug deeper" the wells of his father—comes from *Gevurah*.

Sometimes, the angels of *Gevurah* appear in external experiences, making our lives more difficult. Many of the world's great mystics and religious reformers have been persecuted or, at least, subject to great controversy. Even today, people on a spiritual path

We can never travel beyond the arms of the Divine.
—Dr. Martin Luther King, Jr.[6]

may still encounter opposition or skepticism. More commonly, *Gevurah* appears in the form of great disappointment—for example, in a teacher or friend on whom one had counted—or a physical injury or illness that requires us to confront ourselves. The great spiritual teachers say that everyone on a spiritual path must encounter such challenges at one time or another, because they help us fight the potential for ego-inflation that comes with spiritual growth. As we can see from incidents in the lives of many modern gurus and religious leaders of all denominations, no one is exempt from such dangers.

Every expansion must meet a limitation, just as the lava from the erupting volcano eventually cools in the sea. Our spiritual expansion will be challenged as well. If we accept the challenge, we may encounter important teachings or individuals who can deepen our path. A minor way this happened to me was a shoulder injury that simply would not clear up on its own. After months of resistance to seeking help, I was led to a healer and movement therapist, and the ensuing effort led me to a much deeper connection with my body. People who experience illness or opposition often discover new friends and supporters to help them through their crisis.

When we are visited by the angels of *Gevurah,* we often do best by retiring to our own private container. This can be a place of deep meditation, long walks alone, or soaking in a hot tub with nothing but our own thoughts. When we go on this path, we are defining ourselves by connecting to deeper layers of our unique being. We may feel withdrawn from the world, but close to God. What happens in this withdrawal, this personal *tzimtzum,* is that we can become more in touch with our own unique ways of seeing and experiencing things. We learn to discriminate, giving attention to what is important and reducing our involvement in the trivial. Most importantly, as we learn to hear the messages of angels, we gradually begin to trust God in a more profound way, for we realize that messages are being sent to us all the time.

We also develop a deeper level of what is called "conscience"—a word that was once an important ethical term, but has fallen by the wayside. Literally, it means "knowing-together-with"—a knowing that connects us to the largest realities we can conceive. When we turn to our conscience, we examine ourselves in the light of the highest values we have. We become introspective and discover our true orientation toward life. We create a personal ethic, frequently much more demanding than that of our culture. We become more careful to avoid doing harm to ourselves and others, physically, emotionally, and spiritually. We ask ourselves frequently, "Are we living impeccably—committed and consistent with what we know to be good and what we understand to be God's will?" Sincere, honest self-examination is an important tool for building our self-esteem.

When we develop this characteristic, we can live without fear of human judgment. *Gevurah* is classically regarded as associated with severity and judgment. Too many times, however, we are not so much concerned about what God thinks of us as what humans think. If we know our own conscience, the fear of external judgment vanishes.

On the other hand, our relationship with God also becomes clearer. A famous Hasidic story tells of a certain simple man named Zusya, who lived in poverty and devotion to God. When he was ill, shortly before he died, he cried and cried. His disciples asked him why. "Reb Zusya, you were as kind as Abraham! You were as devoted as Isaac! Surely you don't need to be afraid of judgment by God." Zusya replied, "God is not going to ask me, 'Why weren't you like Abraham? Why weren't you like Isaac?' He's going to ask, 'Why weren't you Zusya?'"

God says to each of us, "I created you in a unique and beautiful way to reflect the Divine image. Where did you fall short of what you could have been?"

Achieving Equanimity

Right understanding ultimately means nondiscrimination—seeing all people as the same, neither good nor bad, neither clever nor foolish; not thinking that honey is sweet and good and some other food is bitter.

—ACHAAN CHAH[7]

Chesed is so fulfilling and supportive that it contains the possibility of grandiosity or ego-inflation. *Gevurah* keeps this in check. It brings us back to humility, which is the only place from which spiritual growth can occur. When we accept as angelic gifts the restraints that are given to us, the result is equanimity.

Many spiritual traditions teach the importance of achieving this quality. *The Code of Jewish Law* begins with the phrase "I keep God before me always," which, the mystics say, can also be read as "I make everything equal before God." Kabbalah teaches that if we are moved one way or the other by events or people, experiencing approval as pleasure and disapproval as pain, we are not yet ready for the advanced spiritual path. Here is a story of a mystical rabbi of the early centuries C.E. that exemplifies this teaching:

> A sage once came to one of the Meditators and asked that he be accepted into their society.
>
> The other replied, "My son, blessed are you to God. Your intentions are good. But tell me, have you attained equanimity or not?"
>
> The sage said, "Master, explain your words."
>
> The Meditator said, "If one man is praising you and another is insulting you, are the two equal in your eyes or not?" He replied, "No, my master, I have pleasure from those who praise me, and pain from those who degrade me. But I do not take revenge or bear a grudge." The other said, "Go in peace my son. . . . You are not prepared for your thoughts to bound on high, that you should come and meditate. Go and increase the humbleness of your heart, and learn to treat everything equally."[8]

Equanimity can develop when we recognize that everything is from God, and we are simply the channel to receive and transform it. The Bible tells a story of King David, who was the object of much controversy and even hatred from his opponents, who considered him a usurper of Saul's throne. One day he was walking with some of his soldiers, and a man standing by the side of the road started cursing him. David's guard, indignant at the man's insults, offered to kill the man.

> But the king said, "What has this to do with you, sons of Zeruiah? If he curses and if the Lord has told him to curse David, who can question it? . . . Let him be, let him curse, for the Lord has told him to do it. But perhaps the Lord will mark my sufferings and bestow a blessing on me in place of the curse laid on me this day." (2 Samuel 16:10–13)

Retaliation for evil is not the answer, but rather faith in God. However, that is often easier said than done. As we experience the energies of *Chesed* and *Gevurah,* we must learn to allow the pain and disappointment simply to *be* what they are. Eventually, we will discover that truly, everything is simply a lesson. With this equanimity comes humility. And humility means recognizing our authentic reality as channels of Divinity in this world. Our *sefirah* of *Tiferet* is then infused with new inner strength.

Running and Returning

The spiritual path does not end with mere acceptance. Equanimity is the stable foundation for deeper, broader, higher explorations. A new level of yearning stirs in our hearts because, in the midst of great blessings and difficult trials, we long to express our gratitude and love to God. We find ourselves seeking to go beyond the flux of ordinary experience and beyond awareness of angelic forces, to connect with God, with our Source, with the One. God becomes the Beloved, the One we are seeking. Yet we find, always, that we are limited in our ability to be with God. We may begin to have experiences of closeness—in Hebrew called *devekut,* or "clinging," to God—but we also find ourselves often separate, feeling far from God.

In the great religious traditions, the themes of union with and separation from God recur often. The *bhakti* (devotional) literature of Hindu tradition speaks of the devotee's love and longing for God, the ecstasy of union, and the drama of separation. The great medieval Sufi poet, Rumi, wrote of this theme constantly. The Song of Songs in the Bible is the Jewish tradition's expression of this profound theme. Traditionally, this poem is understood as an allegory of God's relationship to Israel or, alternatively, God's relationship to humanity. In it we find expressed the awareness of separation:

> Where has your Beloved gone, O fairest of women?
> Which way did your Beloved go, that we may help you seek him?

And of union:

> I am my Beloved's, and my Beloved is mine.

The mystics call this experience *ratzo v'shov,* "running and returning."[9] We "run" toward the Divine, we "return" to our ordinary existence. The moments of "running" in mystical experience energize the higher *sefirot* of *Chochmah* and *Binah,* taking us to levels of illumination and insight that transcend our personal existence. These levels are completely holistic, part of the world of unity, not divisible into individual entities. As we saw in Chapter 2, the Jewish sages said that the upper three *sefirot* are "completely *chesed,*" meaning that when we can experience them, we will know them as completely and unequivocally energies of unconditional Divine love.

Such experiences are rare—but perhaps need not be as rare as we sometimes imagine. We can encounter energies of *Binah* or *Chochmah* through dreams, meditation, or other altered states of consciousness. The illumination of *Chochmah* can come as an experience of light, of awareness, or of love. You might wake up one morning feeling completely and deeply at peace. The experience of *Binah* usually has more specific content. For example you might find, while studying (using the energy of *Da'at*), that the meaning of one of the symbols of your religion becomes transparent and you feel as if you understand it profoundly. Or you might have a special dream that stays with you, giving you a feeling of assurance, even though you do not yet understand it.

It is not easy to hold onto such experiences in ordinary waking life. This difficulty is what the mystics call the aspect of "returning."[10] We often have difficulty remembering our dreams, and we frequently doubt the validity of the "transconscious" experiences we are aware of. As a result, we often do not believe that intuition or inspiration are "real," or that dreams, clairvoyance, or visionary consciousness really do take us into upper realms. But, like the category of angelic experiences, which are helpful messages with an extraordinary quality, intuitive and visionary experiences are also real.

The mystical masters also tell us that these experiences have emotional correlates. We feel love and expansiveness in the phase of running. When we return, we feel our smallness and distance, the nothingness of our ego. In Judaism, these emotions are called *ahavah* and *yirah,* love and awe; they correspond to the sides of *Chesed* and *Gevurah.* The *Tanya* describes them as two wings of a bird, both of which are needed to fly upward, that is, to achieve *devekut.* In love, we can identify with God and long to connect with the Divine. In awe, we stand back at a distance, so to speak—sometimes, as Kierkegaard wrote, in "fear and trembling" for, as we saw earlier, God is sometimes a consuming fire.

These waves of experience are normal. One cannot remain close to God for long periods of time. Even great spiritual masters have times of closeness with God and times of apparent separation, feeling distant from God. We will sometimes feel in touch with revelation or inspiration, or have insight and profound acceptance of the lessons of life. At other times, we will feel as though we are just doing our best to live by the rules and manage our ordinary lives. God is always present, but the nature of existence is such that we are sometimes riding on God's shoulders, so to speak, and sometimes we are part of the axle that makes the wheels go round. These shifts are part of the "mystery of the Chariot," as it is called in Kabbalah. We must conquer any feelings of discouragement that may arise. "Never give up!" said Rabbi Nachman. We may feel we are in front of a brick wall, but soon we will see it is just a doorway. When we are able to open it, new possibilities will appear.

Notice, however, that this description, typical of many explanations of running and returning, suggests that returning is something negative. I want to suggest a different viewpoint. Yes, the mystic yearns for God and feels adrift and alone when life goes along at a "normal" pace. But if he is attached to the idea that true spirituality is the phase of running, his spirituality is feeding his ego! What God wants of us is that we should yearn *just as much* to manifest Godliness in our everyday life as we yearn to have profound illuminations. If we truly understand that God is present in everything everywhere, returning can be just as fulfilling as running.

The Spiral of Loving Consciousness

The love that is astir in you—raise it to its basic potency and its noblest beauty, extend it to all its dimensions, toward every manifestation of the soul that sustains the universe, whose splendor is dimmed only because of the deficiency of the person viewing it.

—Rabbi Abraham Isaac Kook[11]

The realization that running and returning are simply two directions, that one is not less valuable than the other, is crucial to our understanding of Kabbalah. In fact, we can only go "up" (running) by also going "down" (returning). We can deepen inwardly only if we are willing to go out of ourselves, reaching out toward others. We can study, pray, and meditate all we want, but such practices will inevitably become ego-centered if we do not also incorporate compassionate action into our lives. We cannot enter into the higher realms solely by exerting our personal will. Rather, we must be doing God's will. That is why every Jewish mystic is expected to be a practicing Jew, doing the *mitzvot* (commandments) of Torah. That is also why so many mystics have sacrificed themselves caring for the poor and sick, or have challenged the inhumane restrictions of their societies.

Some elements of practice point upward—prayer, study, and meditation to *Da'at, Binah,* and *Chochmah.* Other practices, like charity and caring for one's health, bring energies of compassion and wisdom downward, through *Netzach, Hod,* and *Yesod,* to *Malkhut.* Up or down, they are all simply *practice.* We do them because they are good and they are Godly actions, with as little personal attachment and as much humility as possible. Once we awaken to this realization, a new movement begins among all these *sefirot.* Our ascent also contributes to the elevation of what is below, and our involvement with the energies of the lower *sefirot* awakens deeper yearnings for connection with the higher realms.

As we proceed, we eventually come to see that even the division between "upper" and "lower" is artificial, because all spiritual energies proceed from and return to the heart, our central core, the energy of *Tiferet* manifesting in us. Remember, the *sefirah* of *Tiferet* is the *sefirah* of Divine-human incarnation. As the *Zohar* tells us, it is the bolt that holds everything together, from the highest of heavens to the lowest place on earth. The more we are unified with our practice, the more we find ourselves being transformed into channels for Godliness.

Let us make this point as clear as possible by portraying it on the Tree of Life. The movement of compassionate connection, to God and to the world, is a spiral that moves up, around, and down through all the *sefirot.* Look closely at the diagram below as we follow the flow of energy.

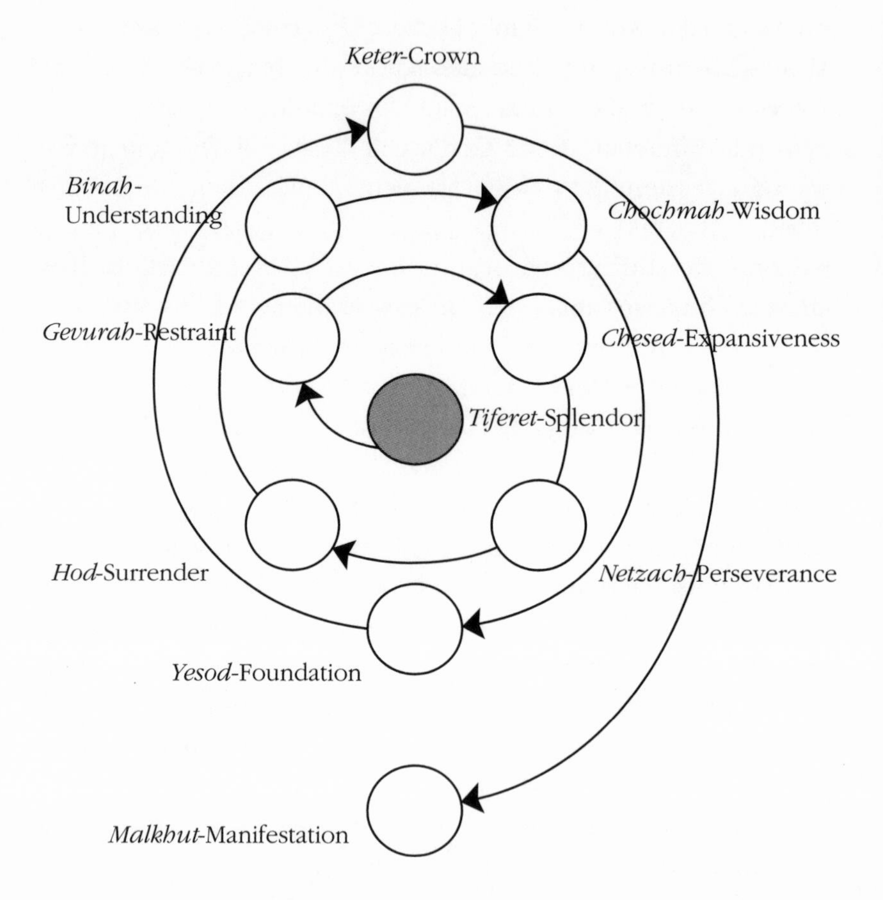

From the heart-center of *Tiferet,* an arrow follows the energy to *Gevurah* and *Chesed*. In our hearts we feel and perceive that we are continuously being directed and supported by *Gevurah* and *Chesed.* This awareness changes our perception of our social environment, our friends, the way we spend our time, and the ways we experience our emotional life. These perceptions thus awaken new energies in the *sefirot* of *Netzach* and *Hod,* as the next arrow suggests.

As we perceive ourselves and our relationships differently, we begin to see more goodness in the world. This shift of consciousness connects to the upper *sefirot,* as the next arrow shows, because it involves an attempt to see the world through God's eyes. On each phase of creating the world, God said, "It is good." Thus Rav Kook wrote, "It is an art of great enlightenment . . . to emulate the eye of God, that focuses only on the good."[12] We, too, want to see the goodness in the world, to see beyond the apparent differences and separations, and to remind ourselves that there is one loving God behind everything that manifests in the universe. This means connecting to *Binah* and *Chochmah.*

With this new sight comes deeper insight from *Binah* and *Chochmah,* enlarging our conception of the cosmos. We begin to recognize that the events and personalities familiar to us are only one small part of a grand design, one that has been unfolding for eons and involves, on this earth, billions of souls. From this perspective, our own story seems different. We can tell the story differently, we can pass on our heritage in a different and larger light—the insights from above affect our connection to *Yesod.* This is represented by the arrow from *Binah* and *Chochmah* to *Yesod.*

Then, the stirring of the deep energies of creativity at *Yesod* spirals upward to *Keter,* following the next arrow. In some forms of yoga, the connection between these two energies is described as a physical experience *(kundalini)* in deep meditation. That it is sometimes described as the uncoiling of a snake parallels the idea of a spiral.

Even this highest energy spirals down again to *Malkhut.* Our deeds in the world then have the potential to be infused with the energy of the Divine. As light rays, as glistening raindrops, we have the ability to bring vitality to the world around us. As manifestations of Divine soul, we can make life meaningful, vibrant, thrilling, joyous. Moreover, as we complete the circuit by acting in the world, the spiral of energy reverses, going up to *Keter,* which then energizes the whole again, returning finally back to the heart, filling it with more love and passion for God and goodness.

This re-description of the dynamics among the *sefirot* is very important. It reminds us that our creative energy spirals out from, and returns to, the heart, the place of *Tiferet,* the Divine image. We must not be tempted by the transcendence of blissful experiences of *Binah*- or *Chochmah*-consciousness to forget our mission to the world. Nor should we trust too much even in *Da'at,* our faculty for study and concentration, for a person can be extremely intelligent but hard-hearted. Rabbi Dessler writes, "God chose . . . the perceptions of the heart. . . . Intellect may fly high but only the heart can influence actions."[13] From the perspective of Kabbalah, the higher levels must be united with the lower, and this can happen only at the heart. *Tiferet* is the place of passion for life and compassion for others, of love for God, for the Divine purpose, and for all creation.

The connection that Kabbalah embodies between the upper and the lower worlds, between the higher reaches of spirit and the ordinary tasks of life, is no accident. In Judaism, mystical techniques were originally developed by the ancient prophets, who demanded of kings, priests, and rich men that they pay attention to what God wanted in the world—to care for the poor and relieve the suffering of the oppressed. Kabbalah, however visionary or esoteric it may have been, is rooted in a tradition of caring for the world. This intense sense of responsibility has sometimes faded into the background, but it is absolutely essential. One can only rise as high as one can bend down. If we are not involved in compassionate action on behalf of our families, communities, and societies, our ability to ascend will be limited. Conversely, if we do not have a spiritual practice that asks us to soar to the heights, we will be restricted by the natural forces of the social and physical worlds in what we can accomplish.

This is the true meaning of "running and returning." Running means going to God; returning means coming back not only to the self, but to discerning, caring involvement in the world. Returning means using our new vision to see anew, using our deeper sensitivity to feel compassionate.

Enhance your ability to feel compassion for others by practicing the "Meditation on Lovingkindness" in Part IV (p. 189).[14]

The Gift of the Soul

Remember that our spiritual growth, like physical growth, does not always go smoothly and evenly. Occasionally, we may find ourselves out of synchrony with parts of our life. Adults on a spiritual path often experience emotional roller coasters that we thought we had left behind with adolescence. For example, when we take on a religious practice, or return to one left behind long ago, our families may be bewildered. We may not feel so certain about what we are doing either. We say to ourselves, "Is it worth it? Maybe I should just forget about it." Or we pretend a certainty we don't really feel, and go around preaching to our friends about how great our new practice is: "You should try meditating—it will help you straighten out your life." In truth, what is being called forth from us is greater compassion, a more heartfelt relation to the world.

Have faith that, as each issue in your life is brought into the light of a spiritual purpose, you will become more in tune with your own Divine essence. It is almost certain that you will be called to go back and review the issues of your personal history to attune everything to a new level. For example, after I began a new level of spiritual work in a dream circle, I had a series of dreams that were very exciting because they seemed to hint at a true spiritual journey. Then I started dreaming about my parents, old friends, and what seemed

You whose day it is, make it beautiful!

Get out your rainbow colors, so it will be beautiful.

—A NOOTKA SONG[15]

to be familiar psychological issues. My dream teacher reassured me that I was not becoming more neurotic but just reintegrating my perception of my parents and childhood into a new picture of myself. I had my doubts, but over time, I saw the same process recur with other dreamers, and found in my own life that what she said was true.

We will eventually come to the place where we no longer feel compelled by the past or anxious about our path into the future. We will become confident—hopefully without arrogance—that we are on the way to manifesting our souls, being who we were meant to be. We don't suddenly become gurus or develop an amazing romantic relationship with our spouses. In fact, we frequently make no obvious external changes at all. Like the Zen priest, we chop wood and carry water. But we take responsibility by making conscious choices in the context of a wholehearted commitment to life: Today, here and now, we will continue polishing our lamps and allow the light of Divinity to shine through us. "Each moment of time presents for each created being a new opportunity to contribute to the Divine revelation."[16]

Usually, as we develop spiritually, we are given more choices to make and more responsibility to carry. This happens to almost every person who begins to demonstrate more trust, faith, and courage in the work of the soul. It is as if God's angels are monitoring our progress in cleaning our lamps of their sediment, and when our lights start to shine a little brighter, we are given more area to illuminate. Thus as we come closer to God, we move to a higher perspective on the mountain, so to speak. We see more work to do, and we feel greater responsibility for it. This shift doesn't necessarily make our lives easier. But the work becomes more interesting, exciting, and fulfilling.

This is the way we bring the gifts of our soul to earth. At the same time, remember that we don't achieve this by directly willing it. The ultimate secret of heaven is that the gift of our soul appears without our conscious volition as we surrender more and more deeply, as we respond to whatever appears before us each day. As many spiritual teachers insist, the work of life is more about getting out of God's way than about doing what we think ought to be done. By the time we finish, at the other end of life, just as at the beginning, we seem to become empty vessels, receiving the Divine energy of our own souls and translating it into earthly reality. When the lamp is completely clear, radiant rainbow colors will shine through you, and you will be able to feel the harmony of your deepest self with Divine purpose. That is the gift of Kabbalah.

Let our spirit fashion for us its creations. We recognize the angel, full of life, who attends to the act of birth, who brings into being his creations. He soars toward us from the great beyond, he draws close to us, he reveals himself in our souls. He has now come.
—RABBI ABRAHAM ISAAC KOOK[17]

On the following page, for your review, are the *sefirot* as we described them in the Path of Remembering.

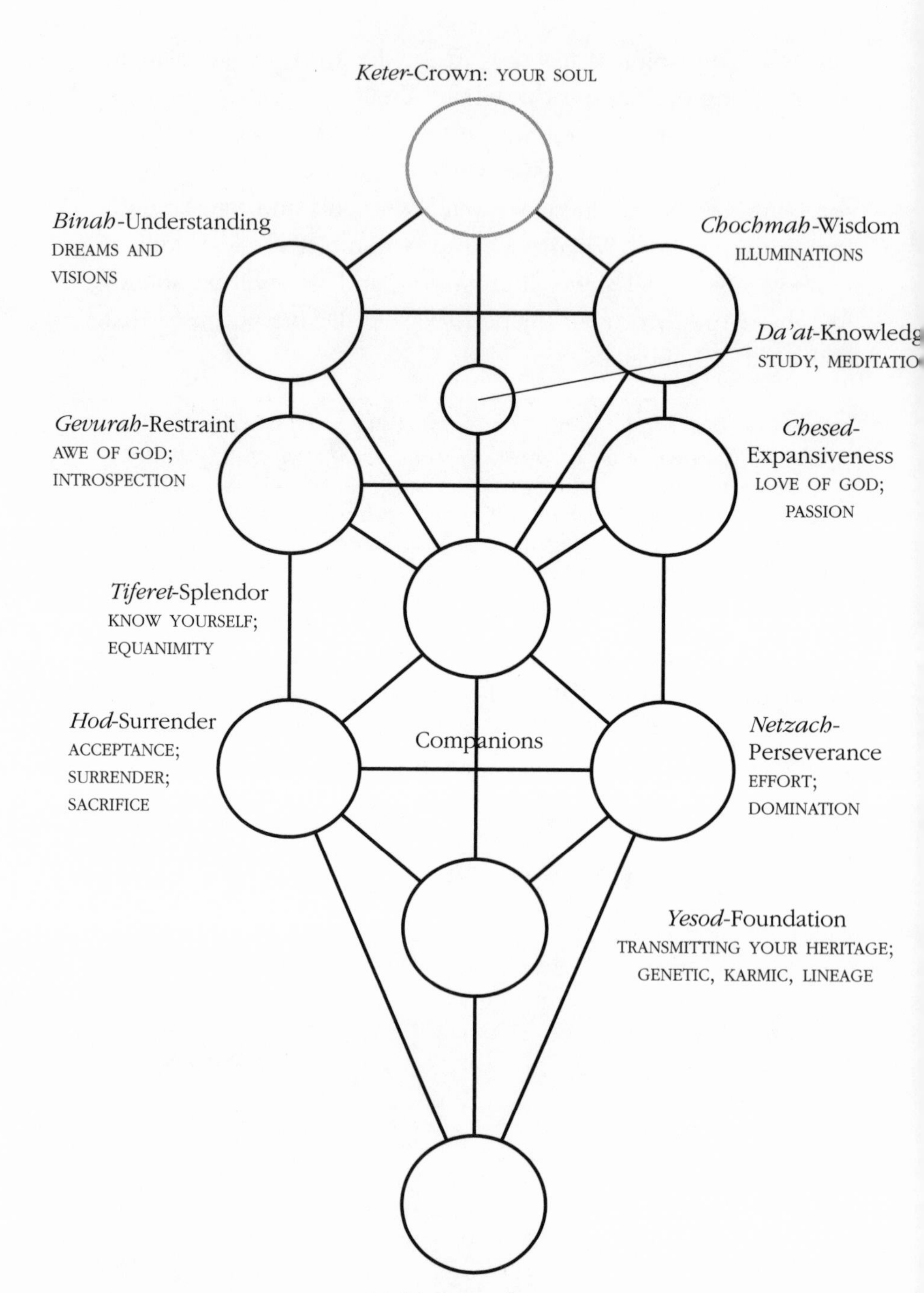

Keter-Crown: YOUR SOUL
Binah-Understanding
DREAMS AND VISIONS
Chochmah-Wisdom
ILLUMINATIONS
Da'at-Knowledg
STUDY, MEDITATIO
Gevurah-Restraint
AWE OF GOD; INTROSPECTION
Chesed-Expansiveness
LOVE OF GOD; PASSION
Tiferet-Splendor
KNOW YOURSELF; EQUANIMITY
Hod-Surrender
ACCEPTANCE; SURRENDER; SACRIFICE
Companions
Netzach-Perseverance
EFFORT; DOMINATION
Yesod-Foundation
TRANSMITTING YOUR HERITAGE; GENETIC, KARMIC, LINEAGE
Malkhut-Manifestation
NAMES AND ROLES; ACTION; MITZVOT

PART IV

PRACTICAL APPLICATIONS OF KABBALAH

Techniques for Spiritual Growth

You may already use certain practices to enrich your spiritual growth, but when you are learning something new, it is especially helpful to introduce a practice that relates specifically to that learning. A simple method is to pray that the learning you are doing will be deeply integrated in yourself. I think, however, that with the intricacies involved in the system of *sefirot,* it is helpful to have practices directly cued to the kabbalistic system. In this section, therefore, I suggest several ways to use the concepts of Kabbalah.

First is a set of affirmations that can be used on a daily or occasional basis. Second is a framework for prayer to help you align yourself along the central pillar of *sefirot.* Third is a series of meditations, based on the concepts presented in this book aligned with specific arrangements of the *sefirot.* Fourth is a practice specified in Jewish tradition, associated with the period between the annual holidays of Passover and *Shavuot,* known as *Sefirat Ha-Omer,* or "Counting the Omer." Fifth is a personal practice of contemplation that I have developed using kabbalistic concepts, originally based on the dream teachings of my colleague Connie Kaplan.

One other practice that I have adopted relating to Kabbalah is a mystical celebration of the holiday *Tu B'Shevat,* the fifteenth of the month of *Shevat* (usually in early February). This day is known as the New Year of the Trees, and the mystics of Safed developed a "seder" for the occasion. Considerations of length prevent me from offering it here, but if you are interested, you can e-mail me at tfrankiel@juno.com to get more information and request a copy (put *"Tu B'Shevat"* in the subject line).

What I offer here is in no way intended to override any existing customs or interpretations, but only to suggest practices that have worked for me and many of my colleagues and students.

Affirmations

An affirmation is a way of creating a positive mindset. Many of us have, over the years, created mental habits that are like ruts in a driveway—we simply go down them without thinking because they're the path of least resistance. Affirmations create new mental habits, a new and more beautiful and expansive road for our minds to travel.

One kind of affirmation is an "I am" meditation. These are specifically about yourself. They work best if they are framed in a way that expresses your *being,* not your *doing.* In other words, they should be "I am" statements, not "I can" statements. Remember that *Anochi,* "I am," is the first word spoken by God in giving the revelation at Sinai to the Jewish people. It is the essence of the *sefirah* of *Chochmah.* When you say "I am," you should try to use words that express your eternal essence, not your temporary frame of mind or feelings. (In daily life, this means it is better to say "I feel tired" rather than "I am tired"; "I feel angry" rather than "I am angry," etc.) It's not always necessary to use "I am" for affirmations, but the sense of being-ness should be prominent.

This first set of affirmations is designed to set up a positive frame of mind, which will allow you to see yourself in the context of the Divine creative energy that sustains the universe at all times, along the framework created by the Tree of Life of the *sefirot.* You may wish to use them individually or say them as a series, after your morning devotions. After you become familiar with the ideas expressed, you may wish to change some of the words so that they feel comfortable.

Keter: I am a spark of God. My essence is Divine.

Chochmah: I emerged from the wild creativity of existence—I am a path worth risking everything for.

Binah: My being—body, mind, and spirit—is aligned with the patterning of the universe. I am a temple for my Divine soul.

Da'at: I am a seeker of higher Divine unity through my mind.

Chesed: I am in touch with the support of the universe, the unconditional love of God.

Gevurah: My limitations and challenges are Divine gifts.

Tiferet: I am a free being, choosing to align my will with God's will.

Netzach: I am a giver, wholeheartedly contributing my effort to creating the world by tending my little part of the universe.

Hod: I am grateful, appreciating and honoring the work of others.

Yesod: I am a channel of transmission, gathering and passing on all that comes to and through me for the good, to other living beings and to the next generation.

Malkhut: I am part of a greater whole, joining with all other beings to express gratitude and praise to the Creator of the universe.

Another kind of affirmation expresses a positive view of the world around you, resetting your world view as you might reset your watch. When we feel victimized or want to blame someone, when we feel disappointed or don't understand why our plans aren't working out, or when we feel overwhelmed, this kind of affirmation can be very helpful. The following list is also correlated with the *sefirot,* to help you at difficult times, when you are experiencing conflicts or when you are having difficulties in seeing the good in what is happening.

Keter: Master of the universe, may Your Will be done.

Chochmah: This world is being infused with Divine intent at every moment.

Binah: Every pattern or design I see is an aspect of Divine reality, revealing itself to me.

Da'at: The path of unification is open to me at any moment by settling my mind.

Chesed: I join the outpouring of Divine love by performing acts of *chesed* and thinking kind thoughts.

Gevurah: What happens is all from the Creator. Now I have an opportunity to re-examine my connection to my spiritual path.

Tiferet: God connects to the world through me; my purpose on earth is being fulfilled even though that may not be apparent to me.

Netzach: My creativity is valued and cherished in the ultimate scheme of Divine unfolding.

Hod: I am willing to sacrifice my personal desires for the general good and for the glory of the Divine.

Yesod: God is Master of time, Creator of coincidences, and Lord of history—whether I can see it or not, there is an evolving design.

Malkhut: God's will is manifest right here and now; everything is exactly as it is supposed to be.

Deepening Your Prayer

Prayer can be a very powerful form of expression when you make an effort to connect to God along the central pillar of the *sefirot*. If you do not already have a prayer form that is comfortable for you, I suggest you experiment with a discipline that orients you physically, emotionally, and mentally through action and visualization, while also using words of prayer to ask for what you need and to pray for others. Follow these steps:

1. *Malkhut:* Begin by standing, then emptying yourself in humility and gratitude. If it is comfortable for you, you may bow, kneel, or prostrate yourself to express humility in a physical way. Choose a prayer that allows you to express those attitudes. A simple prayer that many Jews say on awakening is the *Modeh Ani*: "I give thanks before You, Living and Eternal King [or God], for restoring my soul to me with kindness; great is Your trust in me."[1]
2. *Yesod:* Now, make yourself available as a channel for Divine-human communication, the transmission that is the essence of *Yesod*. Imagine that you are a priest or priestess of the Divine, chosen as this channel. You may wish to say the Priestly Blessing addressed to yourself: "May *Adonai* ['the Lord'] bless and guard you; May *Adonai* make His face to shine upon you and be gracious to you; May *Adonai* lift up His face to you and grant you peace."
3. *Tiferet:* Express the intent to align your will with Divine purpose. Create an image of the harmony and beauty and goodness—*Tiferet*—that God intends. Some of the psalms may help you do this (e.g., Psalm 147).
4. *Da'at:* Meditate on the ultimate unity of God and creation. If you are Jewish you may want to say the *Shema*: *Shema Yisrael, Adonai Eloheinu, Adonai Echad. Baruch shem k'vod malkhuto l'olam va'ed.* ["Hear O Israel, the Lord is our God, the Lord is One. Blessed is the name of the glory of His kingdom forever."]
5. Now you are ready to offer your specific requests. For each thing you want to ask, form a positive image in your mind of *how you will feel,* and *how the object of your prayer will feel,* when your prayer is granted. Take time to make the image as vivid as you can. Breathe deeply and peacefully "into" the image. Then say, as best you can, the words that express your request.

6. *Keter:* End with a statement of positive acceptance such as "Thy Will be done." Jewish prayers end with "May the words of my mouth and the meditations of my heart be acceptable to You, Lord, my Rock and my Redeemer."[2] In Hebrew, this sentence has ten *yuds*—the tenth letter of the Hebrew alphabet—alluding to the ten *sefirot* within ten *sefirot,* all going back to the *yud* that is the first letter of God's holy four-letter name.

Meditative Visualizations

Visualizations are methods to enrich our spiritual imagination. We use our capacity for fantasy all the time, but we often do not realize how much disciplined imagination can enhance our spiritual journey. By visualizing spiritual imagery, we increase our sensitivity and develop our powers of awareness at the same time as we connect positive images to what we are learning.

You can do each of these meditations in one of several ways: (1) Read it over until it is reasonably familiar; then put the book down and do it mentally as best you can remember, without judging yourself. Your own imagery will probably replace some of the specific imagery of the text. (2) Have a friend whose voice you enjoy read it to you. (3) Tape yourself reading the meditation aloud, then play it back whenever you want.

THE HOUSE OF THE WORLDS

This meditation takes you through all the levels of the *sefirot,* organized along the lines of the Four Worlds mentioned on pages 23–24. I have adapted this meditation from one created by Judy Greenfeld for a *Tu B'Shevat* seder; I later heard very similar imagery used in a Hasidic story by Rabbi Yaakov Jacobson. The first level represents *Malkhut* and the lowest world of *Assiyah.* The second represents the six middle *sefirot,* from *Yesod* to *Chesed* (world of *Yetzirah*). The third is *Binah (Beriah)* and the fourth is *Chochmah (Atzilut),* which points toward *Keter.*

* * *

Imagine that you are walking on a path that leads uphill toward an attractive old stone house, several stories high. Allow yourself to enjoy the gentle climb as the path winds through a meadow of grass and flowers.

As you approach the house, the door is open to welcome you. You enter a foyer and look around. A comfortable living room is on the right, and a dining area you can glimpse behind it, while on the left is a hallway probably leading to bedrooms. You walk into the living room. It is comfortable and thoroughly lived-in. There is a television and computer, a stereo, and stacks of newspapers and magazines. As you stroll into the kitchen the timer on the microwave rings, and the scent of fresh coffee is in the air. It seems a pleasant and busy place, and it would be inviting to sit down for breakfast, but you want to explore the whole house.

You return to the foyer and climb the staircase, which has wooden banisters and steps showing signs of wear. At the second floor landing, you find yourself in another set of rooms. On one side is a large room with many paintings on the wall, and an easel set up there tells you it is a studio. Classical music plays in the background. A breeze blows through colorful curtains. On the other side is a room filled with plants, a greenhouse with part of the ceiling extended to capture the light. The plants are full and rich, the flowers like jewels. Light, exotic scents fill the air, and breathing seems easier here. It is tempting to stay—but you will explore more.

The stairs to the next level are of rich olive wood, with deeply carved banisters. Fewer footsteps have worn down the grain here. As you come to the top, you see there is only one room. It appears to be a library. Many shelves fill the walls, and there are cabinets with drawers as well. You walk along the shelves and you see that many of the books are ancient, with leather bindings and gold letters. You carefully take one large volume off the shelf and open it. It is an illuminated manuscript, perhaps several hundred years old, but it looks as though it were copied yesterday.

After returning it to its place, you open a drawer and you see scrolls, even more ancient, with writing you cannot recognize. In between the cabinets are rich tapestries covering most of the walls. Light comes in gently from perfectly placed windows high in the walls, directing the light toward the middle of the room, away from the delicate books yet perfect for reading at the tables in the center. So much wisdom is contained in these archives—you long to spend time with these books, and it is very hard to tear yourself away.

But there is another staircase. This one is quite remarkable—it appears to be made of colored glass. A rainbow emerges beneath your feet at every step, as though the stair was lighting up as you put your foot on it. The light increases as you ascend, until you finally reach a room that is so full of light that it seems to have no walls. Indeed, windows occupy most of the wall area, and a high ceiling arches toward a skylight. But when you look out the window, expecting to see the pathway up the hill you climbed below, instead you have a vista grander than you have ever seen. It is as if this floor of the house extended toward the clouds. You can see the earth stretched beneath you, fields and lakes and mountains and oceans. Though you seem to be looking from a great height, you can see individuals too—people, animals, buildings, even individual trees. Your breathing grows deep and wide. You feel lighter than you ever have in your life. You feel ecstatic with love and blessing.

The realization grows that you are not alone. In this place of light are other beings of light. Their forms come into focus, and they smile at you. You experience them not so much as people but as colors, radiant but gentle. Just being among them makes you feel happy. With a deep breath you realize that here, you could really stay forever. You bask in the light and love. Breathe again, deeply.

After a while, you realize that it is time to go. You glance around and smile at those in the room, then start down the stairs. In the library, you now see there are others present here, too, walking among the shelves and studying at the tables. They look up and smile at you, as though they know you.

At the next level, you see gardeners puttering among the plants, a couple of artists at work in the studio, and you see someone playing a piano you hadn't noticed before. A dog lying on the rug perks up to watch you, and a cat walks by, rubbing itself on your legs and purring. You relax, a friendly smile forms on your face, and you go on down the stairs.

On the first floor, children have just burst through the front door, home from school, and run into the kitchen shouting for their mother. An elderly man sits in the living room reading the newspaper. You greet him, and he nods in return. Then you depart, walking slowly on the path down the hill.

Take a few deep breaths. Remember this place; you can return here again whenever you like. And take the memory with you into your day.

* * *

BREATH IS THE SIGNATURE OF SPIRIT

Virtually every spiritual tradition has a practice that involves working with the breath; Kabbalah is no exception. Breathing exercises are recorded among the kabbalists of medieval times; Rabbi Aryeh Kaplan has traced hints of such exercises back to the prophets of the biblical era.

We can see why breathing would be important because the heart-lung system corresponds to the triangle represented by *Chesed, Gevurah,* and *Tiferet*. *Tiferet* is the crucial link between heaven and earth, between the upper *sefirot* and Divine manifestation. This is suggested in the Bible by the story in Genesis describing how God gave life to inanimate form by breathing into it (Genesis 2:3). When you breathe consciously, you enter directly into the reciprocal rhythm of *Chesed* and *Gevurah* and, as

Rabbi Nachman's story of the Heart and the Spring (Chapter 4) suggests, you nourish your physical and spiritual heart as well.

This meditation asks you to use the breath as a vehicle for expanded consciousness. Be aware of your breath as you practice this meditation, but you do not need to force yourself to breathe in any special way.

• • •

Sit comfortably in a chair with your back supported and your feet on the floor; or take a meditation posture of your choice.

Close your eyes. Focus your attention inward, at the area of your heart, lungs, and solar plexus. Become aware of your breathing, your chest lightly rising and falling.

Visualize in the center of your chest a small light. (If you want to work with the Hebrew alphabet, visualize the light in the shape of the letter *alef*. If not, a circle or the shape of a candle flame will be fine.) Notice how the light intensifies and expands as you breathe in and returns to its original size as you exhale.

Now, with each breath, allow the light to expand a little more. Slowly, let the light fill your entire chest and then grow further to fill your whole body. Sit with the radiant light inside you for several breaths, allowing it to warm you and to send its light to all parts of your body. Imagine that you can feel the warmth and light all over your skin, coming from inside.

Now, with each breath, allow the light to expand still more. Go with the light, allowing your body to expand as well. You are one with the light as it grows.

The light—the circle—the *alef*—you—expand until you fill the room. Breathing, you expand still more, filling the house and going beyond its boundaries. Your light is expanding and rising gently and slowly so that from where you are, in the center of it, you can now see your house, your neighborhood, your city.

Continue to expand, breath by breath, as much as you feel comfortable. You can expand to the edges of the earth, or out into space. When you have gone as far as you are comfortable, rest there a few moments, breathing gently. Feel what it is like to be in this expanded state. Be aware of the earth, moon, planets, stars that each have their own light, just as you do. Allow yourself to be connected to every entity that you can see or feel. Acknowledge the blessing of being part of a vibrant universe of light.

When you are ready, turn your attention to your breathing again, and with each breath, as you exhale, allow your light to begin to condense. Slowly, let the space you occupy become smaller. Return to the earth, to the region above your country, to your city. Slowly return, breath by breath, to your neighborhood, your house. Allow your light slowly to return to the room where you began. Breath by breath, you come back to the boundaries of your body. The light gently returns to being a small circle in the center of your chest.

Take three deep breaths. Gently move your fingers and toes. When you are ready, open your eyes.

* * *

CONTEMPLATING YOUR PLACE IN HISTORY

Yesod is the *sefirah* representing how we transmit our heritage—genetic, cultural, personal—to the rest of the world and the next generation. This is a crucial juncture, but one that it is sometimes difficult to relate to in a deeper way. This meditation may help you. It is adapted from one developed by Connie Kaplan for a seminar we taught together in 1998–99.

* * *

You may sit or stand for this visualization. If you are in a chair, make sure it is positioned so you can turn around.

Imagine that you are facing the future. Now turn around and face the past.

See your mother and father before you. Turn first toward your mother, and contemplate her image for a few moments. See her smiling at you pleasantly. She has brought you a blessing. She extends her hands and places them on your head, giving you her blessing. Accept it. You know in your heart what it is—a gift of some quality of being, or way of approaching life, that you can treasure. You are aware of feelings of gratitude. If you wish, say thank you.

Now see that behind your mother stands her mother. You and your mother both turn toward her, and she is smiling, extending a blessing. She extends her hands and, blowing it with a kiss, sends a blessing to both of you. Then she turns around and you see, behind her, her mother. Again a blessing is sent from mother to daughter, granddaughter, and great-grandchild. As you gaze at them, you see that behind her stands a line of women, a line that seems to extend into the infinite past, all sending their blessings to you.

Now turn toward your father. He smiles and offers you a blessing. He places his hands on your head, and you accept the blessing with gratitude. Then he turns, and behind him you see his father. He gives a blessing, and then your great-grandfather appears with a blessing as well. So it continues, a seemingly endless line of fathers sending their blessing to you. Take your time, seeing as far back as you can.

Think for a moment of all you are receiving from these men and women who have lived through so many centuries. You are the one on whom they have chosen to bestow the choicest of their love, their experiences of ecstasy and suffering, and their knowledge. You are their hope—they want you to take the best of their lives and shape it into a future of life and joy.

Now turn around and face the future. Before you stand your children—your own children if you have them, or, if not, other children that you encounter such as nieces or nephews, children of close friends, neighbors, students. They wait for you to pass the gifts you have received onto them. Give them each a blessing, a quality you want to give to the future.

See each of them grow to adults, and then turn around to face the future. More children appear—their children, one by one—to receive a blessing from those you have blessed. They in turn grow up and turn to face the future, and bless yet another row upon row of children. Once more—they grow up and now a vast number of children appear.

Then, all of them turn back to you—the children and adults who received from you. They all look up to you and speak their gratitude. Hear their voices—"Thank you." "We really appreciate what you did." "We couldn't have done it without you."

Let your heart feel the appreciation and love that comes to you from the future. Know that all your work, all your struggles are worthwhile. You belong to the future, and you live within all the generations to come.

* * *

RELEASING YOUR PAST

I learned the following exercise from Connie Kaplan, who credits Carlos Castaneda with teaching it to her. Over the years, Judy Greenfeld and I have adapted it in connection with helping people work on forgiveness. But even when forgiveness is not required, releasing our ties to events, individuals, and groups helps us work with the energies of *Netzach* and *Hod*. We achieve clarity of intent when we are not perceiving the present in the light of past emotional experiences.

The exercise is demanding but extraordinarily effective. Once you decide to undertake it, be patient with yourself and do not judge yourself if you are not able to follow a regular schedule or complete it when you think you ought to. Simply return to it when you can, knowing that every time you do it has a value in and of itself, even if its effects may not be immediately evident to you.

* * *

Plan to set aside fifteen minutes of time every day for the next few months. At the beginning, you will spend each day's assigned time sitting with paper and pencil, writing down every person you can remember meeting in your whole life. You can begin at the beginning and work forward, or you can begin with today and work backward. If you remember an encounter with someone but can't remember the person's name, just write down a description (e.g., "that kid who pulled my hair in third grade" or "my grouchy neighbor down the street").

After you have made your list (this may take quite a few weeks), begin spending the day's time with each person on your list. Don't start with a difficult person or one with whom you have had many encounters, such as a parent. Take someone whom you met only once, or had slight encounters with. Save the more complicated ones for later.

Visualize the person in front of you, recalling also an incident with him or her. Notice the energy around the memory. What is the feeling? Name it. Tell the person how you feel about the encounter or exchange you are remembering. Recognize their part in the event, and yours. Don't judge yourself or the other person for these events in the past. Focus only on the energy you are still carrying in the present. Thank God—and, if possible, the other person—for the experience, and the clarity to learn from it. Then announce that you are done with this event and ready to recover the energy that has tied you to this person.

Take a deep breath in and then exhale. As you blow out, turn your head slowly to the left, then to the right, releasing your ties to the other person. You may wish to visualize fibers that have connected you and watch them dissolve. Then look at the person's image again. Has it faded or changed to weaker colors? If so, the work is being done. If not, you may wish to repeat this process, today or on another day, because there may still be emotional ties that you have not recognized.

On the next day, do the same process with the next person on the list. When you come to someone with whom you had many experiences, call up each memorable experience or context, one by one.

As you become more practiced, you will recapitulate your memories of some people very quickly. You will probably recognize familiar emotions repeated over and over again with different people. Still, it will take a long time to finish the list—depending on how old you are and how sociable you have been!

When you have completed the list, you will want to continue the same method to review encounters with people, frequently if not daily. You can also apply the same process to groups—for example, the energies you bring home from the meetings you attended or traffic jams you suffered through.

As you work through this process, you will begin to see your emotions as information and you will free yourself from the need to react. You can watch your emotions rise and fall (an important technique taught in Vipassana Buddhist meditation) and know that these feelings are simply the patterns of your emotional being. Once you free yourself from your past ties, in fact, you will see the true "you" ever more clearly.

* * *

MEDITATION ON LOVINGKINDNESS

The rabbis say that *Chesed* or Lovingkindness is the essence of the Torah, and the kabbalists say that the upper worlds are entirely *Chesed.* Many other traditions echo this thought. The Buddhist tradition has a classic meditation on *metta,* or lovingkindness, which I have adapted here from a version given by Andrew Harvey in his book *The Direct Path*. Use it to enhance *Chesed* in your life. It will also strengthen the connection between the upper *sefirot* and *Tiferet,* at your heart.

• • •

Begin with the following prayer. If you are Jewish, you may wish to say first the phrase "May it be Your Will, Lord my God and God of my ancestors, that . . .", which traditionally begins invocations of blessing.

Then say: "Even as a mother watches over and protects her child, her only child, so with a boundless mind may I cherish all living beings, radiating friendliness over the entire world, above, below, and all around without limit. May I cultivate a boundless good will toward the whole world, uncramped and free from ill will or enmity."

Then direct lovingkindness *(chesed)* toward yourself, since this is necessary in order to have compassion for others. Say to yourself:

May I be free from danger
May I have mental happiness
May I have physical happiness
May I have ease of well-being.

You may find it hard to feel that you deserve such blessings. If you have feelings of unworthiness or hear "you have to be kidding" voices, simply continue to breathe deeply and calmly. Look at whatever arises in you without fear or judgment. It can help to imagine someone who loves you very much—a mother, or grandfather, or friend—and recall their love for you. Or imagine a compassionate angel looking at you with unconditional love.

Repeat the four phrases quietly, softly, and with calm feeling. If you wish to change or add to the words to express specific needs (for example, "May I have financial ease," "May I have inspiration in my work"), feel free to do so. Allow yourself to feel compassion for yourself in your needs.

When you feel sincerely that your lovingkindness toward yourself is vivid and warm, begin directing *chesed* to someone who has been good to you. Think of this person with deep gratitude and recite the same four phrases slowly and reverently for him or her.

May _______________ *be free from danger*
May _______________ *have mental happiness*
May _______________ *have physical happiness*
May _______________ *have ease of well-being*

Now choose to direct lovingkindness toward a beloved friend, one whose heart and loyalty you are sure of. Recall the depth and beauty of your friendship, and let yourself be warmed by memories of what it has brought you. Then, as before, recite the four phrases with prayerful tenderness for your friend.

By now your sense of inner abundance and power to love should be strong and secure. You can now direct unconditional lovingkindness toward those who have hurt you or even tried to destroy you.

First, though, choose someone who is neutral in your life. This could be a cashier you see at the supermarket, or a librarian who sometimes checks out your books. While they do serve you, you don't have any particular feelings toward them. Call one of these people to mind and repeat the four phrases for him or her. You may find, the next time you see that person, you will feel a change in your attitude.

Now choose someone who has wanted to harm you in thought, speech, or actual deed. If you succeed in evoking genuine compassion for someone who has wounded you, you will taste the freedom and sublime beauty of the force of unconditional love at the core of your inner nature. This is a direct connection to God within you. Knowing that you will experience love will begin to liberate you from the need to cling to anger or bitterness that may still remain from your past distress.

In practice, however, doing this may be difficult. It may help to visualize the person you have chosen as a vulnerable child, or to focus on some good points in their character, a talent or a past kindness. You may wish to imagine what happened to make them the kind of person they are. Call up the image of the person before you and surround it with a soft light. Recite the four phrases, methodically and slowly, offering up for transformation your own anger or bitterness as well.

If your negative feelings continue, ask yourself, "Who is suffering from this rage? Who is afflicted by this bitterness?" It will immediately become clear that your enemy is not suffering from your anger—you are. You need release. Try repeating this phrase a few times:

Out of compassion for myself, may I let go of all these feelings of anger and resentment forever!

After reciting the four phrases for your enemy and, with your whole heart, directing lovingkindness to him or her, now direct a stream of lovingkindness toward the whole world in all directions. South, west, north, east, up, down—let lovingkindness flow from your heart. Rest in the bliss, peace, joy, and unshakable strength of unconditional compassion. Dedicate all good that comes from this meditation to the benefit of sentient beings everywhere. If you are Jewish, you may wish to end with a traditional closing prayer: "May the words of my mouth and the meditations of my heart be pleasing to You, Lord, my Rock and my Redeemer."[2]

• • •

If you are interested in additional meditations, I suggest consulting Rabbi Aryeh Kaplan's *Innerspace,* David Cooper's *Handbook of Jewish Meditation Practices,* or Andrew Harvey's *The Direct Path* (see the Recommended Readings section). You can also begin creating your own meditations, based on passages from sacred scripture or religious icons that are meaningful to you.

Sefirot in the Jewish Calendar: *Sefirat Ha-Omer* (Counting the Omer)

The Torah stipulates that the Jewish people should count forty-nine days—seven weeks of seven days—beginning with the second day of Passover. Offerings from the new barley harvest (an *omer* is a measure of grain) were brought to the Temple in Jerusalem each day as part of this counting. This counting would lead the people to the time of the wheat harvest, which would begin seven weeks later. Rabbinic tradition noted that this period of time corresponded to the time between the Israelites' leaving Egypt on the fifteenth of the month of *Nisan* and arriving at Sinai to receive the Torah on the sixth of *Sivan*. From this, they concluded that the period between the two holidays was also a period of spiritual preparation.

The mystics elaborated on this notion. Using the seven lower *sefirot* as a basic structure for the seven weeks of seven days, they interpreted this period as an ideal time for specific, focused spiritual work for each individual. Each week would correspond to a *sefirah,* and each day to a *sefirah* within that *sefirah*. Thus the first day would be *Chesed sheb'Chesed,* Expansiveness that is in Expansiveness. The second would be *Gevurah sheb'Chesed,* Restraint that is in Expansiveness; the third, *Tiferet sheb'Chesed,* Splendor in Expansiveness, and so on. The second week would begin with *Chesed sheb'Gevurah,* Expansiveness in Restraint, and so the series would be completed in seven weeks.

This custom has been reintroduced into larger spiritual circles of Jews in the second half of the twentieth century, largely through the outreach influence of Hasidic teachers. How exactly to apply this practice to our personal lives has been a subject of much discussion. I offer here a sketch of one method, using the descriptions of the *sefirot* presented earlier in this book.

THE WEEKS

Here are some ideas for the overall theme of each week. If you are just beginning the practice of *Sefirat Ha-Omer,* this may be enough for you, without getting into complications of the energy of each day within the week. Take the themes as guidelines, not definitive rules as to what to think about. Observe how they work in your life—what things fall into line with the energies described here, and what surprises you find along the way. Make notes for your own future reference next year. Remember, the first week starts on the second day of Passover.

Week 1: *Chesed*-Expansiveness. You are in a mode of receptivity and openness to the love of God. If you are Jewish, you are celebrating Passover, experiencing in your own life the drama of redemption, of going out of Egypt. Try to free yourself from too many external constraints at this time, and use meditations that focus on the support and unconditional love streaming from God.

Week 2: *Gevurah*-Restraint. God sometimes leaves us on our own or gives us challenges. These aren't necessarily big spiritual tests, just reminders of what it's like to be independent. Note whether you feel constrained to do things against your personal will or overwhelmed by too many demands. Do you see your life as undisciplined or too strictly defined?

Week 3: *Tiferet*-Splendor. This is the *sefirah* where your will and the Divine will meet and embrace. Allow yourself to deepen your understanding of your purpose in life. (Remember, it's not about *doing* but about *being*.) Use meditations that direct your gaze upward to God as well as downward to the world that is your sphere of influence. In your prayers and meditations, ask that your own will be in harmony with the Divine.

Week 4: *Netzach*-Perseverance. The theme is building and strengthening the external structures of your life, with focus on actions. This could mean paying attention to your physical space—your home, your room, your office, your garden, your body. Or it may be your spiritual space—your community, your observance of commandments.

Week 5: *Hod*-Surrender. Time to step back and get in touch with feelings. Appreciate what is going on around you and what has been given to you. Take time to sense the energy of other people. At the same time, work on untying yourself from attachments, recognizing that everything is a gift from God.

Week 6: *Yesod*-Foundation. All the work you have been doing is brought together here. Give yourself credit for what you have accomplished. Remind yourself of your ideals and goals for the future. Since *Yesod* is the channel through which all the energies of the higher *sefirot* pass, you may be dealing with those elements of your life that are about transmitting who you are to the world. For example, issues may arise about children, students, or fellow workers.

Week 7: *Malkhut*-Manifestation. What you have learned becomes manifest. Talk about your spiritual work with others. Put yourself wholeheartedly into the roles you have been assigned. Remind yourself that God is working through you, and your main job is to get your ego out of God's way.

THE DAYS

Here are some guidelines for the days within each week.

Week 1: Expansiveness

The Lord said to Avram . . . I will bless you and make your name great, and you shall be a blessing. (Genesis 12:2)

Day 1: *Chesed* in *Chesed.* The second day of Passover, a holiday *(Yom Tov)* when work is forbidden on the traditional Jewish calendar. As a holiday, it is a good time to absorb the Divine energy that is transmitted. Passover is the "courtship" of God with the Jewish people, and during this holiday the biblical book *Shir Ha-Shirim* (Song of Songs) is read as an emblem of the mutual love between God and Israel.

Day 2: *Gevurah* in *Chesed.* While the spirit of God's support and love is in the air all week, today is a day to pay attention to the awesomeness of the event of deliverance. Learn about the restrictions of the intermediate days of Passover that keep us in an attitude of awe and respect.

Day 3: *Tiferet* in *Chesed*. Contemplate what it means to you to be the recipient of God's love. Recognize that God welcomes you into the universe daily, supports you, and places trust in you.

Day 4: *Netzach* in *Chesed*. See your actions and choices as building a world in which Divinity will live—where entities of love, peace, and goodwill will be at home.

Day 5: *Hod* in *Chesed*. Think of all the beings you would invite into the world you are building for God. Welcome them as God welcomes you.

Day 6: *Yesod* in *Chesed*. This is the seventh day of Passover, commemorating the splitting of the sea, when the Israelites walked through the sea on dry land, thus escaping their Egyptian persecutors. In order for this miracle to happen, they had to demonstrate their faith by walking into the water. Put your trust completely in God, knowing that emptying yourself of ego allows more of Divinity to enter.

Day 7: *Malkhut* in *Chesed*. Eighth day of Passover. Think of all the things you are thankful for today, and in recent days. Set aside time to speak to God about them, expressing your thanks aloud as completely as you can.

Week 2: Restraint

And Isaac dug anew the wells . . . (Genesis 26:18)

Day 8: *Chesed* in *Gevurah*. God's apparent withdrawal is effective this week, but Divine love is present here too. Look at how you can experience your own independence as a gift from God.

Day 9: *Gevurah* in *Gevurah*. "The beginning of wisdom is fear of the Lord" (Psalms 111:10). Contemplate the idea that your being is significant only insofar as you are connected to the Divine plan.

Day 10: *Tiferet* in *Gevurah.* We make the most important decisions alone. Reflect on the awesome responsibility that comes with the free choice about how to live your life.

Day 11: *Netzach* in *Gevurah.* Consider whether more discipline—physical, mental, social, or spiritual—might be a valuable addition to your life now.

Day 12: *Hod* in *Gevurah.* What can you give up—as a form of self-sacrifice—for God, your community, or the larger environment? If you have been overindulgent, now is a good time to correct that.

Day 13: *Yesod* in *Gevurah.* We are called to feel sympathy with the suffering of others who may be experiencing pain or deprivation. How can you deepen your connections with people, near or far, who are suffering now?

Day 14: *Malkhut* in *Gevurah.* Pray for humility—the ability to be your authentic self without a trace of arrogance.

Week 3: Splendor

And he said, "No longer will it be said that your name is Jacob, but Israel, for you have wrestled with God and man, and prevailed." (Genesis 32:29)

Day 15: *Chesed* in *Tiferet.* God's love for you as a unique individual is very present—bask in it. Notice all the ways God has provided support specifically for you.

Day 16: *Gevurah* in *Tiferet.* Awe of God and of God's creation is a good focus for meditation. This is an appropriate day to reflect on the place of humanity in the universe, as the Book of Job says: "What is man that You are mindful of him?"

Day 17: *Tiferet* in *Tiferet.* Allow the deep, creative levels of your being to express themselves toward other beings. Be radiant with the inner knowledge that you belong here and you are doing good work.

Day 18: *Netzach* in *Tiferet.* Your mastery over the world can be evident on this day. Contemplate all the things you have accomplished.

Day 19: *Hod* in *Tiferet.* Spend some time withdrawing into deep meditation—this is your imitation of the Divine *tzimtzum* (self-contraction).

Day 20: *Yesod* in *Tiferet.* Contemplate what you see yourself contributing to the world in the future. Write a glorious eulogy for yourself—don't be shy or self-deprecatory. Give yourself credit for everything you have done, no matter how small.

Day 21: *Malkhut* in *Tiferet.* Meditate on the amazing idea that God made human beings in the Divine image. Pray for the ability to manifest that image in every moment of your life.

Week 4: Perseverance

Moses' . . . hands remained steady till sunset. (Exodus 17:12)

Day 22: *Chesed* in *Netzach.* Become aware of God's support for the specific things you are building in your life—health, home, family, means of sustenance.

Day 23: *Gevurah* in *Netzach.* Notice the areas of your life that are difficult for you. What can help you accept the limitations and disappointments that you experience?

Day 24: *Tiferet* in *Netzach.* Take pleasure in the fact that you have the opportunity to express God's will through your actions. Think of a specific practical *mitzvah* that you can add to your practice.

Day 25: *Netzach* in *Netzach.* "Treat God's will as if it were your own will, so that He will treat your will as His will" (Avot 2:4). Be confident that you can accomplish your goals.

Day 26: *Hod* in *Netzach*. Contemplate the interdependence of your work and that of your community, society, and environment. Nurture the relationships that will support your work.

Day 27: *Yesod* in *Netzach*. How does your work contribute to the history of your community, the larger society, the evolution of the universe? How would you like to expand it? Think big—your choices will affect the next millennium.

Day 28: *Malkhut* in *Netzach*. Pray for strength and confidence to do the work required of you today and every day.

Week 5: Surrender

And Aaron was silent. (Leviticus 10:3)

Day 29: *Chesed* in *Hod*. Become aware of the love and support you receive from your "companions," those who are traveling with you on the path right now. Allow yourself to bask in it.

Day 30: *Gevurah* in *Hod*. If there are any ways in which you are feeling restricted or limited in your life, examine them closely. Work on developing a spirit of acceptance.

Day 31: *Tiferet* in *Hod*. Appreciate your unique abilities in the context of the energy of surrender: How do you retreat from the world? What are your special ways of respecting others?

Day 32: *Netzach* in *Hod*. If possible, take an active role in increasing the respect people have for one another among your family or friends, or in your workplace.

Day 33: *Hod* in *Hod*. *Lag b'Omer*. On this minor holiday, Jews commemorate the *yahrzeit* (anniversary of the death) of Rabbi Shimon bar Yochai, one of the great mystics of the second century. At this time also, the period of deaths that had been suffered by thousands of Rabbi Akiva's students (during the Bar Kochba revolution and its aftermath of disease and destruction) finally ceased. It is said that one of the reasons these great scholars had to suffer so much was because they did not pay enough respect to one another. The *sefirah* of *Hod sheb'Hod* reminds us of the importance of the character trait of respect for others. If you haven't yet focused on releasing your emotional ties this week, do it today (see "Releasing Your Past," p. 187).

Day 34: *Yesod* in *Hod*. Think of all the people you have come to respect, even stand in awe of, in your life. Make a gallery of them—pictures, names, memories you jot down. Talk to your children about their ancestors or old family friends to help pass on the awareness of the support you continuously receive from others.

Day 35: *Malkhut* in *Hod*. Meditate today on profound acceptance of everything and everyone just the way they are—and manifest that attitude in your interactions.

Week 6: Foundation

Joseph saw the face of his father Jacob. (*Midrash Rabba* to Genesis 39:9–10)

Day 36: *Chesed* in *Yesod*. Imagine yourself receiving new resources from deep within your lineage and tradition. What gifts would you like from people of your past—your family, your distant relatives, or other eras to which you feel connected?

Day 37: *Gevurah* in *Yesod*. Examine where you feel the restrictions of your past, what you have been willing to accept and what you have rejected.

Day 38: *Tiferet* in *Yesod*. Remember that you are the sole bearer of your unique genetic heritage, and realize that you are also a unique source of your cultural and family heritage as well. Are you called to represent this heritage to the world in any way?

Day 39: *Netzach* in *Yesod*. Consider whether there is some way to take action—in the form of study, speech, or deeds—regarding your tradition and heritage. You may want to call relatives you haven't spoken to in a while, or plan a storytelling about your heritage at a local library.

Day 40: *Hod* in *Yesod*. Contemplate your heritage. You might consider sitting down to look at pictures in a family album or studying something about your history. Ask God for assistance in manifesting who you are as a transmitter of lineage and tradition.

Day 41: *Yesod* in *Yesod*. Now contemplate the broadening and deepening of your concept of heritage, tradition, or lineage. Do you have a multicultural background you would like to affirm? Do you imagine that you have lived past lives that are very different from your current one? Can you think of yourself as a citizen of more than one country, or of planet earth? Remember that each lineage and tradition is embedded in another, and then another, back to the beginning of humankind, and before that to the emergence of the green planet and all its inhabitants.

Day 42: *Malkhut* in *Yesod*. Meditate on the awesome idea that everyone alive today has received their genetic and cultural inheritance from untold numbers of ancestors, and will pass on what they can to untold numbers of future generations. You may wish to do the visualization "Contemplating Your Place in History," p. 185.

Week 7: Manifestation

I am my prayer . . . (Psalms 69:14)

The week of *Malkhut*-Manifestation is the celebration of the *sefirah* that "has nothing of its own," and is totally a channel for Divine Will. The prime example is King David who, despite his royalty and his deep involvement in the world, repeatedly returned to humbling himself before God.

You may find yourself expected to "do" a lot this week in the world of manifestation. All the more important, then, that you take time for meditation and prayer to stay in the realm of "being" and to help you maintain clarity. The items below suggest a focus for your meditation each day. Add your own specific examples to each.

Day 43: *Chesed* in *Malkhut.* The world I see before me is a manifestation of unconditional Divine love.

Day 44: *Gevurah* in *Malkhut.* The world I see before me is a manifestation of Divine withdrawal, or *tzimtzum.*

Day 45: *Tiferet* in *Malkhut.* The world I see before me is a manifestation of the Divine-human encounter.

Day 46: *Netzach* in *Malkhut.* The world I see before me is a manifestation of human beings' persistence and will to survive.

Day 47: *Hod* in *Malkhut.* The world I see before me is a manifestation of human beings' ability to cooperate and create together.

Day 48: *Yesod* in *Malkhut.* The world I see before me is a manifestation of nature's evolution and the human enterprise over time, from generation to generation since the first cell.

Day 49: *Malkhut* in *Malkhut.* The world I see before me is a manifestation of Divine will at this moment.

The fiftieth day is the holiday of Shavuot *("Weeks"), celebrating the giving of the Torah at Mount Sinai. May we all merit to receive a new level of revelation and inspiration.*

Your Personal Tree of Life

Studying the concepts of the *sefirot* helps bring them into your life. However, I have found it far richer to have also a personal connection to the *sefirot* and a growing recognition of how they operate in my own life—to use them to "examine" and "probe" reality, as the *Sefer Yetzirah* says (1:4). I discovered the value of this connection while working with a spiritual teacher, Connie Kaplan, whose concepts of the guiding principles of consciousness dovetail with concepts of the Kabbalah. She has developed a method of identifying principles active in an individual's life—which she calls principles of the individual Soul Contract—by doing a new kind of astrological reading.

The details of her discoveries will appear in a book of her own. What I want to share with you is how this perspective enabled me to open up the *sefirot* in radically new ways.

After you follow the procedures outlined in the following section, you will end up with a diagram you can use for contemplation. It will be your personal Tree of Life, identifying the colors that reveal your soul's potential, as it appears in three levels of reality.[3] Kaplan calls these levels "Ascending," "Connecting or Containing," and "Descending."

In the work of Rabbi Yitzchak Ginsburgh, we find a parallel to this system. In his profound work on the Hebrew letters, *The Alef-Beit,* he has explained that the letters of a person's Hebrew name reveal the nature of his or her soul's manifestation in three levels of reality called "Worlds," "Souls," and "Divinity." Ginsburgh writes:

> Worlds, when rectified, "ascend"; Souls "connect"; Divinity "unifies" all.
>
> At the level of Worlds, one experiences himself as being "below" or "down." All one's effort is set upon ascent from one's initial, relative state of physicality to that of spirituality. This consciousness characterizes all "spiritual searchers." At the level of Souls one senses the primary need for the connection of all souls of Israel as an organic one. Only when connected do the Souls become the Throne of God on earth. "Connection" is a "horizontal" consciousness, for all souls are essentially equal. "Ascent" is a vertical consciousness, the will to climb and achieve ever higher states of awareness.

> At the level of Divinity one experiences God's Absolute will to dwell below, to reveal Himself universally, through the means of the souls of His People Israel. The experience of Divinity and true unification is thus essentially a downward flow.[4]

The correlation between these two frameworks is notable. Kaplan's is the more universal, since it does not require a Jewish identity or Hebrew name. For hers, you need only an astrology chart based on your precise birth time and place.[5]

In an astrological chart, every planet not only has a sign and house placement, but also a degree, ranging from 0 to 29 (because each sign has 30 degrees in it, making 360 degrees for the entire circle of the zodiac). Kaplan's work shows that the 30 degrees can be divided into three groups of ten, degrees 0–9 representing the Ascending qualities, 10–19 the Connecting, and 20–29 the Unifying or Descending. She uses from the astrological chart ten planetary placements (eight planets plus sun and moon), and two sky orientations, Ascendant and Midheaven. The planetary information is then arranged on the Tree of Life to translate the astrological chart into a sefirotic chart. This information is combined with Kaplan's system of colors (to be described below) to give you a personal chart for meditation.

Here's how to do it: Get an accurate astrology chart. On it, each planet's position at the time of your birth will be described in terms of degree and sign, and placed in a house. For example, ☉ 23°18′ ♈ means the sun is at 23 degrees, 18 minutes of the sign of Aries. For this analysis you will *not* pay attention to the zodiac signs and houses—only to the *degree* of each planet, and usually not the minutes unless the reading is 54–59 minutes. In the above example, we would only be concerned with the fact that the sun is at 23 degrees. If the reading were 23°55′, we would read it as 24 degrees. If the reading is retrograde (represented in astrological charts by the letter R), do not round it up to the next degree.

Now, any planetary position can have a reading from 0 to 29 degrees. Each degree is represented by a color, going through the rainbow from violet to red and back again. (One way of describing the *sefirot* is as a "linear 'spectrum' of colors emerging from a point of light,"[6] which here is represented by white and black at degrees 14 and 15.)

DESCENDING—UNIFYING	CONNECTING—CONTAINING	ASCENDING—SEEKING
29 violet	19 green	9 yellow
28 indigo	18 blue	8 orange
27 blue	17 indigo	7 red
26 green	16 violet	6 red
25 yellow	15 black	5 orange
24 orange	14 white	4 yellow
23 red	13 violet	3 green
22 red	12 indigo	2 blue
21 orange	11 blue	1 indigo
20 yellow	10 green	0 violet

Thus, if your sun were at 23 degrees, it would be represented by the color red. If it were 24, by orange, and so on. Each color has a meaning in Kaplan's system as well, but discussion of these is beyond the scope of this book. For now, you are simply constructing a beautiful object for contemplation.

The next step is to find the colors of each of the planets on your chart, plus the Midheaven (the degree at the top of the chart) and the Ascendant (the degree at the far left, at right angles to the Midheaven). Fill in the chart below with that information.

	DEGREE	COLOR (fill in the square with the appropriate color)	
Midheaven	________	________________	☐
Sun	________	________________	☐
Moon	________	________________	☐
Mercury	________	________________	☐
Venus	________	________________	☐
Mars	________	________________	☐
Jupiter	________	________________	☐
Saturn	________	________________	☐
Uranus	________	________________	☐
Neptune	________	________________	☐
Pluto	________	________________	☐
Ascendant	________	________________	☐

The planets and positions correlate to the *sefirot* as follows:

Keter	Midheaven—points upward toward your Source
Chochmah	Uranus—"mind" beyond the conscious
Binah	Mercury—connection to collective patterns of thought
Da'at	Midheaven (use fainter color than for *Keter*)—your power of mental unification
Chesed	Jupiter—your support from the universe
Gevurah	Saturn—your unique structural configuration
Tiferet	Sun—your purpose in this incarnation
Netzach	Mars—physically dominating energy, together with Pluto, the energy that provides victory over death
Hod	Venus—energy of emotional awareness, together with Neptune, your connection to the collective emotional realm
Yesod	Moon—your mastery achieved in past lives
Malkhut	Ascendant—your ego and survival strategies

Now you can plot these colors on your own personal Tree of Life. The *sefirot* are represented by the planets and positions as in the diagram on the following page. Neptune and Pluto are represented as larger circles behind Venus and Mars, respectively, since they represent more collective and deeper versions of the same principles. You can make several copies of this page so you can complete one for yourself and others for family and friends for whom you have astrological data.

Reflect on your chart and notice especially: (1) the color of your sun *(Tiferet),* (2) the color of your moon *(Yesod),* and (3) the color of your Midheaven *(Keter).* If two or more of these are the same color, they are extremely strong in your life, and you can benefit from focusing on that color while contemplating your chart. If they are each different colors, focus on the sun *(Tiferet)* at the center, because that provides the primary focus for you in

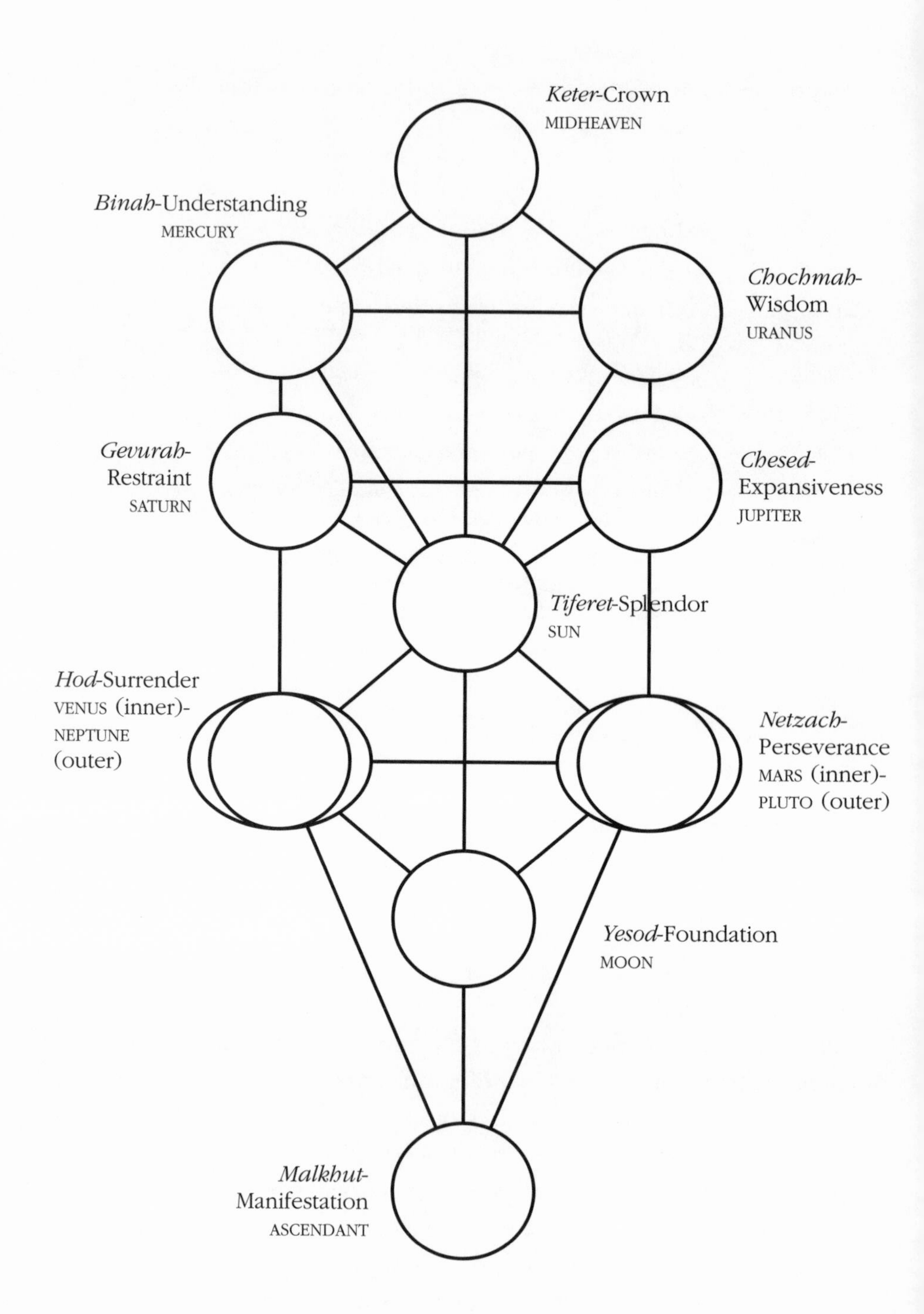
Keter-Crown
MIDHEAVEN
Binah-Understanding
MERCURY
Chochmah-Wisdom
URANUS
Gevurah-Restraint
SATURN
Chesed-Expansiveness
JUPITER
Tiferet-Splendor
SUN
Hod-Surrender
VENUS (inner)-
NEPTUNE (outer)
Netzach-Perseverance
MARS (inner)-
PLUTO (outer)
Yesod-Foundation
MOON
Malkhut-Manifestation
ASCENDANT

this incarnation. If your chart shows other colors appearing with a high frequency—three or more instances of the same color—you may want to concentrate on that color as well.

Here are some specific suggestions for meditation:

In the morning, shortly after waking or during your morning prayers, look at the chart for a few minutes, close your eyes, and imagine yourself being bathed first with your color of *Tiferet,* then with any other dominant colors, then with the color of *Tiferet* again.

In the evening before sleep, look at your chart again. This time, look at the color of *Keter,* because it is the trajectory toward your soul, which is more dominant at night. Close your eyes and imagine yourself being bathed in that color.

As you study the information in this book, you may recognize that certain areas of your life, represented by the various *sefirot,* are coming up for attention. For example, you may find yourself in a position where you are asked to exercise dominance *(Netzach).* If you are having difficulties around that, you may wish to meditate on the colors of your own *sefirah* of *Netzach* (Mars and/or Pluto).

Use of the colors of the *sefirot* in this way will gradually refine your approach to life, as you will be connecting with higher levels—the frequency of waves of color—rather than remaining attached to concrete dimensions of existence.

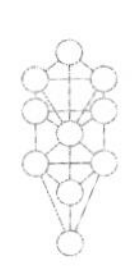

Notes

A Note on the History of Kabbalah

1. See Neil Asher Silberman, *Heavenly Powers: Unraveling the Secret History of the Kabbalah* (New York: Grosset/Putnam, 1998), for a good general history of Jewish mystical movements that concentrates on the culturally radical ideas those movements promulgated.
2. The best-known works by Luzzatto that have been published in English are *Path of the Upright: Mesillat Yesharim* (Northvale, N.J.: Jason Aronson, 1995), *The Knowing Heart* (New York: Philip Feldheim, 1982), and *The Way of God: Pocketbook Edition* (New York: Philip Feldheim, 1999).
3. For example Rabbi Samson Rafael Hirsch, who later became one of the outstanding Torah commentators of the nineteenth century and defender of tradition against Reform Judaism. His writings are not considered mystical, although to the sensitive reader they betray considerable influence from Kabbalah. For an introduction to his thought that sheds great light on the conflict between religion and modernity, see *The Nineteen Letters About Judaism,* trans. Karin Paritsky (New York: Philip Feldheim, 1996). For his philosophy in greater depth, see *Horeb: A Philosophy of Jewish Laws and Observances,* trans. I. Grunfeld (Brooklyn, N.Y.: Soncino, 1994; originally published in 1836).

Chapter 1

1. Rabbi Mordecai Miller, *Sabbath Shiurim* [lectures] (Gateshead, England: Gateshead Foundation for Torah, 1969), p. 86.
2. Rabbi Aryeh Kaplan, *Sefer Yetzirah: The Book of Creation in Theory and Practice,* revised ed. (York Beach, Maine: Samuel Weiser, 1997), p. 41: The *Sefer Yetzirah* "does not tell us to contemplate the *Sefirot* themselves. Rather, it instructs us to use them in developing an inner sight with which to view the world."

3. Robert Frost, "The Trial By Existence," in *The Poetry of Robert Frost,* ed. Edward Connery (New York: Holt, Rinehart and Winston, 1969), p. 21.
4. Abraham Joshua Heschel, *Moral Grandeur and Spiritual Audacity: Essays,* ed. Susannah Heschel (New York: Farrar, Straus & Giroux, 1996), p. 6.
5. Rabbi Schneur Zalman of Liadi, founder of Chabad-Lubavitch, explains in *Likutei Amarim: Tanya* (Brooklyn, N.Y.: Kehot Publication Society, 1981; hereafter cited simply as *Tanya*), 1:23, p. 95, that when a person fulfills God's will by doing one of the *mitzvot* (commandments), the physical action is

   > . . . like a body in relation to the soul, the "soul" being the Supreme Will [of God] to which it is completely surrendered. In this way, the organs of the human body which perform the commandment . . . truly become a vehicle for the Supreme Will; as, for example, the hand that distributes charity to the poor or performs another commandment; or the feet that carry a person toward the performance of a commandment; similarly with the mouth and tongue engaged in uttering the words of the Torah, or the brain engaged in reflecting on the words of the Torah or on the fear of Heaven, or the greatness of God, Blessed-Be-He.

6. Most people are aware that the Torah and rabbinic tradition prescribe many commandments for Jews (the traditional number is 613), but the ancient sages also state that there are seven "Noachide" commandments for non-Jews. These include avoiding idolatry, blasphemy, murder, theft, adultery, and injury to animals, and setting up courts of justice to administer the laws.

Chapter 2

1. This language is similar to that proposed by physicist David Bohm, who speaks about the "implicate" and "explicate" order of things. The universe—or more accurately, the "holomovement"—is "enfolded" in each of us as a holographic image, and "unfolded" as we reveal more and more of its aspects. While Bohm eschews spiritual language, his "holomovement" is similar to the creative force that Kabbalah attributes to God. For a brief discussion of his views, see David Bohm, "Postmodern Science and a Postmodern World," in *The Reenchantment of Science: Postmodern Proposals,* ed. David Ray Griffin (Albany, N.Y.: State University of New York Press, 1988).
2. Rabbi Nachman of Breslov, "The Turkey Prince," in *Rabbi Nachman's Stories,* trans. Rabbi Aryeh Kaplan (Jerusalem: Breslov Research Institute, 1983), pp. 479–480.

3. *Tanya* 1:4, pp. 12ff.
4. Rabbi Eliyahu Dessler, *Strive for Truth!* (New York: Philip Feldheim, 1985), pt. 2, p. 22.
5. Frost, "Trial By Existence," op. cit.
6. See Rabbi Jacob Immanuel Schochet, "Mystical Concepts in Chassidism," chs. 4 and 5, Appendix to *Tanya,* pp. 860–871. For other discussions of the Worlds and *sefirot,* see Rabbi Aryeh Kaplan, *Innerspace: Introduction to Kabbalah, Meditation, and Prophecy* (Brooklyn, N.Y.: Moznaim Publishers, 1990), and Yechiel bar-Lev, *Song of the Soul: Introduction to Kabbalah* (Petach Tikva, 1994).

Chapter 3

1. Rabbi Abraham Isaac Kook, *The Lights of Penitence, The Moral Principles, Lights of Holiness, Essays, Letters and Poems,* trans. Ben Zion Bokser (New York: Paulist Press, 1978), p. 225. As the *Tanya* says, "Let a person shape in his thought and contemplate the subject of God's blessed true Unity" (1:33, p. 147). I highly recommend studying the *Shema* with the insights provided by Rabbi Norman Lamm in *The Shema: Spirituality and Law in Judaism* (Philadelphia: Jewish Publication Society, 1998).
2. Bohm, "Postmodern Science and a Postmodern World," in *Reenchantment of Science,* ed. Griffin, p. 63.
3. Kaplan, *Innerspace,* p. 44.
4. See Rupert Sheldrake, "The Laws of Nature as Habits: A Postmodern Basis for Science," in *Reenchantment of Science,* pp. 81–83.
5. *Tanya* 4:11, p. 447.
6. The ancient source known as the *Bahir* identifies Wisdom as the second *sefirah:* "The second one is *Chochmah* . . . A 'beginning' is nothing other than *Chochmah,* as it is written (Psalms 111:10), 'The beginning is wisdom, the fear of God.'" See *The Bahir: An Ancient Kabbalistic Text Attributed to Rabbi Nehuniah ben HaKana first century C.E.,* trans. Aryeh Kaplan (York Beach, Maine: Samuel Weiser, 1979), no. 142, p. 52. *Chochmah* represents the energy of the highest of the Four Worlds, that of Emanation *(Atzilut),* and is represented by the letter *yud* in God's four-letter name. The *Tanya* (4:5, pp. 407–409) says:

   > For *Chochmah*-Wisdom is the primordium of the intellect, antecedent to apprehension and understanding becoming manifest; rather, still in a state of hiding and concealment, except for some trifle here and there showing forth and issuing from there to the faculty of *Binah*-Understanding, making it possible to understand and to apprehend the hidden intellect. In the holy *Zohar, Chochmah*-Wisdom is therefore referred to as "the dot in the palace."

7. As Swimme and Berry explain:

> To get atoms in the universe to bounce together haphazardly to form a single molecule of an amino acid would require more time than has existed since the beginning, even a hundred times more than fifteen billion years. Yet amino acids formed not only on the planet Earth, but throughout the Milky Way galaxy. . . . In fact, if we consider any of the structures of the large-scale universe, we discover that they are difficult or impossible to account for in a random or unbiased cosmos.

See Brian Swimme and Thomas Berry, *The Universe Story: From the Primordial Flaring Forth to the Ecozoic Era: A Celebration of the Unfolding of the Cosmos* (San Francisco: HarperSanFrancisco, 1994), p. 70 and, for further discussion, pp. 17–25, 66–71. Rabbi Aryeh Kaplan in *Innerspace* describes *Chochmah*-Wisdom as the *sefirah* in which the axioms—more precisely, the conditions of possibility—of the universe are designed (p. 58).

8. Swimme and Berry, *Universe Story,* p. 138.
9. Rabbi Akiva Tatz uses this image for inspiration in his book *Living Inspired* (Jerusalem: Targum Press, 1993), adopting it from Nachmanides, the great thirteenth-century biblical scholar and mystic. A secular example comes from the great nineteenth-century mathematician, Johann Gauss, who wrote this of his discovery of the way to prove a certain arithmetic theorem: "Finally, two days ago, I succeeded, not on account of my painful efforts, but by the grace of God. Like a sudden flash of lightning, the riddle happened to be solved. I myself cannot say what was the conducting thread which connected what I previously knew with what made my success possible." See Willis Harman, *Higher Creativity: Liberating the Unconscious for Breakthrough Insights* (Los Angeles: Tarcher, 1984), p. 48.
10. *Tanya* 1:37, pp. 166–67. The author is commenting on the verse, "To you it was shown, so that you might know that the Lord is God; there is nothing else beside Him" (Deuteronomy 4:35).
11. "The Root of every *nefesh, ruach,* and *neshama,* from the highest of all ranks to the lowest . . . all derive, as it were, from the Supreme Mind which is Supernal *Chochmah*-Wisdom" *Tanya* 1:2, p. 7. Similarly, for "the soul of man and the souls of all the created beings in all the higher and lower worlds, . . . wisdom is the beginning and source of the life-force." *Tanya* 2:8–9, p. 325.
12. Kaplan, *Sefer Yetzirah,* p. 12.
13. Swimme and Berry, *Universe Story,* pp. 43–44.

14. Kook, *Lights of Penitence,* p. 222.
15. *Zohar* 1.15a, quoted by Kaplan, *Sefer Yetzirah,* p. 14.
16. The *Bahir* identifies this as the third *sefirah:* "The third one is the quarry of the Torah, . . . the quarry of the 'spirit of God.'" See *Bahir* 143, p. 52.
17. Rabbi Nachman of Breslov, *Likutei Moharan* (Jerusalem: Breslov Research Institute, 1986–2000), lesson 38.
18. Emmanuel Schochet, "Mystical Concepts in Chassidism," in appendix to *Tanya,* p. 846. For a discussion of different philosophies of Kabbalah, see Rabbi Yitzchak Ginsburgh, "Basics in Kabbalah and Chassidut: Three Stages in the Evolution of Kabbalistic Thought," on http://www.inner.org (Shechem, Israel: 2000).
19. Kaplan, *Sefer Yetzirah,* p. 14.
20. Psalms 89:3.
21. For the fundamental nature of metaphors, see Mark Johnson, *The Body in the Mind: The Bodily Basis of Meaning, Imagination, and Reason* (Chicago: University of Chicago Press, 1987).
22. Harman, *Higher Creativity,* pp. 45, 48.
23. Talmud *Berachot* 61a; cf. Isaiah 6:10: "Their heart will understand and they will return and be healed." According to Rabbi Nachman of Breslov, the *Zohar* connects *Binah* with joy because *Binah,* the mother, receives from *Chochmah*'s 'kindnesses' *(chasadim).* See Nachman of Breslov, *Likutei Moharan* Vol. 1 (1988), Lesson 12, n. 62, p. 224.
24. These are referred to in the *Zohar* (trans. H. Sperling, M. Simon, and P. Levertoff; New York: Soncino Press, 1984) as the "palace above" and the "palace below" (III: 127a, p. 360).
25. See Samson Rafael Hirsch, commentary on the Pentateuch, Exodus 25.
26. Dannion Brinkley with Paul Perry, *Saved by the Light: The True Story of a Man Who Died Twice and the Profound Revelations He Received* (New York: Villard Books, 1994), pp. 26–27.
27. The Jewish mystics hold that not only the heart but also the lower *sefirot* and the lower torso of the body have an intelligence. For example, *Netzach* and *Hod* are associated with the information that comes from prophecy while the kidneys are associated with giving advice (Talmud *Berachot* 61a; cf. Psalms 16:7). See Tamar Frankiel and Judy Greenfeld, *Minding the Temple of the Soul: Balancing Body, Mind, and Spirit Through Traditional Jewish Prayer, Movement and Meditation* (Woodstock, Vt.: Jewish Lights Publishing, 1997), Chapter 3. For a scientific discussion of how the heart has its own "intelligence," see Doc Childre and Howard Martin, *The Heart-Math Solution* (San Francisco: HarperCollins and the Institute of Heart-Math, 1999).
28. Miller, *Sabbath Shiurim,* p. 89.
29. Kook, *Lights of Penitence,* p. 196.

30. Rabbi Nissan Mandel explains that there are really two levels of *Da'at*-Knowledge, one of which is a direct reflection of *Keter* fusing the two other mental *sefirot,* and a lower level that channels the energy of the two into the lower *sefirot.* This adds another level of complexity that we will not consider here. The reader can consult Mandel's introduction to the English version of the *Tanya,* printed at the back of the volume cited herein.
31. Nachman, *Likutei Moharan* Vol. 1 (1988), Lesson 13:1.
32. Rabbi Chaim Kramer with Avraham Sutton, *Anatomy of the Soul* (New York: Breslov Research Institute, 1998), pp. 180, 185.
33. See Kaplan, *Innerspace,* p. 198, n. 19 for a brief discussion of *Da'at.* Rabbi Yechiel Bar-Lev explains that *Da'at* has its roots in the world of *tikkun* and provides a balance between *Binah* and *Chochmah* that was missing in the earlier world of *tohu* (formlessness). See Bar-Lev, *Song of the Soul,* p. 212.

Chapter 4

1. Swimme and Berry, *Universe Story,* pp. 35, 36.
2. As Rabbi Chaim Kramer explains, based on the Maharal (Rabbi Loew of Prague), the Talmudic quotation at the head of this section is to be understood as meaning that reality to us has a bipolar nature. "'Male and female' refer primarily to pairs of conceptual opposites such as heaven and earth, transcendence and immanence, revelation and concealment, mercy and justice, Divine omniscience and human free will, daytime and nighttime, sun and moon, soul and body, next world and this world, etc. . . . They do not define God, but rather the double lens through which we perceive Him." See Kramer, *Anatomy of the Soul,* p. 16.
3. The *Tanya* elaborates (2:5, 297–99):

> *Gevurah* (Might, Restraint) is the quality of *Tzimtzum* . . . and restraining of the spreading forth of the life-force from His *Gedulah* (Expansiveness), preventing it from descending upon and manifesting itself to the creatures, to give them life and existence in a revealed manner, but rather with His Countenance concealed. Thus the life-force conceals itself in the body of the created being and it is as though the body of the created being has independent existence and is not [merely] a spreading forth of the life-force and spirituality—as the diffusion of radiation and light from the sun—but an independently existing entity.

4. Rashi on Genesis 1:1. According to Rabbi Aryeh Kaplan, the Ari (Rabbi Isaac Luria) taught that the original *sefirot* could not hold the Divine

light because they weren't interrelated. Each stood on its own in great perfection, but did not give to or receive from the others. When human beings become givers (through the *mitzvot,* which sustain the spiritual universes), we resemble God. Therefore we can receive the light and hold it. See Kaplan, *Meditation and Kabbalah* (York Beach, Maine: Samuel Weiser, 1982), pp. 212–213.

5. Traditionally, seven male figures are associated with the seven lower *sefirot:* Abraham, Isaac, Jacob, Moses, Aaron, Joseph, and David. I have added female figures to each *sefirah,* the seven prophetesses: Miriam, Hulda, Sarah, Devorah, Chanah, Abigail, and Esther.
6. Harvey, *Direct Path,* pp. 8–9.
7. This portrayal appears in the first blessing before the *Shema* in a traditional Jewish prayer book. However, it should be noted that the angels are also sometimes portrayed as having opposite qualities such as fire and water, which require God's mediation. The liturgical phrase *Oseh shalom bimromav* . . . , "He who makes peace in the heights, may he make peace among us and all Israel," has been interpreted to mean that God sometimes has to make peace among the angels.
8. *Bahir,* Saying #135, p. 50, discusses how "Isaac became worthy of the attribute of Terror *(Gevurah).*"
9. For stunning examples of *Gevurah* in the feminine realm, see Caroline Bynum's excellent work on medieval Christian nuns and female mystics: *Holy Feast and Holy Fast: The Religious Significance of Food to Medieval Women* (Berkeley: University of California Press, 1988) and *Fragmentation and Redemption: Essays on Gender and the Human Body in Medieval Religion* (Cambridge, Mass.: Zone Books, 1991). Some prominent examples in Judaism come from Talmudic accounts of women sacrificing their lives rather than giving in to the Hellenistic Syrian conquerors in the time of the Maccabean war (the victory celebrated by the holiday of Hanukkah); women who insisted on covering their hair more than the law required; and women who followed very strict interpretations of the rules of menstrual purity.
10. Rabbi Nosson Scherman, *The Complete Artscroll Siddur*—Ashkenaz (Brooklyn, N.Y.: Artscroll Mesorah, 1986), pp. 708–709.
11. Moshe Chaim Luzzatto (the Ramchal), *The Knowing Heart [Da'at Tevunot],* trans. Shraga Silverstein (New York: Feldheim, 1982), p. 81.
12. Modern thinkers, such as Rabbi Schneur Zalman of Liadi, harmonize the differences in the two views by saying that God's *essence* is unchanging and all-inclusive, even though the Torah uses human language and thus seems to say that God changes. Perhaps one way to put this is that God, while infinite and unchanging, can include the idea of change as it is experienced by humans.

13. Abraham Joshua Heschel, "The Meaning of This Hour," in *Between God and Man,* ed. Fritz A. Rothschild (New York: Free Press, 1997; orig. 1959), pp. 255–57.
14. *Sefer ha-Ne'elam,* by an anonymous kabbalist quoted in Moshe Idel, *Kabbalah: New Perspectives* (New Haven, Conn.: Yale University Press), p. 180.
15. The Opter Rebbe, *Ohev Yisroel,* Vayetze 15b, quoted in Aryeh Kaplan, *The Light Beyond: Adventures in Hasidic Thought* (New York: Maznaim Publishing, 1981), p. 50.
16. David Ray Griffin, "Of Minds and Molecules: Postmodern Medicine in a Psychosomatic Universe," in *Reenchantment of Science,* p. 143.
17. *Bahir,* #146, says of Tiferet, "The sixth one is the Throne of Glory . . . the house of the World to Come, and its place is in Wisdom. It is thus written, 'And God said, "Let there be light," and there was light'" (p. 53).
18. *Tiferet*-Splendor is also associated with the entire torso, since it is the center of the six middle *sefirot.* See Chaim Kramer's notes to Nachman's *Likutei Moharan* 5, Lesson 41, n. 10, p. 309.
19. Nachman of Breslov, *Rabbi Nachman's Stories,* pp. 385–89.

Chapter 5

1. Kook, *Lights of Penitence,* p. 207.
2. In Judaism, the rabbinic tradition says that since the destruction of the Temple, three things substitute for sacrifice: prayer, giving to charity, and our table (holiness in eating). These are ways of beginning to "obliterate all ego."
3. While the source of illumination and inspiration are in *Chochmah* and *Binah,* the mystical masters tell us that prophecy is also connected with *Netzach* and *Hod.* The way I understand this is that the inspiration must find some physical connection, in the body or its movements, that provides a metaphor or symbol to link the "light" of revelation with an idea that can actually be brought into speech or material form. Similarly, Rabbi Aryeh Kaplan discusses in his book *Innerspace* (pp. 131–134) a "center of imagination" in the part of the body represented by these *sefirot.*
4. See Barbara Ehrenreich, *Blood Rites: The Origins of the Passions of War* (New York: Henry Holt and Company, 1997).
5. Swimme and Berry, *Universe Story,* p. 22.
6. Traditional Kabbalah often placed *Yesod* at the male genitals and referred the next *sefirah, Malkhut* (Kingship), to the womb as well as the feet because *Malkhut* was also identified with the feminine while the previous six *sefirot* were masculine. However, it seems to me that this results from an overlapping of two systems, one having to do with

the progressive development from thought to action, the other referring to the dynamics of dualism in the relations of male and female. (An alternate ancient interpretation was that *Malkhut* was the "mouth" of the male organ.) For purposes of this book, the sexual and/or procreative energies, whether in man or woman, are understood as being at the place of *Yesod.*

7. This interpretation is based on the biblical verse that designates the seven lower *sefirot:* "Yours, O God, are the Greatness, the Strength, the Beauty, the Victory, and the Glory, for All in heaven and in earth; Yours, O God, is the Kingdom . . ." (1 Chronicles 29:11). See Kaplan, *Sefer Yetzirah,* p. 25.
8. However, most kabbalists do not seem to insist that one necessarily incarnates again immediately after completing the round of one's previous life. A soul might reincarnate soon, or not again for centuries.
9. In some Indian teachings, the concept of karma does seem to be used in a negative sense, particularly to justify the caste system (if you are born into a low caste, it's because of your karma). This politicization of the concept is, in my view, unethical.
10. Kenneth Kramer, *World Scriptures: An Introduction to Comparative Religions* (Mahwah, N.J.: Paulist Press, 1986), p. 111.
11. While many people have the impression that Judaism's path is described in the Hebrew Bible (Old Testament), this is actually not the case. Judaism's unique construction is called the *mesorah*—usually translated "tradition." This involves an interpretive community of scholars—the rabbis—who base their decisions on study of the situations and decisions made over some thirty centuries in the framework of the commandments set forth in the written Torah (first five books of the Hebrew Bible). The set of rules called *halacha* has been established for each generation and each individual by the process of scholars responding to questions that arise in the community and seeking answers in the Torah, according to carefully defined procedures and precedents. This is a powerful system that has helped keep the Jewish community alive and vibrant for thousands of years.
12. Kaplan, *Sefer Yetzirah,* commentary to 1:1.
13. Rupert Sheldrake, *The Presence of the Past: Morphic Resonance and the Habits of Nature* (Rochester, Vt.: Inner Traditions, 1995).
14. Many interpreters of Torah state that change is impermissible and that it has not occurred in authentic Judaism. However, it is widely recognized that different applications have been made. For example, the written Torah explicitly permitted a certain form of slavery, while modifying its negative effects by placing strong restrictions on the master. Eventually, rabbinic tradition forbade slavery. Another example is that capital punishment was prescribed for some infringements

of law, but the rabbis created conditions that made it very difficult to apply, so that a Sanhedrin (Supreme Court) that ordered one execution in seventy years was considered a cruel court.

15. *God's Breath: Sacred Scriptures of the World,* eds. John Miller and Aaron Kenedi (New York: Marlowe & Company, 2000), p. 378.
16. Kaplan, *Sefer Yetzirah,* p. 55.
17. *Tanya* 1:4, pp. 15–17.
18. *Tanya* 4:5, p. 415, 4:9, p. 437; emphasis added.
19. For recent discussions, see Wayne Muller, *Sabbath: Restoring the Sacred Rhythm of Rest* (New York: Bantam Doubleday, 1999); and *Olam: One Light for All Mankind,* special issue on Shabbat, November 2000. This magazine is available online at www.olam.org.
20. Rabbi Akiva Tatz, "Ordeals—A Deeper Look at Life's Challenges," lecture for Ohr Sameach International (Los Angeles: May 14, 2000).

Chapter 6

1. Excerpted from E. J. Browne's translation in *Literary History of Persia* (Cambridge: Cambridge University Press, 1909), vol. 1, pp. 436, 439, in Kenneth Cragg and R. Marston Speight, *Islam from Within: Anthology of a Religion* (Belmont, Calif.: Wadsworth Publishing Co., 1980).
2. Rabbi Yitzchak Ginsburgh, *The Alef-Beit: Jewish Thought Revealed Through the Hebrew Letters* (Northvale, N.J.: Jason Aronson, 1995), p. 8.
3. For further insight in this area, see the brilliant work of James Hillman, *The Soul's Code: In Search of Character and Calling* (New York: Warner Books, 1997).
4. Kook, *Lights of Penitence,* p. 223.
5. *Pirke Avot (Sayings of the Fathers)* 1:4, 3:2. Texts describe *Netzach* and *Hod* as represented by "Torah scholars," meaning those who devote themselves full-time to absorbing and transmitting spiritual teachings. See Nachman of Breslov, *Likutei Moharan,* 41:3, and Moshe Cordovero, *Palm Tree of Devorah,* on *Netzach* and *Hod.*
6. This metaphor is from Connie Kaplan; see *The Woman's Book of Dreams: Dreaming as a Spiritual Practice* (Portland, Ore.: Beyond Words, 1999).
7. Quoted in Miller and Kenedi, *God's Breath,* p. 115.
8. The classic expression is in the Torah itself, when the Israelites at Mount Sinai said *Na'aseh venishmah,* "We will do and we will hear." In other words, we will perform the commandments first and then we will integrate them into our being. As Rabbi Chaim Kramer explains, "The basic premise of the commandments is that once we 'act' in

compliance with the objective morality of the Torah, this morality will become part of the spiritual and emotional makeup of the human personality. Thus, the Torah does not directly command us to 'be' but to 'do' . . . its commands are clearly designed by God to impact on our basic character traits, but through our actions." *Anatomy of the Soul,* p. 41.

9. See Carolyn Myss, *Anatomy of the Spirit: The Seven Stages of Power and Healing* (New York: Random House, 1997).

Chapter 7

1. Rashi (Rabbi Shlomo Yitzchak) on Genesis 2:5. The commentary of Rashi is available in most Hebrew Bibles, and several editions now have English translations or paraphrases of his most important comments.
2. Jewish tradition holds that the Land of Israel is a different case, and still depends on the integrity of the actions of Jews and on their prayers. This belief is expressed in the second paragraph of the core affirmation of Judaism, the *Shema,* where God stipulates the conditions for a good harvest in "your land": "And it will come to pass, if you diligently obey [literally, deeply hear or fully understand] My commandments that I command you [plural] today, to love the Lord your God and serve God, with all your heart and with all your soul, I will give rain for your land in its time, the early and the late rain, and you will gather in your grain, your wine, and your oil. And I will give grass in the field for your cattle, and you will eat and be satisfied."
3. Heschel, "On Prayer" in *Moral Grandeur,* p. 260.
4. Some excellent discussions of these issues can be found in Larry Dossey, *Healing Words: The Power of Prayer and the Practice of Medicine* (San Francisco: HarperSanFrancisco, 1993).
5. "Motivating oneself to settle one's mind enables one to connect one's *Daat* to *Keter,* i.e. to the spiritual." Kramer, *Anatomy of the Soul,* p. 193.
6. Reb Natan of Nemirov, *Likutei Halachot, Birkhat HaReiach* 4:14–16, quoted in Kramer, *Anatomy of the Soul,* p. 163. Similar comments come from the non-Hasidic teacher, Rabbi Eliyahu Dessler, who writes that internalizing knowledge, or "returning the knowledge to one's heart," is achieved by use of the imagination. See *Strive for Truth!* pt. 3, p. 235.
7. Kaplan, *Sefer Yetzirah,* p. 89.
8. Hirsch, *Horeb,* pp 427–228.
9. See Aryeh Kaplan, *Meditation and the Bible* (York Beach, Maine: Samuel Weiser, 1988).

10. For a modern interpretation of prayer with movement, see Frankiel and Greenfeld, *Minding the Temple of the Soul.*
11. An excellent discussion appears in Rabbi Dessler's "Being and Having" in *Strive for Truth!* pt. 3, pp. 195–205.
12. Cf. Rabbi Dessler's similar comment on internalizing knowledge: "You shall return it to your heart means making it a reality in your inner self" (*Strive for Truth!* pt. 3, p. 188).
13. Quoted in Miller and Kenedi, *God's Breath,* p. 374.
14. For a preliminary discussion of the "soul contract," see Kaplan, *Woman's Book of Dreams.* While I have not found a reference to this specific idea in Judaism, the basic concept is supported by descriptions of the soul's work found in modern mysticism and Hasidut.
15. Dessler, *Strive for Truth!,* pt. 3, p. 99.
16. Heschel, "To Be a Jew," *Moral Grandeur,* p. 7.

Chapter 8

1. Kook, *Lights of Penitence,* p. 229.
2. Bohm, "Postmodern Science," p. 67.
3. Kaplan, commentary to *Sefer Yetzirah,* p. 79, where he explains that there are different types of angels: *Serafim* are in the world of *Beriah (Binah), chayot* are in *Yetzirah,* and *ofanim* are in *Asiyah.* Many modern discussions, however, refer to angels as rooted in the world of *Yetzirah.*
4. See Tamar Frankiel and Judy Greenfeld, *Entering the Temple of Dreams: Jewish Prayers, Movements, and Meditations for the End of the Day* (Woodstock, Vt.: Jewish Lights Publishing, 2000), ch. 2.
5. See Melvin Morse and Paul Perry, *Parting Visions* (New York: Ballantine Books, 1993).
6. Martin Luther King, Jr., *Strength to Love* (Philadelphia: Fortress Press, 1986), p. 124.
7. *A Still Forest Pool: The Insight Meditation of Achaan Chah,* eds. Jack Kornfield and Paul Breiter (Wheaton, Ill.: Theosophical Publishing House, 1985), p. 34.
8. Kaplan, *Meditation and Kabbalah,* p. 143.
9. The prophet Ezekiel's famous vision of the chariot (Ezekiel 1) contains this profound concept. In the vision, Ezekiel describes angelic beings surrounding and creating a chariot for a Divine figure. One of the types of angels is called *chayot,* usually translated "living creatures." In a verse (which, interestingly, was left out of the Greek translation on which many Christian Bibles are based), the text says simply: "And the living creatures ran and returned like rays of light." This phrase "ran and returned" suggested to the kabbalists that even the angels, who are described as beings that "never swerved in their course" nor

deviated from their mission, did not remain in a fixed relationship to God. They were running and returning, as if they were flashing in and out of existence.

10. See Kaplan, *Innerspace,* p. 115: "Part of the discipline of a prophet is the ability to recapture a spiritual experience that seemingly defies conscious recall."
11. Kook, *Lights of Penitence,* pp. 207–208.
12. Kook, *Lights of Penitence,* p. 236. Conversely, the great mystic Rabbi Schneur Zalman of Liadi taught, regarding the ultimate goodness of God's wisdom, that when we know that creation is occurring constantly at every moment, we will recognize the complete goodness of the universe. As he wrote in the *Tanya* (pt. 4, pp. 445–447):

> When a person will contemplate this in the profundity of his understanding, and will imagine in his mind coming to be *ex nihilo* truly every moment, how can he possibly think he has ever suffered, or had any afflictions related to "children, life and sustenance" or whatever other worldly sufferings. For the Nothingness that is His blessed *Chochmah* is the source of life, welfare, and delight. It is the Eden that transcends the world to come except that, because it is not apprehensible, one imagines [oneself] to have sufferings or afflictions. In fact, however, no evil descends from above and everything is good, though it is not apprehended because of its immense and abundant goodness. And this is the essence of the faith for which man was created: to believe that "There is no place void of Him" and "In the light of the King's countenance there is life," and conclusively, "Strength and gladness are in His place," because He is but good all the time.

13. Dessler, *Strive for Truth!* pt. 3, p. 235.
14. This is adapted from Andrew Harvey's version in *The Direct Path,* pp. 157–160.
15. This phrase from a Nootka (Native American) song is inscribed on a wall of the Denver Art Museum.
16. Dessler, *Strive for Truth!* pt. 3, p. 232.
17. Kook, *Lights of Penitence,* p. 213.

Part IV

1. Alternatively, try some of the movements and meditations in Frankiel and Greenfeld, *Minding the Temple of the Soul.* The *Mah Tovu* prayer is especially appropriate to begin your private prayers.

2. This phrase of ten Hebrew words, *Y'hiyu l'ratzon imri fi v'higion lebi lefanecha, Adonai tzuri vegoali,* is kabbalistically very significant. In addition to the "tens" mentioned in the text, the letter *yud* stands for the *sefirah* of *Chochmah,* and the point of the *yud* for *Keter.*
3. Visualization of the *sefirot* in different colors was known among the Spanish kabbalists of the thirteenth and fourteenth centuries. Moshe Idel quotes Rabbi David ben Yehudah ha-Hasid as insisting that the *sefirot* be visualized with colors and/or verses from the prayers. As specific colors are not mentioned, Idel thinks they are correlated with the *sefirot* through the imagination of the mystic. This visualization enabled the "imaginative faculty" to ascend to a higher level, from which the mystic could draw down the Divine flow into the world. Idel also discusses the importance of colors in the work of one Rabbi Joseph ha-'Arokh. See Idel, *Kabbalah,* pp. 104, 106.
4. Ginsburgh, *Alef-Beit,* 17–18. These levels are also discussed in Kaplan, *Sefer Yetzirah,* commentary to Chapter 1.
5. The connection of Kabbalah to astrology was very strong. The Talmud taught that there is a *mazal* (Divine influence) over each hour, as well as an angel named *Lailah* that oversees birth, so that one's birth time and place was highly significant. Planets, paths on the Tree of Life, and letters of the alphabet were coordinated with times and qualities. See Kaplan on *Sefer Yetzirah,* Chapters 4 and 5, especially pp. 171, 180ff. There were, however, a number of different systems that did not agree with one another. The lack of authoritative direction in this area suggests that it was open to interpretation, probably according to the contemplative understanding a person achieved. The system offered herein is in the same spirit—use it as a basis for your own contemplation, not as an authoritative system.

   It should be noted that traditional Judaism has generally disapproved the use of astrology for predicting the future, because the future is totally in the hands of God and cannot be predicted; nor can a person's "fate" be determined.
6. Ginsburgh, *Alef-Beit,* p. 20.

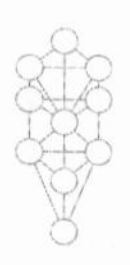

Glossary

Asiyah: "Action." The fourth and lowest of the Four Worlds according to Kabbalah, namely, the world of action and material form.

Atzilut: "Emanation." The first and highest of the Four Worlds according to Kabbalah, in which God began creating the world by emanating Divine energy.

Bahir: "Brilliance." A well-known mystical text, probably from the eleventh century but possibly much earlier, which describes the structure of the system of *sefirot* almost as they are known today.

Beriah: "Creation." The second of the Four Worlds according to Kabbalah, where God's energy began to take the form of thought.

Binah: "Understanding." The *sefirah* of the left temple, representing the Divine template or matrix of thought forms; nourishes and develops flashes of inspiration from *Chochmah*.

chayot: "Wild beasts" or "living creatures." Angelic beings with animal faces, seen in a vision by the prophet Ezekiel.

Chesed: "Lovingkindness." The *sefirah* of the right arm, with the quality of expansiveness and outgoing love.

Chochmah: "Wisdom." The *sefirah* of the right temple, with the quality of surprising creativity, like a lightning-bolt flash of inspiration.

Da'at: "Knowledge." The *sefirah* located at the brain stem, with the quality of internalizing and unifying knowledge, connecting mind with the lower *sefirot*.

devekut: "Clinging." A state of mystical elevation in which the practitioner achieves a profound closeness to God.

Gevurah: "Strength." The *sefirah* of the left arm, with the qualities of restraint, discipline, and withdrawal.

halacha: "The walking." The general term for Jewish law.

Hasidism: A popular Jewish religious movement that began in late-eighteenth-century Eastern Europe, fully within the Orthodox framework, emphasizing devotion in prayer, love of one's fellow, and strong relationships between teacher and disciple. Hasidic teachers were noted for their ability to transmit difficult concepts of mysticism to the ordinary person.

Hod: "Glory." The *sefirah* of the left hip and leg, with the quality of sensing and processing emotional information.

Kabbalah: "Received." Generally, the Jewish mystical tradition from about the second century C.E. to the present.

kaddish: A prayer said in honor of the dead, during the first year of mourning and annually thereafter. In different forms, the *kaddish* also serves to mark different sections of the Jewish congregational prayer service.

kedushah: "Sanctification." A very sacred congregational prayer, led by the cantor while members of the congregation are standing, traditionally in a manner that "imitates the angels."

Malkhut: "Kingship." The tenth of the *sefirot,* at the feet, expressing the world as it is normally perceived; also regarded as the final manifestation of Divine will.

midah (*plural,* midot): Literally, "measure." A quality or attribute of a person or of God. In mystical contexts, the word usually refers to one of the six middle *sefirot (Chesed, Gevurah, Tiferet, Netzach, Hod, Yesod).*

midrash: The general term for the collections of homiletic and inspirational interpretations of scripture, particularly using stories and word associations, produced during the third to eighth centuries C.E.

mitzvah (*plural,* mitzvot): "Commandment."

Netzach: "Victory." The *sefirah* of the right hip and leg, expressing perseverance and motion.

ofanim: "Wheels." Angelic beings that bore the Divine Chariot seen in a vision by the prophet Ezekiel.

Sefer Yetzirah: "Book of Creation." An ancient and influential Jewish mystical text, possibly written in an early form in the second century C.E., remarkable for its intricate numerological and alphabetical correlations.

sefirah (*plural,* sefirot): The ten Divine energies manifested in every process of creation.

seraphim: Angelic beings of an intense, fiery appearance, described by the prophet Isaiah.

Talmud: The records of extensive discussions of Jewish sages on topics of Jewish law and practice, from the third to the sixth centuries, which form the textual core of Judaism from that time onward. While Talmuds were collected and edited in both the Babylonian and Israelite (Jerusalem) communities, the word "Talmud" usually refers to the more complete Babylonian Talmud unless otherwise noted.

Tanya: "It has been taught . . ." The first word and common title of the *Sefer Shel Benonim,* or "Book for the Average Person," written by Rabbi Schneur Zalman of Liadi at the turn of the nineteenth century. Originally written for his disciples in the Chabad-Lubavitch group, it is now regarded as a classic of Hasidic philosophy and a great work on spiritual self-improvement.

Tiferet: "Splendor." The *sefirah* of the heart, expressing the Divine-human union of vision and purpose.

tzimtzum: "Contraction." The withdrawal of Divine energy into Itself at the beginning of creation, allowing a space to be "vacated" in which a universe could emerge. Metaphorically, the word can mean personal withdrawal of energy.

Yesod: "Foundation." The *sefirah* of the pelvic region, with the quality of channeling and transmitting sexual, karmic, and social energy.

Yetzirah: "Formation." The third of the Four Worlds of Kabbalah, denoting the stage of creation in which things are given their distinct energetic qualities.

Zohar: "Radiance." A classic mystical text whose sources are claimed to go back to a famous second-century rabbi, Shimon bar Yochai. It was published and widely circulated beginning in the thirteenth century, and provides the foundation for most modern Jewish mystical schools of thought.

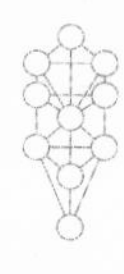

Recommended Readings

Cooper, David. *The Handbook of Jewish Meditation Practices: A Guide for Enriching the Sabbath and Other Days of Your Life*. Woodstock, Vt.: Jewish Lights Publishing, 2000.

Frankiel, Tamar, and Judy Greenfeld. *Entering the Temple of Dreams: Jewish Prayers, Movements, and Meditations for the End of the Day*. Woodstock, Vt.: Jewish Lights Publishing, 2000.

______. *Minding the Temple of the Soul: Balancing Body, Mind, and Spirit Through Traditional Jewish Prayer, Movement, and Meditation*. Woodstock, Vt.: Jewish Lights Publishing, 1997.

Gefen, Nan Fink. *Discovering Jewish Meditation*. Woodstock, Vt.: Jewish Lights Publishing, 1999.

Ginsburgh, Yitzchak, *The Alef-Beit: Jewish Thought Revealed Through the Hebrew Letters*. Northvale, N.J.: Jason Aronson, 1995.

Greenbaum, Avraham. *Under the Table and How to Get Up: Pathways to Jewish Spiritual Growth*. Jerusalem: Breslov Research Institute, 1991.

Griffin, David Ray, ed. *The Reenchantment of Science: Postmodern Proposals*. Albany, N.Y.: State University of New York Press, 1988.

Harvey, Andrew. *The Direct Path: Creating a Journey to the Divine Using the World's Mystical Traditions*. New York: Broadway Books, 2000.

Hirsch, Samson Rafael. *The Nineteen Letters About Judaism*, translated by Karin Paritsky. New York: Philip Feldheim, 1996.

Kaplan, Aryeh. *Innerspace: Introduction to Kabbalah, Meditation, and Prophecy*. Brooklyn, N.Y.: Moznaim Publishers, 1990.

———. *Meditation and Kabbalah*. York Beach, Maine: Samuel Weiser, 1982.

———. *Sefer Yetzirah: The Book of Creation in Theory and Practice*. Revised edition. York Beach, Maine: Samuel Weiser, 1997.

Kaplan, Connie Cockrell. *The Woman's Book of Dreams*. Portland, Ore: Beyond Words, 1999.

Kook, Abraham Isaac. *The Lights of Penitence, The Moral Principles, Lights of Holiness, Essays, Letters and Poems*, translated by Ben Zion Bokser. New York: Paulist Press, 1978.

Kramer, Chaim, with Avraham Sutton. *Anatomy of the Soul*. Jerusalem: Breslov Research Institute, 1998.

Kushner, Lawrence. *The Way Into Jewish Mystical Tradition*. Woodstock, Vt.: Jewish Lights Publishing, 2000.

Lamm, Norman. *The Shema: Spirituality and Law in Judaism*. Philadelphia: Jewish Publication Society, 1998.

Nachman of Breslov. *Likutei Moharan*. Jerusalem: Breslov Research Institute, 1986–2000.

———. *Rabbi Nachman's Stories*. Translated by Rabbi Aryeh Kaplan. Jerusalem: Breslov Research Institute, 1983.

Schneur Zalman of Liadi. *Tanya: Likutei Amarim*. Brooklyn, N.Y.: Kehot Publication Society, 1981.

Swimme, Brian, and Thomas Berry. *The Universe Story: From the Primal Flaring Forth to the Ecozoic Era: A Celebration of the Unfolding of the Cosmos* (San Francisco: HarperSan-Francisco, 1994).

Steinsaltz, Adin. *The Thirteen Petalled Rose: A Discourse on the Essence of Jewish Existence and Belief*. New York: Basic Books, 1980.

Tatz, Akiva. *Living Inspired*. Jerusalem: Targum Press, 1993.

———. *Worldmask*. Jerusalem: Targum Press, 1995.

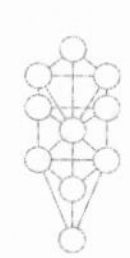

About JEWISH LIGHTS Publishing

People of all faiths and backgrounds yearn for books that attract, engage, educate and spiritually inspire.

Our principal goal is to stimulate thought and help all people learn about who the Jewish People are, where they come from, and what the future can be made to hold. While people of our diverse Jewish heritage are the primary audience, our books speak to people in the Christian world as well and will broaden their understanding of Judaism and the roots of their own faith.

We bring to you authors who are at the forefront of spiritual thought and experience. While each has something different to say, they all say it in a voice that you can hear.

Our books are designed to welcome you and then to engage, stimulate and inspire. We judge our success not only by whether or not our books are beautiful and commercially successful, but by whether or not they make a difference in your life.

We at Jewish Lights take great care to produce beautiful books that present meaningful spiritual content in a form that reflects the art of making high quality books. Therefore, we want to acknowledge those who contributed to the production of this book.

Stuart M. Matlins, Publisher

PRODUCTION
Marian B. Wallace & Bridgett Taylor

EDITORIAL
Sandra Korinchak, Emily Wichland,
Martha McKinney & Amanda Dupuis

JACKET DESIGN
Graciela Galup, Cambridge, Massachusetts

TEXT DESIGN
Susan Ramundo, SR Desktop Services, Ridge, New York

JACKET / TEXT PRINTING & BINDING
Lake Book, Melrose Park, Illinois

Healing/Wellness/Recovery

Jewish Pastoral Care
A Practical Handbook from Traditional and Contemporary Sources

Ed. by *Rabbi Dayle A. Friedman*

Gives today's Jewish pastoral counselors practical guidelines based in the Jewish tradition.
6 x 9, 464 pp, HC, ISBN 1-58023-078-4 **$35.00**

Healing of Soul, Healing of Body
Spiritual Leaders Unfold the Strength & Solace in Psalms

Ed. by *Rabbi Simkha Y. Weintraub, CSW,* for The National Center for Jewish Healing

A source of solace for those who are facing illness, as well as those who care for them. Provides a wellspring of strength with inspiring introductions and commentaries by eminent spiritual leaders reflecting all Jewish movements.
6 x 9, 128 pp, Quality PB, Illus., 2-color text, ISBN 1-879045-31-1 **$14.95**

Jewish Paths toward Healing and Wholeness
A Personal Guide to Dealing with Suffering

by *Rabbi Kerry M. Olitzky*; Foreword by *Debbie Friedman*

Why me? Why do we suffer? How can we heal? Grounded in personal experience with illness and Jewish spiritual traditions, this book provides healing rituals, psalms and prayers that help readers initiate a dialogue with God, to guide them along the complicated path of healing and wholeness.
6 x 9, 192 pp, Quality PB, ISBN 1-58023-068-7 **$15.95**

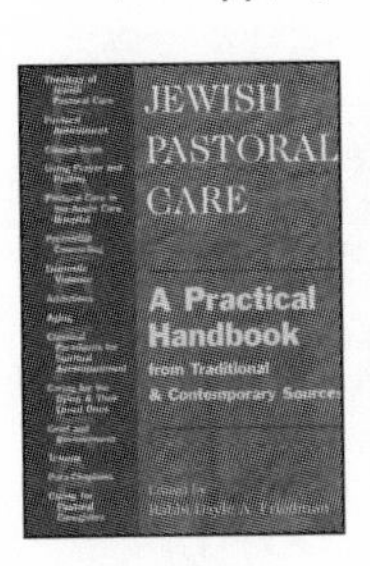

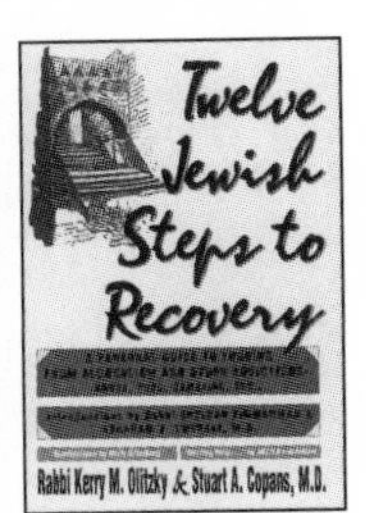

Twelve Jewish Steps to Recovery: *A Personal Guide to Turning from Alcoholism & Other Addictions . . . Drugs, Food, Gambling, Sex . . .* by Rabbi Kerry M. Olitzky & Stuart A. Copans, M.D. Preface by Abraham J. Twerski, M.D.; Intro. by Rabbi Sheldon Zimmerman; "Getting Help" by JACS Foundation 6 x 9, 144 pp, Quality PB, ISBN 1-879045-09-5 **$13.95**

One Hundred Blessings Every Day: *Daily Twelve Step Recovery Affirmations, Exercises for Personal Growth & Renewal Reflecting Seasons of the Jewish Year* by Rabbi Kerry M. Olitzky 4½ x 6½, 432 pp, Quality PB, ISBN 1-879045-30-3 **$14.95**

Recovery from Codependence: *A Jewish Twelve Steps Guide to Healing Your Soul* by Rabbi Kerry M. Olitzky 6 x 9, 160 pp, Quality PB, ISBN 1-879045-32-X **$13.95**; HC, ISBN 1-879045-27-3 **$21.95**

Renewed Each Day: *Daily Twelve Step Recovery Meditations Based on the Bible* by Rabbi Kerry M. Olitzky & Aaron Z. *Vol. I: Genesis & Exodus*; *Vol. II: Leviticus, Numbers and Deuteronomy*
Vol. I: 6 x 9, 224 pp, Quality PB, ISBN 1-879045-12-5 **$14.95**
Vol. II: 6 x 9, 280 pp, Quality PB, ISBN 1-879045-13-3 **$14.95**

Spirituality

My People's Prayer Book: *Traditional Prayers, Modern Commentaries*

Ed. by *Dr. Lawrence A. Hoffman*

Provides a diverse and exciting commentary to the traditional liturgy, helping modern men and women find new wisdom in Jewish prayer, and bring liturgy into their lives. Each book includes Hebrew text, modern translation, and commentaries *from all perspectives* of the Jewish world.

Vol. 1—*The Sh'ma and Its Blessings,* 7 x 10, 168 pp, HC, ISBN 1-879045-79-6 **$23.95**
Vol. 2—*The Amidah,* 7 x 10, 240 pp, HC, ISBN 1-879045-80-X **$23.95**
Vol. 3—*P'sukei D'zimrah* (Morning Psalms), 7 x 10, 240 pp, HC, ISBN 1-879045-81-8 **$23.95**
Vol. 4—*Seder K'riat Hatorah* (The Torah Service), 7 x 10, 264 pp, ISBN 1-879045-82-6 **$23.95**
Vol. 5—*Birkhot Hashachar* (Morning Blessings), 7 x 10, 240 pp (est), ISBN 1-879045-83-4 **$24.95**
(Avail. Fall 2001)

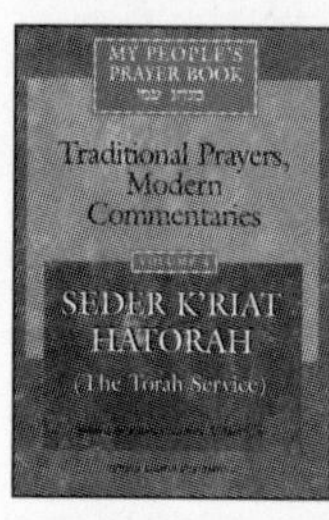

Becoming a Congregation of Learners
Learning as a Key to Revitalizing Congregational Life by Isa Aron, Ph.D.; Foreword by Rabbi Lawrence A. Hoffman, Co-Developer, Synagogue 2000
6 x 9, 304 pp, Quality PB, ISBN 1-58023-089-X **$19.95**

Self, Struggle & Change
Family Conflict Stories in Genesis and Their Healing Insights for Our Lives
by Dr. Norman J. Cohen 6 x 9, 224 pp, Quality PB, ISBN 1-879045-66-4 **$16.95**; HC, ISBN 1-879045-19-2 **$21.95**

Voices from Genesis: ***Guiding Us through the Stages of Life***
by Dr. Norman J. Cohen 6 x 9, 192 pp, Quality PB, ISBN 1-58023-118-7 **$16.95**; HC, ISBN 1-879045-75-3 **$21.95**

God Whispers: ***Stories of the Soul, Lessons of the Heart***
by Rabbi Karyn D. Kedar 6 x 9, 176 pp, Quality PB, ISBN 1-58023-088-1 **$15.95**

The Business Bible: ***10 New Commandments for Bringing Spirituality & Ethical Values into the Workplace***
by Rabbi Wayne Dosick 5½ x 8½, 208 pp, Quality PB, ISBN 1-58023-101-2 **$14.95**

Being God's Partner: ***How to Find the Hidden Link Between Spirituality and Your Work***
by Rabbi Jeffrey K. Salkin; Intro. by Norman Lear **AWARD WINNER!**
6 x 9, 192 pp, Quality PB, ISBN 1-879045-65-6 **$16.95**; HC, ISBN 1-879045-37-0 **$19.95**

God & the Big Bang
Discovering Harmony Between Science & Spirituality **AWARD WINNER!**
by Daniel C. Matt
6 x 9, 224 pp, Quality PB, ISBN 1-879045-89-3 **$16.95**

Soul Judaism: ***Dancing with God into a New Era***
by Rabbi Wayne Dosick 5½ x 8½, 304 pp, Quality PB, ISBN 1-58023-053-9 **$16.95**

Finding Joy: ***A Practical Spiritual Guide to Happiness*** **AWARD WINNER!**
by Rabbi Dannel I. Schwartz with Mark Hass
6 x 9, 192 pp, Quality PB, ISBN 1-58023-009-1 **$14.95**; HC, ISBN 1-879045-53-2 **$19.95**

Spirituality—The Kushner Series

Books by Lawrence Kushner

The Way Into Jewish Mystical Tradition

Explains the principles of Jewish mystical thinking, their religious and spiritual significance, and how they relate to our lives. A book that allows us to experience and understand the Jewish mystical approach to our place in the world. 6 x 9, 224 pp, HC, ISBN 1-58023-029-6 **$21.95**

Eyes Remade for Wonder
The Way of Jewish Mysticism and Sacred Living

A Lawrence Kushner Reader Intro. by *Thomas Moore*

Whether you are new to Kushner or a devoted fan, you'll find inspiration here. With samplings from each of Kushner's works, and a generous amount of new material, this book is to be read and reread, each time discovering deeper layers of meaning in our lives.
6 x 9, 240 pp, Quality PB, ISBN 1-58023-042-3 **$16.95**; HC, ISBN 1-58023-014-8 **$23.95**

Because Nothing Looks Like God

by *Lawrence and Karen Kushner;* Full-color illus. by *Dawn W. Majewski*

What is God like? The first collaborative work by husband-and-wife team Lawrence and Karen Kushner introduces children to the possibilities of spiritual life with three poetic spiritual stories. Real-life examples of happiness and sadness—from goodnight stories, to the hope and fear felt the first time at bat, to the closing moments of life—invite us to explore, together with our children, the questions we all have about God, no matter what our age. **For ages 4 & up**
11 x 8½, 32 pp, HC, Full-color illus., ISBN 1-58023-092-X **$16.95**

Invisible Lines of Connection: *Sacred Stories of the Ordinary* AWARD WINNER!
6 x 9, 160 pp, Quality PB, ISBN 1-879045-98-2 **$15.95**; HC, ISBN 1-879045-52-4 **$21.95**

Honey from the Rock SPECIAL ANNIVERSARY EDITION
An Introduction to Jewish Mysticism 6 x 9, 176 pp, Quality PB, ISBN 1-58023-073-3 **$15.95**

The Book of Letters: *A Mystical Hebrew Alphabet* AWARD WINNER!
Popular HC Edition, 6 x 9, 80 pp, 2-color text, ISBN 1-879045-00-1 **$24.95**; *Deluxe Gift Edition,* 9 x 12, 80 pp, HC, 2-color text, ornamentation, slipcase, ISBN 1-879045-01-X **$79.95**; *Collector's Limited Edition,* 9 x 12, 80 pp, HC, gold-embossed pages, hand-assembled slipcase. With silkscreened print. Limited to 500 signed and numbered copies, ISBN 1-879045-04-4 **$349.00**

The Book of Words: *Talking Spiritual Life, Living Spiritual Talk* AWARD WINNER!
6 x 9, 160 pp, Quality PB, 2-color text, ISBN 1-58023-020-2 **$16.95**;
152 pp, HC, ISBN 1-879045-35-4 **$21.95**

God Was in This Place & I, i Did Not Know
Finding Self, Spirituality and Ultimate Meaning
6 x 9, 192 pp, Quality PB, ISBN 1-879045-33-8 **$16.95**

The River of Light: *Jewish Mystical Awareness* SPECIAL ANNIVERSARY EDITION
6 x 9, 192 pp, Quality PB, ISBN 1-58023-096-2 **$16.95**

Spirituality & More

The Jewish Lights Spirituality Handbook
A Guide to Understanding, Exploring & Living a Spiritual Life

Ed. by *Stuart M. Matlins, Editor-in-Chief, Jewish Lights Publishing*

Rich, creative material from over 50 spiritual leaders on every aspect of Jewish spirituality today: prayer, meditation, mysticism, study, rituals, special days, the everyday, and more. 6 x 9, 304 pp, Quality PB, ISBN 1-58023-093-8 **$16.95**; HC, ISBN 1-58023-100-4 **$24.95**

Six Jewish Spiritual Paths: *A Rationalist Looks at Spirituality*

by *Rabbi Rifat Sonsino*

The quest for spirituality is universal, but which path to spirituality is right *for you*? A straightforward, objective discussion of the many ways—each valid and authentic—for seekers to gain a richer spiritual life within Judaism. 6 x 9, 208 pp, HC, ISBN 1-58023-095-4 **$21.95**

Restful Reflections: *Nighttime Inspiration to Calm the Soul, Based on Jewish Wisdom* by *Rabbi Kerry M. Olitzky* and *Rabbi Lori Forman*

Wisdom to "sleep on." For each night of the year, an inspiring quote from a Jewish source and a personal reflection on it from an insightful spiritual leader help you to focus on your spiritual life and the lessons your day has offered. The companion to *Sacred Intentions: Daily Inspiration to Strengthen the Spirit, Based on Jewish Wisdom* (see below).
4½ x 6½, 448 pp, Quality PB, ISBN 1-58023-091-1 **$15.95**

Sacred Intentions: *Daily Inspiration to Strengthen the Spirit, Based on Jewish Wisdom*
by Rabbi Kerry M. Olitzky and Rabbi Lori Forman
4½ x 6½, 448 pp, Quality PB, ISBN 1-58023-061-X **$15.95**

The Enneagram and Kabbalah: *Reading Your Soul*
by Rabbi Howard A. Addison 6 x 9, 176 pp, Quality PB, ISBN 1-58023-001-6 **$15.95**

Embracing the Covenant: *Converts to Judaism Talk About Why & How*
Ed. and with Intros. by Rabbi Allan L. Berkowitz and Patti Moskovitz
6 x 9, 192 pp, Quality PB, ISBN 1-879045-50-8 **$15.95**

Mystery Midrash: *An Anthology of Jewish Mystery & Detective Fiction* AWARD WINNER!
Ed. by Lawrence W. Raphael 6 x 9, 304 pp, Quality PB, ISBN 1-58023-055-5 **$16.95**

Wandering Stars: *An Anthology of Jewish Fantasy & Science Fiction* Ed. by Jack Dann; Intro. by Isaac Asimov 6 x 9, 272 pp, Quality PB, ISBN 1-58023-005-9 **$16.95**

Israel—A Spiritual Travel Guide AWARD WINNER!
A Companion for the Modern Jewish Pilgrim
by Rabbi Lawrence A. Hoffman 4¾ x 10, 256 pp, Quality PB, ISBN 1-879045-56-7 **$18.95**

Spirituality/Jewish Meditation

Discovering Jewish Meditation
Instruction & Guidance for Learning an Ancient Spiritual Practice

by *Nan Fink Gefen*

Gives readers of any level of understanding the tools to learn the practice of Jewish meditation on your own, starting you on the path to a deep spiritual and personal connection to God and to greater insight about your life. 6 x 9, 208 pp, Quality PB, ISBN 1-58023-067-9 **$16.95**

Entering the Temple of Dreams: *Jewish Prayers, Movements, and Meditations for the End of the Day*

by *Tamar Frankiel* and *Judy Greenfeld*

Nighttime spirituality is much more than bedtime prayers! Here, you'll uncover deeper meaning to familiar nighttime prayers—and learn to combine the prayers with movements and meditations to enhance your physical and psychological well-being.
7 x 10, 192 pp, Quality PB, Illus., ISBN 1-58023-079-2 **$16.95**

One God Clapping: *The Spiritual Path of a Zen Rabbi* AWARD WINNER!

by *Alan Lew* & *Sherril Jaffe*

A fascinating personal story of a Jewish meditation expert's roundabout spiritual journey from Zen Buddhist practitioner to rabbi. 5½ x 8½, 336 pp, Quality PB, ISBN 1-58023-115-2 **$16.95**

The Handbook of Jewish Meditation Practices
A Guide for Enriching the Sabbath and Other Days of Your Life

by *Rabbi David A. Cooper*

Gives us ancient and modern Jewish tools—Jewish practices and traditions, easy-to-use meditation exercises, and contemplative study of Jewish sacred texts. 6 x 9, 208 pp, Quality PB, ISBN 1-58023-102-0 **$16.95**

Stepping Stones to Jewish Spiritual Living: ***Walking the Path Morning, Noon, and Night***
by Rabbi James L. Mirel & Karen Bonnell Werth
6 x 9, 240 pp, Quality PB, ISBN 1-58023-074-1 **$16.95**

Meditation from the Heart of Judaism
Today's Teachers Share Their Practices, Techniques, and Faith
Ed. by Avram Davis 6 x 9, 256 pp, Quality PB, ISBN 1-58023-049-0 **$16.95**;
HC, ISBN 1-879045-77-X **$21.95**

The Way of Flame: ***A Guide to the Forgotten Mystical Tradition of Jewish Meditation***
by Avram Davis 4½ x 8, 176 pp, Quality PB, ISBN 1-58023-060-1 **$15.95**

Minding the Temple of the Soul: ***Balancing Body, Mind, and Spirit through Traditional Jewish Prayer, Movement, and Meditation***
by Tamar Frankiel and Judy Greenfeld 7 x 10, 184 pp, Quality PB, Illus.,
ISBN 1-879045-64-8 **$16.95**; Audiotape of the Blessings and Meditations (60-min. cassette), JN01 **$9.95**; Videotape of the Movements and Meditations (46-min.), S507 **$20.00**